The Life Of
HORSES

The Life Of
HORSES

JANE HOLDERNESS-RODDAM

Bounty Books

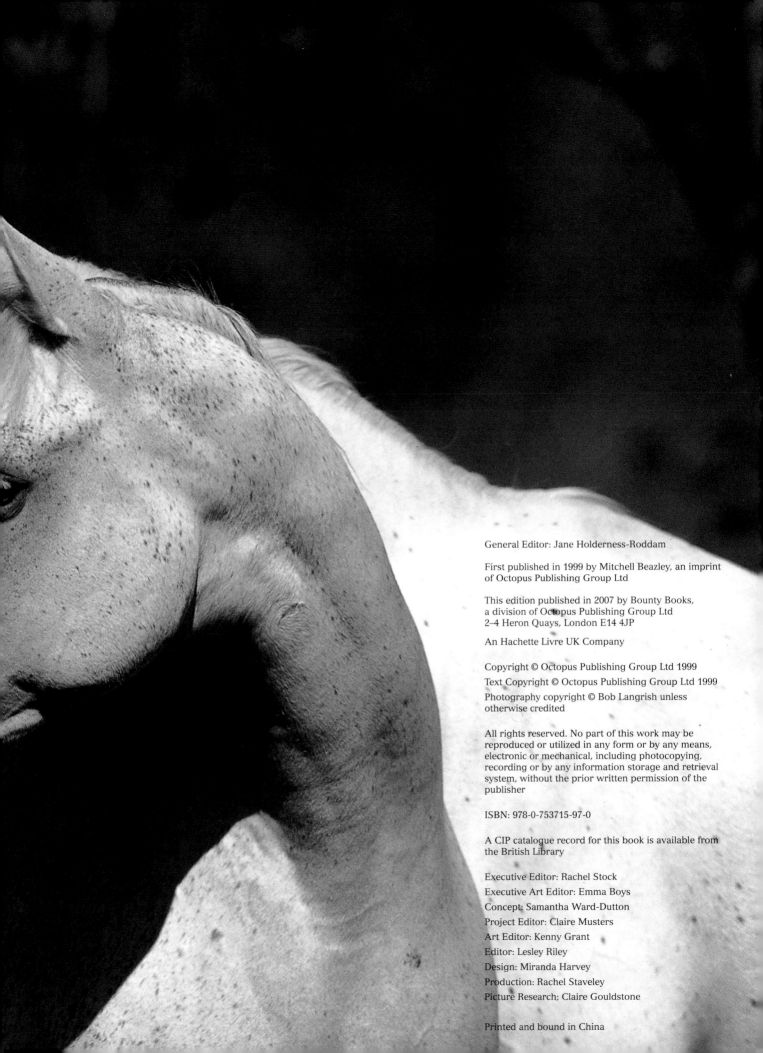

General Editor: Jane Holderness-Roddam

First published in 1999 by Mitchell Beazley, an imprint
of Octopus Publishing Group Ltd

This edition published in 2007 by Bounty Books,
a division of Octopus Publishing Group Ltd
2–4 Heron Quays, London E14 4JP

An Hachette Livre UK Company

ISBN: 978-0-753715-97-0

A CIP catalogue record for this book is available from
the British Library

Executive Editor: Rachel Stock
Executive Art Editor: Emma Boys
Concept: Samantha Ward-Dutton
Project Editor: Claire Musters
Art Editor: Kenny Grant
Editor: Lesley Riley
Design: Miranda Harvey
Production: Rachel Staveley
Picture Research: Claire Gouldstone

Printed and bound in China

Contents

8 **Introduction**
Jane Holderness-Roddam

16 **Understanding Horses**
Susan McBane
18 The evolving horse
20 Essential features
24 Horse needs
30 Interpreting behaviour
36 Education for life
38 A day in the life
of a groom
Nadine Ronan
44 Breaking in a young horse
Jennie Loriston-Clarke

46 **Horse Breeds**
Moira C Harris and Jane Kidd
PONIES
48 Riding Pony
Jane Holderness-Roddam
50 Dales Pony
51 Fell Pony
52 Dartmoor Pony

53 Exmoor Pony
54 New Forest Pony
55 Connemara Pony
56 Shetland Pony
57 Highland Pony
58 Welsh Pony and Cob
60 Haflinger
62 Norwegian Fjord
63 Icelandic Horse
64 Basuto Pony
65 Mongolian Pony
66 Pony of the Americas
68 A day at Pony Club camp
Louisa Brassey
SPORT HORSES
70 Thoroughbred
74 Cleveland Bay
76 Warmbloods
80 French Trotter
82 Selle Français
84 Hanoverian
86 Holstein
88 Oldenburg
90 Westphalian

92 Trakehner
94 Andalusian
96 Friesian
98 Irish Draught
100 Lipizzaner
102 Canadian Horse
104 Appaloosa
106 Morgan
108 Missouri Fox Trotter
110 Mustang
112 Quarter Horse
114 American Saddlebred
116 Standardbred
118 Tennessee Walking Horse
120 Criollo
121 Paso Fino
122 Akhal-Teke
124 Kabardin
125 Orlov Trotter
126 Australian Stock Horse
128 Arabian
132 Barb
134 Palomino
135 Pinto

136 A day in the life of a
physiotherapist
Amanda Sutton
WORK HORSES
138 Clydesdale
140 Shire
142 Suffolk
144 Brabant
146 Ardennes
148 Percheron
150 Dutch Draught
152 A day in the life of
a draught horse
Kevin Flynn

154 Competitive Sports
156 Eventing
Andrew Hoy
166 The three day event
Bettina Overesch
168 Dressage
Bernadette Faurie
174 A dressage lesson
Carl Hester

176 Showjumping
Pamela Carruthers
182 The jump-off
Jos Lansink
184 Racing
Ian Balding
192 A day at the races
Austin Brown
194 Driving
John Richards
202 Western riding
Moira Harris
208 Rodeo
Moira Harris
210 A day at the rodeo
Gavin Ehringer
212 Endurance
Marcy Pavord
216 A vet check at an endurance ride
Tony Pavord
218 Vaulting
Jenny Leggate
220 Polo
Lord Patrick Beresford

224 A day in the life of
a polo pony
Chrissie Kieley
226 Pony Club
Tadzik Kopanski
230 Mounted games
Tadzik Kopanski

**232 Ceremonial and Working
Horses**
Sylvia Stanier
242 A day in the life of
a police horse
Dennis Colton

244 Leisure Activities
Jane Holderness-Roddam
246 Showing
248 Hunting
250 Riding holidays

252 Contributor biographies
and acknowledgements
254 Index

INTRODUCTION

The start of a successful relationship

The horse has been instrumental in developing man's way of life since these two beings first came together many millennia ago. Originally seen as a source of food, the horse evolved over time into a large enough creature for early humans to realize the potential of domestication. The early lives of horses with humans have been variously recorded throughout the ages; many ancient cave paintings, biblical writings, and architectural frieze of early civilizations have given an insight into the great bond between man and horse that has continued to influence our daily lives ever since.

During the later stages of the Ice Age horses were purely a source of food but by 9000 BC humans had begun an agricultural lifestyle, using cattle as pack animals. These were then replaced by horses.

It is generally thought that horses were first tamed in Eurasia at least 6000 years ago. For humans the horse was an ideal choice – it was one of the few animals that was able to survive on a variety of foods, was not migratory, was relatively non-territorial, and understood dominant and submissive relationships. This meant that the nomadic people could herd them wherever they wanted.

A mutual adaption?

It is normally assumed that humans seized upon the opportunity to tame the wild horses that then proved to be so useful to them. However, it is possible that there was a mutual recognition of the compatibility between our species. The animals that spent their time living near human settlements may have gained a lot from the arrangement. Some of them were indeed killed and eaten but many more of them flourished on the human crops and within the protection from other predators that they gained by being near humans.

Horses evolved into suitable animals for domestication a long time before our relationship with them began. Their size, weight, and feeding needs were incredibly adaptable, and they were the only animal of their size and strength without dangerous horns or antlers. It could be seen then that, until we began breeding horses in captivity, our intervention was really minimal, and that it was a natural, mutual need for survival that brought the lives of horses and humans together.

Riding horses into war

No one knows exactly who the first person was who decided to try sitting on a horse, or when that took place, but once tribes had learned to ride horses and got them to carry packs, it made an enormous impact on their lives. Now their speed of mobility was hugely increased and they could reach a much greater range of feeding grounds. This could only be good news for both humans and horses alike.

The domestication of horses spread across the world and for the next 2000 years the horse could be seen as the single most important element in developing the civilized world as it remained the swiftest and most efficient form of transport.

The Egyptians are known to have been using horses to pull chariots as early as 3000 BC. The invention of such wheeled vehicles marked a big change in the relationship of horses and humans. With horse-driven chariots, men could have much greater mobility during battle. Horses helped one people fight and eventually dominate another. This tradition continued with the advent of the cavalry – the Greeks used mounted troops when they expelled the Persians out of their land. It was the notable Greek general, Xenophon, who wrote *The Cavalry Commander*, which shows us just how well the Greeks had mastered the use of cavalry troops.

Breeding horses

The horse's intelligence, and therefore trainability, has allowed this beautiful creature to be developed to fulfil many roles worldwide. Methods of training and breeding spread throughout the ancient world and it was thanks to the observations of such notable trainers as Xenophen that we we now have the foundation of today's teachings.

Breeding began to be directed towards producing the ideal horse for particular roles. Egyptians used horses extensively for transport and, later, for riding as well. The Romans produced specific horses for hunting, racing, war, and work, as well as for parading. For them, the horse also became a political tool – they put on chariot racing displays to divert potentially rebellious people. At all times, the cost of owning and breeding horses has meant that it has been the occupation of the aristocracy. Indeed, throughout history, horses have been seen as status symbols and have often been given as gifts from one royal family to another.

The Renaissance era

Within the Renaissance, more refined methods of training horses were met with enthusiasm and classical equitation became an art form. In the 15th and 16th centuries riding in a school arena became a mandatory part of a gentleman's education. Riding schools were set up throughout Europe and many of their principles are still in use today. The French trainer de la Guérinière wrote *Ecole de Cavaliere*, which became the bible of equitation, and his teaching is still in place at the world-renowned Spanish Riding School in Vienna.

A lot of the movements that were, and still are, practised by such riding schools were derived from those used in war to escape the enemy. Most are based on movements the horse would naturally use to escape trouble.

Breeding for specific purposes

The horse was bred for war in huge numbers to mount large armies, particularly throughout Eurasia, since well before the early crusades. The first great studs (breeding centres) in Europe seem to date from the 12th century and these studs have now turned breeding into an international

Who can resist the enduring qualities of the horse who, even as a foal, can express trust, willingness, intelligence, and beauty.

business. Two centuries ago, breeders were producing general purpose agricultural horses that could also be used as coach horses when necessary. Then, the importance of cavalry and carriage horses increased. After that, the advent of motorized transport in the early 20th century meant that the need for strong carriage horses diminished rapidly. Breeds were then adapted to become the lighter types that are required for general riding and the equestrian sports that were becoming more and more popular.

The age of mechanization

The world's economy depended almost entirely on horsepower right up until the early part of the 20th century. Even today, in some rural parts of the world, it is still an essential backbone to the community's economy.

Even when the Industrial Revolution arrived, working horses did not just disappear. In Britain, horses became an immensely important part of the railway business and railway companies became the biggest employees of horses. Cheaper and more efficient than steam engines, horses were employed to move goods and transport the coal needed to fuel engines. During the same era, horses were used in North America to haul large quantities of timber.

With the population explosion in cities in the 19th century, horses were put to use. They delivered mail and other goods, and also pulled carriages. In an age of pollution and overcrowding, horses were not often treated well and in 1822 British Parliament passed an act to protect animals and ensure they were humanely treated.

Eventually, as electrical devices were invented that could take the place of horses, the need for horse drawn trams, horses as tugs for canal boats on tow paths, and strong heavy horse breeds for agricultural work all but disappeared. They are also no longer needed to pull delivery vehicles in cities that are teeming with motor vehicles. However, in most countries the tourist industry is now a priority and many cities encourage big brewery or transport firms to continue to keep horses as a marketing ploy to demonstrate the historic use of these noble creatures.

Breeding is big business

Due to the changing roles of the horse in society, there is no real need for the many breeds of all shapes and sizes we can find around the world today. Too often there is unnecessary and indiscriminate breeding that results in too many animals with no outlet except the meat market. This is a situation that many of the welfare charities such as the International League for the Protection of Horses (ILPH) are working hard to redress through education and discussion at governmental level when necessary. They arrange and run seminars in cities for those who need help and train the local people to shoe their horses correctly, as well as instructing them in the current, more humane, methods of care.

Throughout the modern world different methods and practices occur in the way horses and ponies are bred, reared, trained, and ridden, and inevitably some of these are controversial. Today horses are used and bred increasingly for sport and leisure. The sport of racing has been well established worldwide for several hundred years. There are generations of Thoroughbreds where selective breeding has been used to increase speed or stamina to win different races.

Breeders of sport horses have also worked hard to produce the best traits to ensure trainability as well as performance. The Warmblood is

Perfect balance is learned as this competition horse is trained indoors to perform in one of the disclplines for which it was specifically bred.

specifically produced to excel in the competitive disciplines – where it now commands enormous prices.

Many breeders have stuck to a strict selective system but others have not and have lost many distinctive features in their horses as a result. A few breeders have experimented with size and colour, some successfully, but others purely for misguided economic reasons. It should be remembered that human interference has not always been to the advantage of the horse and the development of some breeds may in fact just be pandering to the modern craze for wanting something new and different.

The changing face of the sports world
The many sporting activities that involve horses today are now international pastimes and many sport horses are sold worldwide. Thanks to the media and television it is also possible for everyone to enjoy many sports in different countries.

Inevitably there are and always will be casualties and injuries occurring in all sports. The veterinary profession and animal welfare charities spend millions on horse care projects and research on ways to make all sport safer or less stressful. There are numerous areas where huge strides have been made in the treatment and

Traditional agricultural methods are still used in parts of the world but these magnificent heavy horses are competing in a ploughing competition.

care of injuries. They include shoeing, travel, feeding, and fitness exercise. Today's owners have superb facilities and remedial treatments available to them. Both technological advances and the increasing use of natural remedies ensure that their horses perform to the very best of their abilities.

We all have a responsibility to ensure that the horse is understood and properly cared for while we also meet modern expectations and demands. We must resist the temptation to

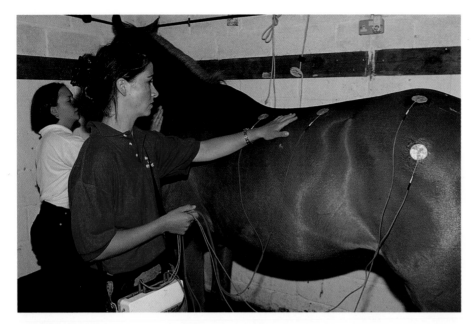

Left: Modern technology ensures today's sport horses benefit from numerous therapies and treatments previously only available to humans.

Right: Concentration and timing play a vital role in the arena, which is where all the hard work and training pays off.

exploit this willing creature in the sporting world where sponsorship opportunities and media and television coverage place huge demands on those running the various activities. What is reasonable and what is exploitation is difficult to define as the domesticated horse responds remarkably well to almost everything it is expected to perform. However, it is important that we do not allow commercialism to continue to dominate the way all equestrian sport is run, as this will inevitably have a detrimental effect on the welfare of the horses involved.

Having said that, top competition horses are probably the best cared for animals in the world but there are still those who would seek to abolish all sport as cruel. Within our very commercial and competitive world perhaps we should consider what the horse itself would prefer – to exist in a paddock to be looked at, fed, and watered, and allowed just enough freedom in a now so restricted world to exist unnaturally but without any exploitation at all? Or should education and understanding of horses' needs be increased to ensure a balance is reached so that horses and all their admirers can still enjoy their talents in the numerous different fields in which they currently enrich our lives?

In my experience horses really enjoy working with humans as long as they are properly understood, given the time to mature and learn whatever they are bred or taught to perform, and are

looked after sensibly. Those familiar with horses cannot ignore the sight of a racehorse proudly entering the winners enclosure after a hard fought finish, the showjumper collecting its sash of honour after a brilliant round, or the winner in the show ring. They know they have done well and revel in the adulation.

Using this book

The Life of Horses is a unique guide to the world of horses and has been written by some of the most eminent international personalities in equestrian circles today. These authors have all been closely involved with their particular subject, and their experience is exceptional; having not only performed themselves in the sports, many are currently involved in the running of them also. It is extremely rare to find so many stars of the horse world writing in a single volume and the book reflects the benefits of their extensive knowledge.

The book firstly explains the evolution of the horse as well as exploring its current needs. It goes on to give detailed information on most of the popular breeds from around the world. The unique qualities of each breed are highlighted and comparisons with other breeds given, and a cross-referencing system will lead you to related subjects in other parts of the book. Most of the breeds we have included are those particularly popular for the sports covered in the book or

are important to their country of origin as a work horse. Many are pony breeds especially suitable for childrens' activities; for each breed you are shown their greatest attributes and uses.

The sports included in the book are the six Federation Equestrian International (FEI) disciplines of dressage, eventing, showjumping, driving, endurance, and vaulting. We have also included racing, polo, Western riding, Pony Club and mounted games, ceremonial and working horses, and leisure riding.

Each of the sports begins with a history, and goes on to look at the scene as it is today, how the sport is run, and what is required of those who wish to participate in it. The special information on key people gives the reader a glimpse of what goes on behind the scenes and how many people are involved.

A further feature of the book is the reportage spreads that give a unique look at the different careers of those who have chosen to work with horses, as well as horses that are involved in specific sports. You can read, for example, about a day in the life of a physiotherapist, what it is like to be a groom, a top showjumper, riding in a jump off, a day at the races, and what it is like to be a police horse. These are just a taster of the exciting articles interspersed throughout the book that will give you an even greater idea of all that is involved in the world of horses.

Horses are a way of life

I first sat on the back of a horse before I could even walk and since then, being with horses has become a way of life for me. I have had the opportunity of learning about horses' remarkable character and the amazing powers of endurance and athletic ability that enable them to perform a wide variety of activities unique to their species. My horses have taken me to the very top competitively, enabling me to experience the exhilaration of winning

at some of the world's most prestigious venues. But more importantly, I have learned the humility necessary to bring out the best in my horses through patient, careful training and to appreciate that without their generosity, co-operation, and ability none of this would have been possible.

As a competitor I learned that it is the partnership and understanding between the horse and human that really make stars. I hope after reading this book you will be able to appreciate a little of what is involved in the many and varied roles with which horses are associated today. Our relationship with horses has survived and developed over the centuries not only because of the knowledge our ancestors passed down to us, but also because of the horse's special adaptability and willingness. It is this unique partnership between horses and humans that we now celebrate here.

Left: Horses are quite competitive and many will try to race one another. These two are well controlled during a training and fitness session.

Below: A charming study of companionship. As horses are herd animals, they are never happier than when they are together.

Understanding Horses

THE EVOLVING HORSE

The ancestors of the modern horse first walked the Earth more than than 50 million years ago. The earliest of these, *Eohippus* – the 'horse from the dawn of time' – evolved into many forms. *Equus*, the family that includes the horse we know today, is the sole survivor of these numerous, now extinct, equines.

Development of the horse family

Eohippus, the so-called Dawn Horse, is also known as *Hyracotherium* because it had a skull like a hare's, and was believed to be related to the small, rabbit-like hyrax. *Eohippus* appeared about 55 million years ago, at the start of the Eocene epoch, in what is now North America.

At that time, the land was mainly swampy, tropical forest. *Eohippus* was about the size of a fox, with a rounded back. Its small teeth were not strong but suitable for browsing – eating the leaves and fruits from trees and bushes. *Eohippus* had four hooved toes on its front feet, and three toes on the back, with a central pad as on a dog's paw.

It was probably timid, escaping predators by hiding in dense undergrowth rather than by running away. Its coat was probably mottled and/or striped, which provided camouflage in the dappled forest light.

FEWER TOES – BIGGER TEETH The horse's next direct ancestors were three-toed browsers. The best known, *Mesohippus*, appeared about 38 million years ago during the Oligocene epoch. *Mesohippus* had the same body shape as *Eohippus* but stood about 60cm (24in) tall at the shoulder. The central toe was bigger and stronger, carrying more weight than the other two. The change was an advantage as the climate became drier and the ground firmer. Grasses were just evolving, and

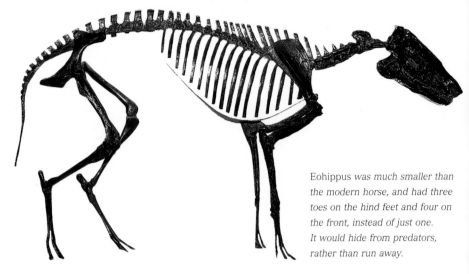

Eohippus *was much smaller than the modern horse, and had three toes on the hind feet and four on the front, instead of just one. It would hide from predators, rather than run away.*

Mesohippus had developed bigger, stronger teeth, too, to deal with the tougher vegetation. *Mesohippus'* habits and temperament were probably much the same as those of *Eohippus*.

A DOUBLE DIET As the Oligocene gave way to the Miocene epoch about 25 million years ago, large grasslands had just begun to form in North America. *Parahippus* appeared about five million years later. It was taller than *Mesohippus* and, with bigger teeth and a bigger, more horse-like head to accommodate its large, strong jaw muscles, it was adapted both to browse on the trees and to graze the new grass. Although the creature still had three toes on each foot, the side toes now bore little weight except in fast gaits – *Parahippus* was a runner with longer legs and a more horse-shaped back than its predecessors. It would have been inclined to run from predators on the developing grassy plains rather than hide among trees. Although its coat colouring would have been plainer, for better camouflage in the open, *Parahippus* was easily visible to predators on the prairie; but for the

species as a whole, there is safety in numbers, and herding instincts would have been developing by now.

THE FIRST GRASS EATERS The next important group among the modern horse's ancestors were the three-toed grazers: *Merychippus* is their main representative, which lived in North America from about 18 million years ago. It had many variants; from it, the immediate ancestor of *Equus*, *Dinohippus*, evolved about 12 million years ago, and survived up to about four million years ago.

These animals were really beginning to look like horses. They stood about a metre (40in) high, and weighed about 200kg (440lb). Their side toes bore none of this weight. They had large, strong teeth that enabled them to grind the tough fibres of grass that formed the main part of their diet.

ENTER EQUUS Finally, about four million years ago, there emerged one-toed grazers. These members of the *Equus* family had specialized, tough, running hooves, a longer neck, and a longer, heavier skull than their forebears, to

PRE	40 MYA		30 MYA		20 MYA		10 MYA		PRESENT

| Eocene (55–38 million years ago) *Eohippus* appeared (55 mya), followed by *Orohippus* (55–47 mya) and *Epihippus* (47–38 mya). | Oligocene (38–24.6 million years ago) *Mesohippus* (38–32 mya), followed by *Miohippus* (35–27 mya). | Miocene (24.6–5.1 million years ago) *Parahippus* (20–12 mya), followed by *Merychippus* (18–12 mya) and *Dinohippus* (12–4 mya). | Pliocene (5.1–2 million years ago) *Equus* appeared (4 mya). | Pleistocene (2 million to 10,000 years ago) Modern species evolved (1 mya). | Recent (10,000 years ago to present) *Equus* domesticated (4000 BC). |

hold strong, grazing teeth and the muscles to power big jaws – and they would have had all the instincts of modern equines. Standing around 1.4m (54in) tall, they would have been about the height of a modern small pony. The *Equus* species we know today – horses, asses and onagers, and zebras – finally emerged about a million years ago.

Spread of horse types

North America is the ancestral home of true horse types. No fossils of animals related to the horse have been found in Australasia, which parted from the Earth's main land mass very early in prehistory. In South America the horse-like *Hippidions* that developed five million years ago had become extinct by about one million years ago. True horse types then migrated south when the Isthmus of Panama was created during land movement.

For millions of years, Europe and Asia were linked to North America by land where the Bering Straits (off Alaska) are today. During the Eocene, *Eohippus* migrated continually over the Bering land bridge to Asia and Europe, followed over millions of years by other horse-like animals, all now extinct. From about three million years ago, there was a huge migration from North America of *Equus* itself, and it became abundant in both New and Old worlds.

Two momentous events occurred just before the end of the Pleistocene – the arrival of humans in the Americas about 15,000 years ago, followed by the disappearance of the horse from its birthplace. The reasons for this extinction are not clear. Possibly, hunters reduced the population beyond hope of recovery; perhaps, too, climatic changes at the end of the last Ice Age left the horse unable to adapt to feed on the changing vegetation. By then, the land bridges over which *Equus* had migrated were below sea level. The Americas were not repopulated

Horses from cold climates, like the Norwegian Fjord, evolved features to help retain heat – long, thick coat, bushy mane and tail, and short limbs.

The zebra has retained its camouflage stripes and some horse breeds with ancient origins show evidence of this on their legs to this day.

with horses until the conquistadores arrived in the late 15th century.

Equus flourished in Eurasia and Africa, however, evolving into horses in Asia and Europe, asses in Africa and Asia, onagers in Asia around present-day Iran and Iraq, and zebras in Africa.

UNEVEN EVOLUTION

Evolutionists long thought that plants and animals evolved gradually and steadily, over eons of time. Since the 1970s, however, many have recognized that this smooth progress can be interrupted and altered by chance events. Unpredictable happenings – such as changes in climate, famine, or an increase in predation by animals and humans – have wiped out many families of horse-like animals that, like *Equus*, have *Eohippus* as a distant common ancestor. *Equus* itself died out in North America only 10,000 years ago.

The survival of *Equus* was not a forgone conclusion. During the late Miocene era, for instance, as many as 16 different families of horses were thriving at the same time, some browsing, some grazing, and with various numbers of toes. Of these animals, only *Dinohippus*, *Equus*' immediate ancestor, did not become extinct. And only through good fortune did *Equus* survive into the modern world. Some 6000 years ago, the horse population was reduced to a few thousand, eking out an existence on the Asian steppes as the grasslands shrank before the renewed march of forest. Then, in the Ukraine, a tribe of hunters adopted and domesticated wild horses. Within 2000 years, they were once again everywhere in Europe and Asia. Rescued from the brink of oblivion, today's horses number 60 million worldwide.

ESSENTIAL FEATURES

Although the horse, as a mammal, follows the basic design of all mammals and other vertebrates, it evolved certain physical features ideally suited for its life on the high plains and steppes. Its specialities are lightning standing starts to escape sudden danger, speed, stamina, and the ability to rest, and even sleep, standing up.

The legs

The legs, particularly in breeds noted for speed such as Arabians, Akhal-Tekes, and Thoroughbreds, are proportionately long and light relative to the body size. There are no muscles below the knee and hock, and the feet are fairly small and light, particularly in fast types. Muscle is heavy, so the nearer it is to the source of movement (the shoulder and hip), and the less weight there is to be moved in those parts moving furthest (the lower limb), the faster the horse can go with the least energy consumption.

The horse's legs are so long because it is standing virtually on the tips of its toes: the horse's knee equates to our wrist, and the hock to our ankle. The legs are supported by long ligaments and tendons, as taut as cello strings when the horse is standing; these provide a slight elastic recoil when the leg and foot bear weight, which helps to propel it forwards and saves a little energy, as well as absorbing some concussion. There are 'pulley' or sesamoid bones in the stifle, lower legs, and feet over which the tendons run, making their movement easier and the tissues less prone to wear.

THE HOOF Rather like our own toenails, the horse's hooves protect the delicate structure of the foot from injury. The horn of the hoof grows from the coronet down, and it takes roughly a year to grow from coronet to ground at the toe. Regular trimming is essential as many horses' feet have rather poor horn that becomes soft in the often moist conditions of the domestic paddock, and tends to crack on hard, rough ground. Working on roads also

POINTS OF THE HORSE

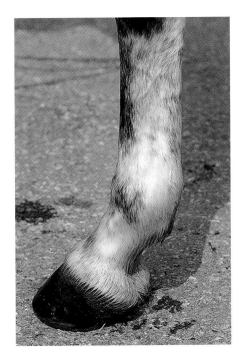

Balanced anatomy of the legs and feet is most important for the modern sport horse, to enable it to withstand the rigours of competition.

wears the hooves, leaving the horse footsore, hence the need for shoeing.

THORACIC SLING Unlike humans the horse has no shoulder joint or collar bone. The ribcage is supported between the shoulder blades and humerus (the bone above the elbow) by soft tissue such as ligament, connective tissue, and muscle, in a system popularly called the thoracic sling. Each time weight is borne by the forehand – as the horse's forelegs land following a stride or jump – this sling of soft but firm tissue absorbs the jar. At fast gaits, therefore, this saves the horse from a good deal of concussion.

HIP JOINT The horse's hip joint (deep inside the hindquarters and not the 'point of hip' normally shown on diagrams of the points of the horse, which is actually part of the pelvis) is an elongated version of a ball and socket joint, made to move the leg mainly in a forwards–backwards plane.

Although horses can obviously move their hind legs sideways to a small extent, they can suffer considerable discomfort if forced to hold a leg flexed and sideways for long periods, such as during shoeing. A considerate farrier will allow the horse to keep its leg

beneath it and, particularly with older horses, allow it frequent rests.

When transported facing the direction of travel, horses habitually spread their hind legs for balance. This unnatural stance significantly stresses the muscles and other soft tissues of the hindquarters, and is very uncomfortable for the horse. Scientific studies show that it can result in a build up of lactic acid (a toxin that causes pain and tiredness) in the muscles, in quantities equivalent to those present after a fast sprint – and this is before the horse even begins to work. Many horses seem to find it easier to travel sideways, across the horsebox, or backwards, tail to the engine.

STAY APPARATUS The horse has a crucial adaptation that enables it to rest and sleep, quite relaxed, while standing up, usually resting one hind leg at a time, with joints flexed, and weight on the toe. It has been shown that a horse uses about 10 per cent less energy standing up than when lying flat out.

A 'locking' system of bones, ligaments, and muscles fixes the elbow, knee, and stifle in place so that the leg can support the horse's weight without using the muscles. This means that the horse can remain on its feet, ready to flee in an instant should danger wake it, without expending any energy. Once on the move, the horse can reach its top speed – of about 70kmph (45mph) – in less than five seconds.

The senses
The horse's five senses are differently attuned from ours, to suit the circumstances in which it evolved – as a prey animal on open grassland.

HEARING The ears move, often independently, in an almost 180° arc, picking up sounds from all around. Most horses become disturbed or distressed in noisy environments.

SIGHT The eyes, placed high up on the sides of the head, give the horse virtually all-round vision, with two small blind spots, immediately in front and behind. Horses prefer dim light to darkness, and research suggests that they have limited colour vision, probably seeing reds and blues very well, but other colours less distinctly.

TASTE Horses have taste buds (sensor cells) on the tongue, palate, and in the throat. They can detect sweet and salt (which they like) and bitter and sour (which they do not). Horses are usually suspicious of new tastes, which is one reason why any changes in diet should always be made gradually.

SMELL Strange-smelling foods often put a horse off eating. Horses use smell to identify and bond with one another, as well as with people.

TOUCH Nerve endings in the skin detect pressure, pain, irritation, heat, and cold. The horse is extremely sensitive to touch and can feel something as light as a fly landing on its side.

The vibrissae, or coarse whiskers around the muzzle and eyes, are important 'feelers' for horses, enabling them to judge distance and texture, and it is a peculiarity of many horse owners to clip them off for the show ring. When they are removed the horse sometimes goes off its food and may become temporarily headshy. More enlightened owners leave these whiskers on, and a growing number of equestrian organizations are forbidding their removal in show animals.

The coat
Different breeds have different types of coat, depending on the region in which they developed. Those that evolved in hot areas of the world have short, fine coats, which facilitate heat loss, and those that evolved in cold climates have long, thick coats, which retain heat. The length of the coat also varies from season to season.

The hairs of the coat have tiny erector muscles at their root, which raise the hairs when the horse is cold, trapping an insulating layer of air next to the skin. The longer the hairs, the greater the overlap between them and the thicker the warm-air layer. In hot weather, the hairs lie flat, reducing the thickness of the warm-air layer and allowing heat to pass more easily from the body to keep the horse cool.

The long winter coat is cast in late winter or spring, and replaced by the shorter summer coat, cast in autumn, so that the horse is always equipped with a suitable coat for the time of year. If moved to cold regions, 'hot-blooded',

fine-skinned horses grow a slightly thicker coat than they would in their natural environment, but never as long and thick as those indigenous to a cold region, such as British native ponies.

CLIPPING Long-coated horses retain more body heat and sweat more than those with a short coat, which is why horses in work are normally at least partly clipped in winter. However, there is no scientific or practical evidence that horses are harmed or 'sweat off condition' by not being clipped.

MANE AND TAIL The hairs of the mane and tail come out more easily in spring and autumn, but are not cast like the coat hair (with occasional breed exceptions such as the Bashkir). The mane and forelock help protect the horse against flies, and the tail is particularly useful since it can be flicked easily at flies all over the back half of the body.

Digestive system

The horse's digestive system is geared to processing low-nutrient, high-fibre foods (quite opposite to the diet many receive) and to have a little food passing through it most of the time.

The food is chewed very thoroughly, with repeated sweeps of the jaws, before being passed to the stomach, where it is pummelled by the muscular walls, and acid digestive juices, enzymes, and a few microbes start to break it down. From here it passes into the small intestine, which is where the concentrated part of the feed (grain and cubes or nuts) is digested, and the nutrients absorbed through its walls.

It is in a section of the large intestine called the caecum that the vital fibre portion of the horse's diet (usually grass, hay, or haylage) is broken down. Billions of micro-organisms living here process the food into a form the horse can readily digest. The fermentation that takes place in the caecum is comparable to the rumination of cattle and sheep, but in these animals the process takes place earlier in the system and is much more efficient than in the horse.

The horse is notoriously fussy about the grass it eats, often overgrazing one area of a field and leaving another untouched.

The horse's digestive system is also very sensitive, and digestive disorders in domestic horses fed inappropriately (with too much concentrated food, insufficient fibre, and erratic, widely spaced feeding times) are very common. A particular 'black spot' is a narrow turning point in the large intestine, which can be prone to blockages if horses are fed too much indigestible fibre (such as straw, poor quality hay, or coarse, dry grass).

THE TEETH Because the horse's top jaw is wider than the bottom one, the chewing action can result in sharp edges and hooks on the back teeth, both top and bottom, which can injure the mouth. Many problems can be traced back to a failure to accept the bit because of a sore mouth. Every horse should have its teeth checked by a vet or equine dentist at least once a year, more often for young and old animals.

Reproduction

The horse's reproductive cycle is almost exclusively controlled by day length. Females come into season in early spring, a few weeks after the brain detects an increase in the hours of daylight, and, once their newly awakened hormones have settled down, they are in season roughly every three weeks until autumn.

Foals conceived in one year are born in spring or summer the following year, when the weather is usually kind and the grass rich, providing nourishment during the most nutritionally demanding time for the mare – the last three months of pregnancy and the first three months of lactation.

Many fillies and mares become moody, more sensitive, 'difficult', and distracted when they are in season. Some become much more affectionate towards everyone – horses, other animals, and humans alike. Allowances must be made for this natural behaviour, and owners who cannot tolerate it would be better off buying a gelding. Gelding male horses normally makes them less 'sharp' and easier to handle, as well as less inclined to nip and bite; but it does not, in many cases, entirely remove stallion-like instincts. Geldings are, however, easier for owners who keep their horse at livery, as many yards will not accept stallions.

Below, from the top: The mouth of a young foal, the teeth of a seven-year-old, and the longer, sloping teeth of an elderly horse (aged 20 plus) are examined.

DENTITION
AT A MONTH OLD foals have four temporary incisor teeth and six temporary premolars in each jaw and can start nibbling solid food. By nine months, two more temporary incisors appear in each jaw, with the first pair of permanent molars.
BETWEEN 2 AND 4 YEARS the temporary teeth are gradually shed. By five years, all permanent teeth are mature, with each jaw having six incisors, six premolars, and six molars and, in males, two tushes or canines.
UP TO EIGHT YEARS the flat surfaces of the incisors carry a changing dark pattern, which helps to determine the age of the horse.
AS HORSES AGE the incisors lengthen, slope forwards, and become prism shaped. At about 10 years, a brown vertical groove (Galvayne's groove) appears on each of the upper corner incisors, next to the gum. At 15, it is halfway down the tooth, at 20 it reaches the bottom; at 25 it is no longer visible on the upper half, and by 30 has disappeared altogether.

HORSE NEEDS

A horse's personal wants are reasonable and simple. It wants to be physically comfortable and mentally content – and that is it.

Physical comfort depends on protection from the elements, lack of hunger and thirst, freedom of movement, and lack of prolonged pain, discomfort, or sickness. Mental contentment results partly from feeling physically comfortable and partly from feeling safe, which involves social acceptance and space.

PROTECTION FROM THE ELEMENTS
Although horses evolved as 'outdoor' animals, many show clearly that they do not want to be exposed to extremes of weather.

Horses and ponies are of different types, from the thin-skinned, fine-haired 'hot bloods' to thick-skinned, woolly coated 'cold bloods'. All, however, use natural or artificial shelter when they need to – as long as they are not frightened off by, say, a bullying herd mate, a muddy or stony approach to the shelter, or a small, dark entrance or interior, if a shed.

In summer, most animals seek out shade to escape prolonged hot sunshine and will find the breezier, cooler spots where there will also be fewer flies. We can help keep insects at bay with the judicious use of fly repellents, by not over-pulling (thinning) the mane and tail, and by fitting a fly fringe to the headcollar.

In winter, horses love cold, dry, still days and playing in fresh snow; they detest wind, rain, sleet, hail, and prolonged snow. The places they choose for sheltering often become seriously muddy or 'poached', which can bring on sore, infected legs (mud fever or scratches). While a waterproof turnout rug can help to keep the horse warm and dry, it is no substitute for an effective field shelter, or for being able to get back to the stable.

All horses that are left out for more than a few hours at a time need a shed or barn into which they can escape, unless the natural shelter and ground conditions are exceptionally good.

LACK OF HUNGER AND THIRST In nature, a horse's food is all around. The animal eats for many hours a day, and feelings of hunger are not only unnatural but also dangerous.

Most feeding problems in domestic horses occur in those stabled and, particularly, those whose fibre intake is rationed. Although the nutrients a horse needs can be supplied in concentrated feeds (grain or pellets) and supplements, these do not provide that satisfied, 'full up' feeling, occupy the mind as foraging does, or fulfil the horse's known psychological need to chew for long periods.

High-nutrient forage feeds (usually based on alfalfa or lucerne), good quality hay or haylage, soaked sugar–beet pulp (which is high in both nutrients and fibre), and other succulents (if grass is unavailable) can provide much of a working horse's nutritional requirement without overloading it with concentrates, or causing hunger because of insufficient fibre. They should also be liberally fed to outdoor horses when grass is scarce.

Plenty of clean water should always be available. Hard-working horses, especially in hot weather, can consume up to about 55 litres (12 gal) of water a day, and in normally comfortable weather will need around half to two thirds of this amount, depending on the individual. If the container is often nearly empty when checked, the horse is not being given enough. If you use an automatic watering system, check at least twice daily that it is clean and working properly.

Natural water sources such as ponds or streams are nowadays often polluted by fertilizers and pesticides; if you want to use them, it is important to have the quality of the water checked regularly, to be sure that it is safe to drink.

FREEDOM OF MOVEMENT There is no question that stabled horses need more than the daily two hours' exercise or less that most receive. Exercise is crucial to good health and body function and every effort should be made to devise ways of exercising stabled (and so very restricted) horses in addition to their normal work.

Turning out two or more ideally on grass, or a surfaced manège if hay is also supplied, will keep them moving and eating for several hours. A horse can be led from another being ridden, long-reined, round lanes and tracks, led out in hand, or put on a mechanical horse walker. Lungeing can provide extra exercise, but should always be

All horses need exercise and periods of freedom. If they are unable to be turned out into a field, an area such as this will be a welcome alternative.

done on large circles or ovals, mainly at a brisk walk. Many people, when lungeing, do not let the rein out fully, forcing the horse to move in stressful, small circles; they also do too much work at trot.

Look for spare areas around the premises that can be made into 'play pens' so that horses can be allowed extra movement with little expenditure of owners' resources.

LACK OF PAIN, DISCOMFORT, OR SICKNESS Lameness and colic are probably the most common causes of pain in domestic horses, both often being the result of work and poor management. It is the owner's responsibility to summon veterinary help in such cases, to devise with the vet a programme of good management and preventative medicine and, if problems persist, to change the horse's regime and work.

Owners should accept the vet's advice if he or she believes a horse will be in severe, prolonged pain or discomfort, to the point where the quality of life is seriously reduced. If, after a thorough and honest assessment, the vet feels that euthanasia is truly in the horse's best interests, this should be carried out humanely at the horse's home.

SOCIAL ACCEPTANCE This is critical to the peace of mind of most horses and ponies. Sadly, many live alone and although they may appear to be alright, when ultimately given congenial company the difference in their demeanour and general health is usually appreciable. Although horses do pal up with animals of other species, there is nothing like another horse or pony for instilling a feeling of real contentment and security.

There is no better way of burning off a little extra energy than a spell in a paddock. It must be safely fenced and free of dangerous objects.

Throwing a newcomer straight into an established herd is asking for trouble; it will almost certainly be rejected immediately and possibly injured, and after this perceived intrusion, the herd will take a long time to accept the new member, if indeed they ever really do so.

The best way to introduce an animal to the herd (however small) is to stable the new horse next to a friendly herd member, introduce them in hand, perhaps ride them together, then turn them loose together before gradually introducing others into the field. This way, the newcomer will already have one friend in the herd, and so will be much more readily accepted by the others. Companions should be chosen

carefully: boisterous youngsters, for instance, will not be suitable herd mates for frail pensioners.

Bullies and aggressors should be removed from the main bunch to avoid injury and to promote peace and calm. Watch your herd carefully to see what the real relationships among individuals are.

SPACE Domestic equines tend to be desperately short of space. Most of us do not have many acres of land, but reasonable turnout space is vital to under-worked leisure horses, which usually spend far too much time stabled. Studies indicate that they are most relaxed in fields of 4 hectares

(10 acres) or more – although any open space is better than nothing.

Research shows that, ideally, horses should have stables of not less than about 4m (15ft) square. This is because horses' 'personal space', into which they permit friends of various species, extends to roughly 3m (10ft) around them; they feel threatened if this space is invaded by any non-accepted being (a fact that some trainers use as a means of dominating the horse).

Few horses have stables as large as this so, for their contentment, they should be stabled only next to accepted colleagues. Unfriendly neighbours will adversely affect a horse's mental and physical health. Despite partitions, each

Mineral and salt licks are often valuable additions to a paddock, especially if grass is in short supply or of poor quality.

will be aware of the other's presence, and the invisible boundary will constantly be breached.

Horses feel safest when they have an all-round, distant view, so – again ideally – stables should have an open aspect, with more than one outlook.

From the human point of view

As well as meeting horses' immediate personal needs, owners must attend to a number of other factors that contribute to their horses' longer-term, overall well-being.

GROOMING Horses groom themselves and each other naturally, by rolling, rubbing themselves on hedges, trees, and fence posts, and scraping each other with their teeth. Outdoor horses are obviously rained on and their coats, although dirty compared to those of stabled horses, are usually healthy, unless skin parasites get a hold.

Working, stabled horses are groomed and often washed to remove the excessive grease and dried sweat that otherwise accumulates in their coats. Washing with shampoos should not be overdone as this can remove natural oils, resulting in dry, itchy skin and a dull coat. Clear water is often enough. In cold weather, horses should be dried thoroughly, particularly the lower legs and heels. If allowed to remain wet, the skin can become chapped and prone to infection, particularly in horses with white socks and pink skin beneath.

Grooming brushes should be washed often and each horse have its own to prevent the spread of skin disease. If a rug or blanket is worn to help keep the horse clean or protect it from the elements, this should be very regularly laundered and not allowed to become caked with grease, hair, and muck, which can cause skin irritations.

FARRIERY Part of grooming involves picking debris out of the feet at least twice daily and certainly before and after each ride. The application of ordinary hoof oils is not now advised as they can hamper the natural permeability of the horn, making it either soft or brittle.

Shoes should be checked daily for fit, wear, and whether they are coming loose. Most horses working on hard, rough ground, or high-performance horses needing extra purchase or the facility to fit studs, need trimming and shoeing roughly every six weeks. Those working on smooth or soft surfaces may not need shoes, but will need expert trimming to maintain comfort and balance.

MANURE Piles of droppings and soiled bedding attract flies, which lay eggs that develop into more flies. Flies

Many horses will pair up for a back scratch when out at grass. This is especially appreciated when the coat is changing and feeling itchy.

greatly irritate horses and some bite them, causing swellings and infected sores, jarred legs and broken feet as a result of galloping in desperate attempts to escape them, and inflamed, even ulcerated eyes. Many horses suffer untold misery due to 'fly strike' several months of the year.

In stables and barns, rotting manure gives off ammonia, a toxic gas that irritates the mucous membranes of the respiratory system, making the horse prone to infection and causing foot disease.

Horses should certainly not be made to live among their own excreta so its removal from stables and shelters is a matter of basic hygiene. Stabled horses should, ideally, be mucked out fully every day, although many working owners keep their horses on semi-deep litter, topping up with fresh bedding daily and mucking out at weekends. A few still use full deep litter, mucking out completely only every few months, although this system is now out of favour with many vets unless in exceptionally well-ventilated buildings.

Removing droppings from paddocks at least every two or three days greatly helps to prevent infestation with intestinal parasites.

Drying off the legs when the horse comes in from the field helps to prevent mud fever, a bacterial infection that causes painful eczema-like scabs.

GRASSLAND CARE Good grassland management can cut significant sums off your feed bills, amounting to much more than the cost of care and fertilizing. Weeds should be removed and herbs sown and nurtured along with a mixture of palatable grasses, so the horses can enjoy a naturally wide variety of food. Devise a paddock-rotation programme so that land can be used and rested in turn; all grazing areas should be rested for a continuous period of six months in each 12, with three as an absolute minimum.

The programme starts with two to four weeks' walking, depending on the level of fitness ultimately required. Start with 30 minutes a day, four to six days a week, increasing to about two hours' brisk walking at the end of the initial period. Introduce two five-minute spells of trotting after this, increasing to two or three of about 10 minutes by the end of, say, the fifth week. Then you can start careful canters and easy jumping, so by the end of the sixth or seventh week the horse can canter easily for 15 minutes twice per session.

Such a programme can be continued on the same lines, with the rider using common sense to introduce longer canters, more difficult jumping, and fast work up to 12 or even 16 weeks, if required. By this time you should have a horse that is fit enough for a three day event! To maintain any level of fitness, simply reduce the work slightly.

VETERINARY CARE Whether you prefer mainstream medicine, complementary medicine, or a combination of the two, your vet can be a tremendous asset to the well-being of your horses and your peace of mind. He or she will devise a health maintenance programme including vaccinations, worming, and an annual check-up, perhaps with an equine blood profile to monitor your horses' state of health.

The vet will also keep you up to date on the recommended contents of your first-aid cupboard. All owners must know how to tell when a horse is off-colour or actually sick or injured, should know how to apply general first

A good relationship with your vet is invaluable, enabling him to get to know your horse as an individual, and give it the best possible care.

aid, how to check temperature, pulse, and respiration rate, and be willing to call the vet when needed.

FITNESS AND FEEDING FOR ATHLETES Most leisure horses cannot be described as working athletes. Indeed, most do not receive enough exercise even to keep them healthily fit. Perhaps owners do not realize just how much work a horse can do, indeed that it needs to do in order to remain mentally content and essentially healthy.

Feral horses are known to cover about 25–40km (15–25 miles) daily; horses who spend most of their time in generous domestic paddocks cover roughly the same. A two-hour active hack can put 15km (10 miles) under a horse's hooves, and half a day's hunting rather more. There is much to be said for owners spending less time on yard chores and more on giving the horse what it really needs and enjoys – exercise and work.

BASIC FITNESS PROGRAMME It usually takes about six weeks for a horse to progress from being completely 'soft' (unfit) to becoming what is called half fit (when it will be suitable for showing, half a day's hunting, half an hour's schooling or instruction, easy jumping, an organized pleasure ride, or a couple of hours' hacking).

INTERVAL TRAINING This is usually introduced after the first six weeks of the fitness programme, or from the start of trot work. It involves repeated short spells of work, between which the horse recovers almost to its pre-work, warmed-up pulse rate. Because the body is only slightly more stressed each time, it is believed, the horse does not experience the greater stress associated with traditional high-level training, and so becomes fit quicker with less risk of injury. The system relies on constant pulse-rate monitoring.

Start interval training by covering a stretch of ground, at least 400m (1300ft) long and as straight as possible, twice in a brisk, controlled trot, with a three minute walk on a long rein in between. Each stint may take about 90 seconds depending on your horse's natural speed. Check the pulse rate, then walk for 10 minutes, and check the rate again, by which time it should be back to its warm-up level of 60–80 beats per minute if the horse is fit enough for this level of work. If so, add a third stint next training session (which should be four days later) and build up from there. Once you start interval training in canter, your horse should cover the distance in about a minute.

Regular exercise is essential to the horse's well-being and fitness. All conditioning work must follow a strict routine and build up gradually.

FEEDING FOR FITNESS

Weigh your horse from a starting condition where you can easily feel but not see its ribs. Use a weigh tape or weighbridge. Branded feeds are easiest to use as they usually state their energy levels in megajoules (MJ) of digestible energy (DE) on the analysis panel. The following are suggested rations for a Warmblood or Thoroughbred:

LIGHT WORK Feed 2–2.5 per cent of body weight daily. Energy 8–8.5MJ of DE per kg; protein 8 per cent; fibre:concentrate ratio 75:25, if concentrates needed.

MODERATE WORK Feed 2.5 per cent of body weight daily. Energy up to 10MJ of DE per kg; protein 8.5 per cent; fibre:concentrate ratio 75:25 to 65:35.

HARD OR FAST WORK Feed 3 per cent of body weight daily, possibly adding oil to the diet. Energy 12–13MJ of DE per kg; protein 8.5 per cent; fibre:concentrate ratio 65:35 to 50:50 minimum.

INTERPRETING BEHAVIOUR

Certain aspects of a horse's behaviour are instinctive, programmed into its genes in the course of evolution. These are fundamental to the horse's existence – even after thousands of years of domestication.

Herd instinct

The modern horse's earliest ancestor, *Eohippus,* was a timid, solitary animal. Its best defence against predators was to hide in the forest that then covered much of the northern hemisphere (where *Eohippus* originated). This habit of hiding in fear created an essentially wary nature, and a few horses still hide from danger when they can.

As the Earth's climate changed, the forest gave way to more open plains, where hiding places were few and far between. For most herbivorous, running animals like the primeval horse, herd living was found to be far safer than a solitary existence.

Predators tend to find the presence of several potential meals in one place, milling around, or galloping headlong, very confusing; and this, combined with a speed well matched to that of the predator, makes for a good survival rate among hunted animals. Moreover, if you are one of many, there is always the chance that another victim will be chosen – not you. Herd living benefits the species, too: since predators usually take the slowest, weakest individuals from the group, only the stronger, fitter animals survive and pass on their genes to future generations.

Living in herds in this way gave horses their strong instinct to be in the company of others, preferably of their own kind, which remains with them today. Some domestic horses refuse to leave a stable yard without other horses, or need a lead from another horse over an obstacle or difficult ground. If left alone, some race around the field or stable, calling worriedly for others; they may sweat profusely, and refuse to eat.

Flight-or-fight instinct

This is very familiar to most horse people. Because horses are prey animals they are constantly alert to

danger and ready to run at the first sign of trouble. This does not mean that they are nervous wrecks, just that most tend to be easily startled – by real or imagined danger.

If a horse is frightened when in an enclosed space, it may crash through fences, into trees or buildings, or simply charge round the stable with complete disregard for any human in there too. If restrained when frightened or, indeed, frightened by restraint, a horse will struggle violently, biting and kicking if need be, trying to get away. As an average riding horse weighs around half a tonne and is unbelievably strong, it is obvious that no mere human can hold a horse when it is in such a state.

Equines survive predation in the wild fairly well, most predators being successful in only about one attempt in four. If a predator (such as a leopard or mountain lion, wolf, or dingo) is detected about 20m (65ft) away, the horse's lightning standing start and ability to reach top sprinting speed of around 70kmph (45mph) – slightly above the top speed of most predators – in three or four seconds will mean it should remain safely out of reach. So staying alert pays off.

The qualities we prize in horses – speed, stamina, and toughness – are the very ones that they evolved to survive in the wild.

Eating habits

The most obvious behavioural trait of the horse that remains from its life in the wild is its wanting to eat almost constantly. Because its natural diet is high-fibre, sometimes high-moisture but usually low-nutrient vegetation, an animal this big needs to eat a lot of food to obtain enough nourishment, and this takes a long time. Horses evolved to eat for around 16 hours a day and they do this, if they can, regardless of the nutrient level of the food. Eating its natural diet for this long nourishes and satisfies the horse, and keeps it mentally occupied.

In their wild state horses will tend to remain with the herd. Those seen out on their own can generally be expected to be unwell or injured.

Stallions can be very territorial, and may be extremely aggressive towards other males invading their perceived territory.

In domestic circumstances, specifically when individually stabled and fed a cereal-based diet with restricted roughage, horses can suffer not only digestive disorders but also psychological distress caused by excess energy, unnatural hunger, deprivation of chewing action, and boredom.

It is bad management to supply the horse with enough nutrients for its needs without also ensuring it feels replete and is occupied mentally in selecting and chewing a range of fibrous feeds for much of its time.

Most nutritionists recommend that fibre (from grass, hay, haylage, fodder straws, or forage feed) should form at least 50 per cent of the diet, even for fit equine athletes, and some advise not less than two-thirds fibre.

Today, with our choice of high-nutrient forage feeds, we should be able to provide a more natural diet even for high-performance horses. Turning competition horses out to grass for several hours daily, a real taboo in some yards, is now possible without giving them heavy bellies to haul around. A few commercial seed companies now market mixes of grasses with relatively low protein and low sugar, but with highly digestible cellulose (fibre), and these complement rather than interfere with the diet of a competition horse.

These improvements in equine feeding can help all horses, including hard-working ones, to lead more natural, comfortable lives – and this can only be good for all concerned.

Life in the herd

The traditional idea of a 'normal' herd of feral horses (there are no truly wild horses left) is a mature stallion, as many as four or five adult mares, their female offspring, and their pre-pubertal male offspring. The stallion is regarded as being in charge, deciding where to graze and rest, when to move on, who enters or stays in his herd, and who leaves. He is also supposed to protect his herd from predators and from other stallions wanting to 'steal' females.

Observations made by scientists and other 'horse watchers' suggest that, in reality, things are rather different.

Herds usually consist of fairly small groups of females plus their young offspring. There is usually a stallion with each herd but he is by no means always the 'boss'. The core of the herd comprises the females, who form strong bonds for life unless they are abducted by another stallion or leave voluntarily to join another band.

Stallions usually hold sway for only a few years. While a colt may reach puberty at around 12 months of age, he will not be strong enough to defeat a mature stallion and take over his herd for another few years, unless the stallion is ailing. (The colt may, however, sneak in the odd mating with a mare if the stallion is not looking.) One researcher described the stallion as a 'lodger' and the females as 'permanent residents' in the herd. Interestingly, it is not known for a herd to reject a new stallion after a successful take-over bid, but feral stallions and 'resident' mares have been known to refuse to accept new mares into their herds.

Males are often ousted from a herd when they reach puberty. They then join roaming bachelor bands, making attempts during the mating season to form harems of their own or to steal another stallion's. It is not unknown, however, for some stallions to tolerate a sexually mature male on the fringes of their herd if they regard him as no threat. Some, but not all, stallions also reject their post-pubertal fillies.

The herd's true decision-maker appears to be a senior mare. While a stallion will herd his harem away from other males, decisions about whether to move on to find fresh grazing and water, finding shelter, and good ground for resting, and so on, seem usually to be made by the matriarch.

Stallions do not protect their families from predators, although they may try to drive the herd away. A mare will usually defend her foal, but other horses are left to fend for themselves.

HERD HIERARCHY The issue of 'herd hierarchy' or 'dominance' is a favourite topic among 'horse watchers'. Feral

Group living is ideal for foals as they can eat, sleep, and play together and, later on, be weaned with the minimum amount of trauma.

Horses, especially youngsters, enjoy the company of other animals. However, they may chase or strike out at dogs if they run.

horses seem to show little evidence of a strong herd hierarchy other than normal tolerance and disciplining from older horses and the submission and respect shown by youngsters. However, the existence of a hierarchy within some domestic herds cannot be denied. Perhaps stress-related friction and contests for dominance arise in domestic horses because they are usually kept in relatively small fields and in stables, and also have their diets and social lives controlled. The fact that their exercise is often severely restricted may also contribute.

Body language

Horses are not particularly vocal animals: they do use sounds, but their main means of communication is body language, often the merest hint of a position or expression.

TAIL Mood and intention are indicated by the tail. A high-held tail generally indicates superiority, excitement, and interest. If the tail is held low but relaxed, so is the horse. In action, a relaxed, swinging tail indicates a horse physically and mentally comfortable with its work and rider. A tail clamped down between the buttocks, however, can indicate anger and stubbornness. If it is being thrashed around, this means the horse is greatly distressed or angry.

EARS The direction of the horse's attention is reflected in the way the ears point. They tend to be pricked forwards if the horse is startled, or has noticed something of interest. When flattened hard back they indicate concentration or aggression (particularly if the head is lowered,

with the muzzle pointing outwards, and angry eyes). One ear forwards and one back shows the animal's attention is divided. Both relaxed sideways is a sign of calmness, dozing, or sickness.

NOSTRILS If the nostrils are wrinkled upwards, the horse is in pain or distress, or may be angry; when flared out into a circle they indicate excitement, fear, or curiosity.

PAWING A horse that paws the ground hard with the front feet tends to be distressed or irritated. However, foals and youngsters often use their front feet to explore strange objects or to attract the attention of their dam or another horse that is lying down.

MOUTHING Foals and yearlings can often be seen snapping their mouths open and shut when in the presence of a senior horse. This means the youngster is submissive, inviting acceptance, and

asking not to be hurt. Mares in season can also sometimes be seen mouthing to stallions.

FLEHMEN When a horse raises its head high and curls up its top lip showing its teeth, it is investigating some unusual or particularly attractive smell. Curling the lip partly closes off the nostrils, trapping the odour in the nasal passages where it can then be assessed by what is known as the Jacobson's organ. Stallions nearly always perform *flehmen* when presented with a mare in season; youngsters do it often when exploring their surroundings.

Communication with others

Horses use the same language whatever species of creature they are 'talking' to – the same flick of an ear,

*Lip curl (*flehmen*) is a common response in stallions in particular. It concentrates an odour in the nasal passages so that it can be identified.*

light in the eye, head position, body attitude, or lift of a leg indicates the same to one and all. Many observers, however, have noticed that horses often give up on humans who do not take in the finer points of equine language. So many humans are not even interested in absorbing their horse's messages – they only want the horse to learn, and obey.

At the same time, horses learn other species' languages very quickly. Wild and feral equines pick up on other creatures' attitudes, alarm sounds, or startled behaviour – and react accordingly. They also detect whether these represent 'internal' interactions (squabbles, mating, bonding) and so are irrelevant to them, or whether they represent an 'exterior', inter-species warning of a predator looking for a meal from any available quarter.

Our language is mainly vocal, unlike theirs, with a distinct lack of horse-type body language, yet horses learn, re-learn, and retain it quickly and well, which surely proves how adaptable and intelligent they are. They must be truly frustrated at our failure to learn their language, and it is not surprising that there is so much apparent lack of co-operation (which is really lack of mutual communication) between horse and human, and so much fascination among humans with the topic we call

'problem horses'. Horses certainly do have problems – with us: our problems must lie within ourselves.

Sleep patterns

Horses do not sleep for long stretches as humans do, but in snatches that usually last about half an hour at a time. The total amount they take varies between about four and eight hours every 24 hours.

As prey animals, it is dangerous for them to spend long periods lying down, even when among the herd. In a line of stables, one or two horses always

Above: A horse needs to spend a certain amount of time lying down if it is to sleep deeply, but it also has the ability to sleep standing up.

Below: To a horse, rolling is one of life's great pleasures, although it can also be an indication of stomach pain (colic) if associated with discomfort.

remain standing 'on guard', ready to warn of danger, so the herd can be up and off in a few seconds. When others stand, they take their turn lying down.

The special arrangement of ligaments and joints in their legs enables horses to sleep lightly while standing up. They

also sleep lying on their breast bones, but to sleep deeply they need to lie flat out for short periods.

Some horses never lie down to sleep, perhaps through insecurity, or fear of pain or of being unable to get up again. If your horse is reluctant to lie down, check that it is not stabled next to a dominant horse, which may be making it anxious. Ask the vet to examine the horse, to determine the cause. A deep, cushioning bed on a slip-resistant flooring should reassure the horse that it will be able to get up again safely.

Rolling

Horses clearly love rolling. It stimulates the skin and is a natural form of grooming, especially valuable for areas they cannot otherwise reach; it helps dry them when wet, and the dust in their coats helps deter skin parasites. Dried-on mud helps protect them against wind, which many hate.

Rolling also plays an important role in herd bonding. Horses often queue up to use a communal 'rolling patch', which is imbued with the herd scent comprising the mixed scents of the individual animals. This herd scent is an important recognition and 'acceptance' factor among equines.

Most horses like rolling on soft ground, and many ponies like rolling in water, even under saddle – which is obviously dangerous for the rider. If the pony lowers its head, it may be just to have a drink, but if it starts to paw the water or buckle at the knees, rolling is imminent – and quick thinking and strong riding will be needed to get the pony moving.

Reflex actions

These are lightning nervous reactions that the horse cannot control and are part of its survival mechanism. Common examples are reactions to sudden pain (caused by treading on a sharp stone or brushing against barbed wire) and to unexpected noises.

Sensory nerve endings detect the pain and send a message to the central nervous system, which sends messages back to move away from the cause of the pain. The ears detect a sound and the nervous system immediately puts the horse's flight instinct into operation: it will run without thinking where it is going.

It takes a well-schooled horse and a cool-headed rider or handler to counteract reflex actions.

Stable vices

'Vices' or 'stereotypies' are repetitive, unproductive actions – such as walking constantly around the stable, or weaving backwards and forwards at the stable door – thought to impair health and performance, and reduce the horse's value. No feral or wild equines have been reported performing stereotypies. However, about half to two-thirds of conventionally kept (stabled, 'corn-fed') domestic horses in the western hemisphere exhibit some kind of abnormal behaviour.

CAUSE AND EFFECT It is now fairly certain that such behaviour is triggered by horses spending too long alone in their stables, a lack of interaction with other horses (merely being able to see them is not enough), or large amounts of high-energy, cereal-based feeds, together with insufficient fibre.

Repeated physical action in some individuals stimulates production of endorphins and encephalins, natural pain-killing, 'feel-good' chemicals. The horse gradually becomes addicted to them, and so repeats the action that produces them.

PREVENTION Most people try physically to stop their horse performing a vice, such as by fitting a grille to the stable door or using a restrictive collar. This plainly addresses only the symptoms of the problem. Instead, we must remove the horse's need to perform the vice, by changing the conditions in which it is kept: turning it out for longer periods, providing a suitable stable companion, changing the diet to include plenty of bulky, low-energy food. This type of management can help to modify even an established vice, reducing the frequency with which it is performed.

Research in the USA indicates that physical prevention actually makes the horse more distressed by removing the outlet for its frustration (so depriving it of the calm-inducing endorphins the behaviour releases). Instead, the animal

Crib biting – grabbing the top of a door with the teeth – often leads on to wind sucking, when the horse gulps in air. Both are considered 'vices'.

COMMON VICES

CRIB BITING: the horse grasps a protrusion such as the stable door with its teeth, arches its neck, and gulps in air with a grunt.
WIND SUCKING: as crib biting but without grasping anything.
WEAVING: the horse repeatedly rocks sideways from one foreleg to the other, the head and neck swaying from side to side.
BOX WALKING: the horse walks ceaselessly round the stable, often at speed.
RUG TEARING: the horse consistently damages or removes its rug.
Other behaviour commonly regarded as 'vices' includes: biting and kicking; unprovoked rearing; bolting or running away; napping (evading the rider's aids) or setting (planting the feet); chronic shying or spooking; slipping the collar (in harness); being dangerous in the stable or to groom. Some feel that being unsafe in traffic should be classified as a vice.

may find another vice, or develop stress-related illnesses such as digestive disorders, high blood pressure, depression, or respiratory disease. Those allowed to perform their 'vices' cope better with life, it seems.

Vices rarely cause serious problems – many competition horses succeed despite them. We need to adjust our own attitudes to such behaviour. Most importantly we need to make our horses more content by implementing a form of care that reflects much more their natural way of life.

EDUCATION FOR LIFE

Attitudes towards training horses have varied throughout time. No one system has been adopted worldwide as being the best way of educating, subduing, or socializing horses to humans. Even the ancients differed in their views on this. Early civilizations used obviously harsh methods, yet one of the authorities best known to us, the ancient Greek cavalry commander Xenophon (c.430–350 BC), advocated fair and kind methods to get the best from a horse.

Methods many regard as brutal are still practised all over the world. These are based on a premise that the horse's spirit must be completely subdued, even 'broken', by irresistibly hard methods calculated to frighten the horse and show it how helpless it is in human hands. The horse must, these practitioners claim, be 'disciplined' (even before it has done 'wrong' trying to defend itself), 'shown who's boss', and terrified into submission.

Young horses often have little contact with humans until they are nearly full grown, when they are able to put up a daunting fight against their handlers. Hence the barbarous methods used. These involve restraint by tethering, trussing up, tying down, throwing the horse to the ground (terrifying for a flight animal), whipping, 'sacking out' by rubbing empty sacks all over the horse while it is restrained, until it 'realizes' they will not hurt (at least, not physically), and even tying the animal to a motor vehicle and dragging it along, sometimes off its feet, or pulling it over backwards to 'teach it a lesson'.

Apart from being scared witless by these methods (which truly merit the term 'breaking in'), some animals are seriously injured and killed in the process, particularly in countries where horses are numerous and 'dispensable'.

Conventional 'breaking'

Considerably less harsh methods (still, however, usually called 'breaking in') are based on the traditional 'English' way. These involve handling the foal kindly, firmly, and thoroughly from its early days, teaching it to obey spoken commands, getting it used to wearing a headcollar, teaching it to lead in hand and move around as requested in the stable and outside, have its feet picked out, and be groomed.

When roughly two, three, or four years old, the youngster is taught, without undue restraint or distress, to work on the lunge and/or long reins, usually wearing a roller and side reins, to carry a saddle, and to be 'backed', allowing a person at first to lie across the saddle, then slide a leg across, and finally to sit up and begin 'riding the horse away'. This work is often initially done on the lunge, with the trainer on the ground helping the horse learn to associate familiar spoken aids with physical ones from legs, seat, and reins so that these can ultimately take over.

The youngster is then said to have been 'broken in'. Although some

Native Americans' natural balance enabled them to control a galloping horse with their legs and weight, leaving both hands free for weapons.

trainers can be harsh and demanding, this system is generally much more humane than the first one described; but it does take much longer.

The new approach

Now, as the millennium turns, we are seeing a welcome revival and development of methods that are based on our 'going to the horse' rather than expecting the horse to do all the learning and giving. These techniques specifically require our learning to understand horse language and society, and using this information to persuade the horse to regard us as its herd leader, following our lead enthusiastically because we are 'speaking' the right language and behaving in a way the horse sees as rational and normal.

There are several methods promoted by different individuals (usually, perhaps strangely in view of traditional 'cowboy' methods, from a background in the American West). These use the horse's body language, visual and tactile, to relate to it. First the horse is rejected, then accepted. This results in what is variously known as 'bonding', 'joining', or 'joining up', depending on

the system. The technique places us firmly in the horse's mind as its leader. Then, further use and refinement of its language and social customs enable us to achieve certain levels of training in a remarkably short time, on the ground or under saddle. Most importantly, no force is applied. Although the horse suffers some distress during the rejection phases leading up to bonding or joining, this is nothing like the terror experienced in some styles of breaking. The horse joins up with the human (who is clearly speaking its language) to avoid the distress of rejection.

In essence, these methods aim to help us achieve a true partnership, with the horse willingly regarding the human as the senior partner. As most horses are followers, not leaders, this ultimate aim mirrors equine society perfectly.

Many of these methods are derived logically from natural equine behaviour, which is why they can be so successful. They are by no means new but stem, at least in part, from earlier times and civilizations that understood the importance of this approach. Their aims and humane techniques are a welcome move towards enriched lives for horse and rider alike.

Above: Conventional 'backing' involves progressive training to prepare the horse mentally and physically to accept the saddle.

Below: Monty Roberts has travelled extensively giving demonstrations of using the horse's own body language as a means of communication.

A day in the life of a groom

A groom is responsible for all aspects of horse care – feeding, grooming, health care, exercising, and training. Whether the horses belong to the yard or are livery horses, a groom is trained to shape the development of every individual under his or her care through close daily contact.

Working as a groom can be the first step of a career in the horse world. A groom who wishes to go on to ride competitively will decide which discipline to pursue, find a suitable yard to work in as a groom, and then begin training for competition in the chosen field. Nadine Ronan has worked at Church Farm in Wiltshire, England, for two years. She is training for her first intermediate event when she will ride one of the yard's most experienced horses, Jerry. As well as caring for Jerry, she is also responsible for four other horses. She looks after all their daily needs as well as checking that they are up to date with general health needs such as worming, teeth care, and shoeing.

◄ **6.30am** 'We all have an early rise to feed, water, and muck out the horses. Each of the six grooms here has their own line of five horses to look after for six days out of every seven. We cover each other's responsibilities when we take it in turns to have our day off.'

▼ **8.00am** 'All the grooms breakfast together – we discuss the plans for the day. We also check the noticeboard that indicates daily any special arrangements for an event or any particular training away from the yard.'

▲ **9.15am** 'I tack up the first horse I will be riding. I often have to exercise all of the horses in my care so, to save time, I may "ride and lead" – I normally ride Jerry around the block to warm him up for about 15 minutes, and lead another horse alongside him.'

12.00pm 'All training is over and there is an hour before lunch to check that the yard is clean, skip out each box, and top up the horses' hay.'

▼ **2.00pm** 'The afternoon is set aside for grooming. Any preparation for an event that is taking place the next day is done now, such as washing and pulling the tail and mane, or cleaning stud holes. I also deal with minor injuries that may have occurred during training and any ongoing health problems. I must decide when it is appropriate to call the vet out to the yard.'

▲ **9.45am** 'Fitness training starts. Each groom is responsible for exercising their horses, but twice a week we have a training session with one of the more experienced trainers or riders. This enables the yard owner to chart the progress of every horse and rider and to decide when each is ready to compete.'

▶ **10.15am** 'No horse is given more than an hour's intensive training a day. After washing Jerry down, I school some of the other horses. This gives me the chance to practise dressage, cross country, or showjumping on a daily basis.'

▲ **4.00pm** 'Skipping out, watering, and feeding the horses is done again. The yard is also swept and I load up wheelbarrows with hay and straw for the following morning. We all try to finish at 5pm as it is such a long day.'

8.00pm 'We make sure that our horses are settled: each gets an extra slice of hay before we leave them for the night. I normally then soak in the bath and get to bed early ready for the next day.'

LIVING AND LEARNING

In our society, most domestic horses have to fit in with humans if they are to have a reasonable lifespan and any chance of an enjoyable life – but even then, sadly, these things are not guaranteed. Even horses with a naturally good temperament can be ruined by inappropriate handling. Over-harsh or too-soft handling both produce horses that are petulant, bossy, 'spoilt', defensive, or aggressive.

As described earlier, horses can be left until they are three or older before training starts, without that training needing to be physically forceful and painful. The 'joining' or 'bonding' methods based on using the horse's language and social principles aim to get the animal's willing co-operation from the start; even many older horses with long-established 'bad habits' have been reformed by these methods.

Traditional English and continental European methods (with the possible exception of those practised in Iberia and the Camargue in southern France), also used in other countries, rely on starting when a foal is very young to get it, gently but firmly, to realize that humans are leaders who can be benevolent, like equine leaders, provided you behave yourself. The aim is the same as with the 'bonding' methods described earlier but the route is longer and different.

Training foals

Ideally, training should begin on the foal's first day or soon afterwards, and it should be one long, logical progression throughout life.

Inexperienced owners often treat foals like pets and play with them, allowing them to stand with hooves on their shoulders, turn tail to a human for a scratch on the bottom, and get away with playful nips. The foal will naturally assume that all this is acceptable (horses learn, for better and for worse, in one 'take'); but by the time the foal is a yearling, such behaviour will be extremely dangerous. When humans, incomprehensibly to the horse, change tack and start to impose discipline, it will become justifiably confused and annoyed – and the seeds of a bad temperament will have been sown.

IMPRINT TRAINING In the 1970s American veterinarian Robert Miller began to develop a system he called 'imprint training', having noticed that foals that had had problems at birth, needing frequent attention and veterinary treatment, grew up easy to handle and well socialized to humans. Imprinting is the biological process by which a newborn animal learns who its mother is and bonds with her.

With imprint training, foals are handled all over for about an hour immediately after birth, then periodically for up to two weeks. They may be exposed to strange noises, to accustom them to sounds they will have to face in later life, and they may be 'bitted' by having a finger placed repeatedly in the mouth. Obviously, most of the time mare and foal are left in peace to cement the bond between them. (No one wants a foal to believe it is human.) This method produces relaxed, confident foals with a positive, accepting, and respectful attitude towards humans that lasts throughout their lives – and they do prove very easy to train.

NATURAL DISCIPLINE It is best, if rarely done, for foals to be brought up with their dams in mixed groups of horses of all ages – ideally, some claim, with the herd stallion. In this way, just as in nature, the foals learn all aspects of horse behaviour and discipline. If, in the course of their upbringing, the herd associates regularly with humans,

The newborn foal is often up on its feet within an hour of birth. In imprint training, the process of socialization with humans begins immediately.

A foal will quickly learn to follow a routine and will proudly walk on the halter once it realizes what is required. This one looks very confident.

youngsters will readily accept them, regarding them as a normal part of their lives.

Discipline meted out by other, usually older, horses is both fairer and harsher than any measures humans can take. Horses raised this way do seem easier to handle and train. Unfortunately most stud owners are set in their traditional ways, and this method is little used.

WEANING Conventionally, a foal is weaned from its mother at the age of six months (or even earlier), usually because the mare is pregnant again. However, the view is slowly spreading that conventional weaning without good reason (such as the dam having little milk or savaging her foal, or the foal being too much for the dam to cope with physically) leaves permanent psychological scars with resultant behaviour problems in horses. The process of suddenly and completely separating dam and foal, then stabling foals alone (even in pairs) is undeniably highly unnatural and distressing for both parties; even though its proponents claim 'they soon get over it', many researchers and behaviourists now believe that they do not, particularly the foals.

Gradual methods of weaning are now more in favour and growing numbers of breeders feel that, with today's improved feeds and knowledge, there is no need to wean foals as early as six months. Most healthy, pregnant mares can easily maintain a suckling foal until shortly before foaling. This is when, in nature, a mare would wean the foal herself, and by this time – at nearly 11 months old – it will be taking very little milk in any case. If she is not pregnant, the foal can stay on with her longer if the two agree.

Yearlings onwards

Horses reach puberty around 12 months of age, when they are in theory capable of breeding. Advocates of natural rearing methods then remove colts from the herd and put them into all-age bachelor bands, such as they would form in the wild; fillies are left with their families unless the herd stallion (if one is present) proves unfriendly or becomes sexually interested in them.

Traditional methods dictate that yearlings are separated by sex into pairs or groups from then on. Those colts intended for racing or breeding may begin the artificial life of a domestic stallion – mostly stabled, and often alone – from this very young age.

KEEPING THEM BUSY Young horses, like young humans, are boisterous and need stimulating, occupying, guiding, and disciplining. A good deal can be gained by walking yearlings out and about, in hand initially then on long reins, around the stud or in the immediate neighbourhood, broadening the range of their experience and getting them used to other sights and sounds. An older, familiar horse can accompany them at first, to show them how to move over different kinds of terrain and around jumps and cones. This can continue until it is time for 'starting' ('backing' or 'breaking in').

Gently pulling the ears through the hand brings comfort to the horse. It is also a good indication of temperature: cold ears mean a cold horse.

A WIDER VIEW

The horse world, it seems, is firmly compartmentalized, with practitioners of one discipline having little interest in others. Each develops its own narrow outlook on how best to train a horse, often refusing to consider what could be learned and how much could be gained by studying and practising others' techniques. It would be a huge, enlightened leap forward if we could all experience a wider horse world, even if only for long enough to show us the benefits and disadvantages of others' methods.

Basic education

All horses need to be well trained in the manners expected of them by handlers on the ground, to learn, for example, to lead obediently in hand, to move over in the stable, to have their feet picked up and handled, as well as not to barge into humans or dive into feed. However, some never reach even this standard, but not through any fault of their own. Many horses and ponies are not disciplined properly, and if they are, the discipline is often insufficient and too late. A dam disciplining her foal, or any mature horse disciplining a youngster, gives an *immediate*, very short and very sharp kick or bite. The immediacy is crucial, since the horse's brain is not capable of connecting the discipline with its behaviour unless the two follow very quickly. Wait two seconds and you have waited too long, say the behaviourists. Disciplining a horse after this time results only in confusion.

Riding horses need to accept a saddle, bridle, and bit – although many never fully accept the latter. The tenet of classical equitation that horses should be and go 'calm, forward, and straight' holds true for horses in any discipline. These three qualities are a basic requirement; without them, other movements cannot be performed well.

Whether you want to cut cattle, ride over a course of jumps, execute a dressage test, or tackle an endurance

Western riding – like all forms of equitation – requires a thorough basic education if the horse and its rider are to communicate well.

ride, you will find it far more enjoyable and fulfilling if your horse is calm, forward, and straight. In fact, if your horse is not calm, it will learn nothing and will barely listen to you. If your horse does not 'go forward', willingly and immediately obeying your seat and leg aids, it will be much harder to

FOAL		YEARLING		2-YEAR-OLD		3-YEAR-OLD	4-YEAR-OLD		5-YEAR-OLD	

Within the first few months of life, a foal should be willing to be handled all over; wear a foal slip, stand quietly in hand, eventually learn to be tied up; be led, turned out, and caught; have its feet trimmed and be lightly groomed; spend short periods without its dam when older.

At the age of two, the horse should be introduced to long reins, walking and trotting out on excursions, over poles and varied terrain; it could be introduced to the bit ('mouthed') and/or the saddle for extra discipline.

Now the young horse can start competing in ridden show classes; learn to take small jumps when ridden; have its first introduction to hounds.

When a year old, the horse should be taught stable manners – moving forwards, backwards, and to the side, and standing to attention when asked. It should stand tied up for short periods; lead willingly out and about; be amenable to grooming; be used to traffic and travelling.

At this age, the horse should be mouthed and backed if not already; jump low obstacles on the lunge rein or loose; probably learn to be shod. Light riding may start, going on outings for experience.

At five years old, the horse can begin light adult work. Horses of this age are often 'overfaced'; physically they are almost, or fully, mature, depending on breed, but mentally young.

control and may even be dangerous to ride. If the horse is not straight, with its hind feet following exactly the same track as its forefeet, it will not use its energy effectively, and will not develop to its full potential.

CLASSICAL TECHNIQUES In some countries, there is increasing interest in what is termed classical equitation. This has come to be synonymous with a lighter, more harmonious, even controlled form of riding that stresses a relaxed, balanced posture with much more emphasis on the use of seat and back and less on leg and hand. It also emphasizes sitting still by going with the horse, not hampering its efforts by means of contrary movements.

This type of equitation began to be developed in continental Europe at the time of the Renaissance (14th–16th centuries) and thrived until about the

middle of the 19th century. Early exponents used harsh methods but later ones, the most prominent being François Robichon de la Guérinière of France in the 18th century and, in our own time, the Portuguese maestro, Nuno Oliveira, stressed humanity, aiming for a willing horse responding to light aids in a harmonious, not coercive, partnership.

Forms of equitation stemming from the similar Iberian methods include the famous Western cowboy style of riding, the South American gaucho seat and, to a lesser extent, the Australian stock seat. Certainly the best exponents of the two former styles rarely touch their horses' mouths, using balance and neckreining instead, and ride with a natural, upright posture, absorbing the horse's movements through smooth, compensatory movements of the pelvis and hip joints.

It seems that horses and riders alike would benefit by receiving at least a basic education in forms of equitation other than their own. Imagine, for example, the benefits of a hunter who, having been taught to ground-tie Western-style, did not gallop off with the field if you took a tumble but stood and waited for you. How much pleasanter riding would be if a light contact were once again taught as standard rather than the heavier, more forceful contact so common now. How many cross-country horses would cease to pull out their riders' arms, or take off with them, or at least be more willing and able to 'come back' to them, if they had received 'classical' rather than current conventional schooling?

Lungeing over poles on the ground helps to improve the balance and co-ordination of the horse. Poles must be set a suitable distance apart.

Breaking in a young horse

Training horses is hard work but it is also very rewarding. Every pony is different and will require a personal approach, depending on how much it trusts its trainer. The initial breaking in (or backing) of a young horse can only take place after it has become accustomed to being handled and is also used to the feel of a bit in its mouth and a saddle on its back. The art of being a good trainer is to concentrate on the horse and its needs throughout the lesson so that you get the best out of it and teach it to listen to your commands through patient repetition.

Jennie Loriston-Clarke began her career with horses in the Pony Club, progressing on to showing, eventing, and point-to-pointing before riding in five Olympic Games – she went on to win the World Bronze Medal for dressage in 1978.

Jennie is now a world-renowned horse trainer. Her day usually starts at 7am, when she rides her own horses. She then trains throughout the day – often up until 7pm. She believes that all work with horses is really as rewarding as the effort that you put into it. She feels it is important to work so closely with each horse that you become one with it because there is nothing like the satisfaction of feeling a horse working with you.

▲ 3 'The horse's ears are showing a little anxiety and fear, and it is at these times that my presence is so important. I always reassure the horse by stroking its neck and soothing it with my voice. When he is ready, I walk him forward a few steps until he is confident. I then move a few more on a circle as on a lunge, using my voice for "walk" and "whoa" with the rider sitting passively. A neck strap, breast plate, or strap over the front of the saddle can be useful for the rider. Some horses will settle on the first day that they are ridden, others will require more time, so I never rush this stage of their training. It may take several days before a horse is confident to go it alone.'

▲ 1 'When I feel a horse is happy with a saddle, I can introduce a side rein. We then practise walks and trots until the horse accepts slight contact. Then I can introduce it to a rider. It is very useful to have a second helper at this stage if at all possible.'

► 2 'The rider is given a leg up. The rider gets on and off several times to give the horse the chance to get used to them. Here, the horse's ears are out sideways, which tells me that he is happy and confident and is ready for the rider to go fully astride.'

▲ 4 'The horse is now working happily in trot, listening to its rider, who is taking over the words of command. When the rider wishes to walk, she will steady her upper body position and allow the horse to walk.'

▶ 5 'A confident horse learns to accept the aids of seat, leg, and reins. Once straight lines and circles have been mastered in walk and trot, we will ask it to canter. The leg aids can be reinforced with a touch of the whip and the command to ''canter''. When the horse is obedient to turning aids, it can be asked to change direction.'

◀ 6 'This young horse is now ready to start hacking in company. I find it is best to start in a field, progressing to a field beside a road before riding in traffic – and a quiet horse for company always helps. My main work with this horse is over; it is now the rider's responsibility to think well ahead and avoid mistakes. If anything does go wrong, they must put it right straight away, so that the horse has the correct thoughts in his head when the ride finishes.'

Riding Pony

The Riding Pony is one of Britain's great success stories, although its breeding came about more through chance than careful selection. Today these ponies are bred all over the world especially for the show ring. Classes for show ponies are divided into various heights and types, including jumping for the hunter divisions. There are also classes for ponies ridden side-saddle, on the leading rein, and for brood mares and young stock in hand.

Breed characteristics

The Riding Pony is an elegant miniature horse, but maintains the true pony characteristics of a small, intelligent head with a bold eye, good shoulders and front, but not too wide, and strong limbs with tough feet. A good pony should stand 'four square' and be in proportion, with a comfortable gait and carriage. Ponies are renowned for their strength in relation to their size, but constant cross-breeding with lighter breeds has diluted this trait, so that the modern Riding Pony is more refined and better equipped for today's sporting activities. Above all, Riding Ponies must be sufficiently calm and equable for children to ride.

There are essentially three different types of Riding Pony: the show pony type (a super-elegant, miniature show hack, with pony features); the show hunter pony (which has more substance); and the working hunter pony (which is a stockier, more workmanlike type).

History of the Riding Pony

In Britain, until the early 20th century, children's ponies were mainly the local native breeds, used simply for riding and hunting. There was little real interest in breeding anything special. With the advent of pony classes at horse shows, in the early 1920s, enthusiastic breeders had the idea of crossing the attractive Welsh and Dartmoor breeds with small Thoroughbreds and Arabians. The result was the elegant riding ponies whose descendants we see in the show ring today.

The Polo Pony Stud Book Society had been formed in 1893 to encourage the breeding of high-class riding and polo ponies. Six years later there were over 100 stallions and nearly 600 mares registered, almost half of which were of the native pony breeds. The name of the society was changed in 1903 to the Polo Pony and Riding Pony Stud Book Society, and again in 1913 when it became the National Pony Society (NPS). Over the years all the native breeds formed their own societies, and the NPS register became dedicated to the British Riding Pony. Since 1994 foreign-bred ponies have been listed in a separate register.

In the USA, another special show breed developed in the 1950s in the form of the Pony of the Americas, with its spectacular Appaloosa markings, while in France the Poney Français de Selle (bred on similar lines to the British pony) emerged in the 1970s.

The Riding Pony today

The Riding Pony has been exported all over the world since the 1950s, and most countries now breed their own ponies, using mainly registered Riding Pony mares and stallions, or import frozen semen to use on their own mares to vary the bloodlines and improve the quality of the stock.

In Britain, the National Pony Society runs numerous classes for Riding

Above: Many Riding Ponies are exceptional jumpers, often clearing huge obstacles in relation to their size.

Right: These two winners epitomize champions, both having great presence, a well-balanced physique, and a neat, attractive head.

Ponies at its various shows, but it is the British Show Pony Society and Ponies UK that hold shows with the greatest number of classes. Similar events are organized by the American Horse Shows Association in the USA.

Ponies have their own status in the competitive disciplines under rules laid down by the International Equestrian Federation (FEI), and there is a growing demand for top-class Riding Ponies to perform in dressage, eventing, and showjumping.

PRE	1900			1950		2000
1893 Polo Pony Stud Book started in Britain.	**1913** National Pony Society regulates and registers ponies bred in Britain.	**1920–30s** Native breeds crossed with small Thoroughbreds result in elegant show ponies.	**1930–50s** Some Arabian blood occasionally introduced to improve stamina and refinement.	**1950s** Show ponies well established and exported worldwide.		**1990s** Ponies recognized by FEI disciplines.

MAIN FEATURES
- supremely elegant
- small head with small, neat ears
- compact and well balanced
- good shoulders, and not too wide
- great presence
- tough feet

CHARACTER
- affectionate
- docile
- kind
- willing
- intelligent

COLOURS
All colours are found, including Palomino and Pinto.

HEIGHT
122–52cm (12–15hh)

COUNTRY OF ORIGIN
Britain

COMPARISON BREED
Pony of the Americas
This is another elegant, miniature horse that was developed as a riding pony and it has similar characteristics. Its spotted colouring on the coat is particularly attractive.

RELATED TOPICS
Dartmoor Pony   52
Welsh Pony Cob   58
Pony of the Americas   66
Thoroughbred   70
Arabian   128
Showing   246

MAIN FEATURES
stocky body
arched neck
long mane and tail
silky feather on legs
tough, blue-horned hoof
sure footed
bold movement
great stamina
good trotter

CHARACTER
even tempered
sensible
intelligent

COLOURS
Most are black or dark
brown, but some are grey
or bay.

HEIGHT
137–47cm (13.2–14.2hh)

COUNTRY OF ORIGIN
Britain (Yorkshire Dales)

COMPARISON BREED
Fell Pony
Very like the Dales but
slightly smaller, with less
feather, the Fell belongs to
the western side of the
Pennine hills, the Dales to
the eastern side.

RELATED TOPICS
Fell Pony   51
Welsh Pony and Cob   58
Clydesdale   138
Dressage   168
Driving   194
Pony Club   226
Riding holidays   250

Dales Pony

A hardy pony native to the eastern Pennines of northern Britain, the Dales has tremendous stamina and a long history of serving humans as a pack and work pony. Today the Dales is known for its brilliance in harness and its eye-catching presence under saddle.

Breed characteristics

Dales Ponies are very economical to keep and are prized for their great endurance and soundness. They are typically dark brown or black, with sturdy legs with dense, flat bone. The close-coupled body has strong loins and deep, powerful hindquarters. The high knee and hock action gives the pony its signature movement.

The hardy disposition and the docile temperament of the Dales Pony make it suitable for several different uses.

History of the Dales Pony

Developed from the native Pennine Pony, the Dales drew many of its traits from the now-extinct Scottish Galloway, which was quick, nimble, and strong, and infused with Friesian blood. The equally sturdy Dales were originally bred to be pack ponies, primarily to carry heavy loads of lead through formidable countryside under adverse weather conditions.

With its agility, power, and speed, the Dales proved not only a huge success in the trotting races that became so popular in the 18th century, but also a worthy mount during organized hunts. Because they could survive – even flourish – in a harsh climate, they found use as utility animals, serving with the British army as pack and mountain artillery ponies.

During the 18th and 19th centuries, Dales blood was mixed with that of other breeds, including Clydesdales, Norfolk Trotters, Yorkshire Roadsters, and Welsh Cobs. In 1916, the Dales Pony Improvement Society began its campaign to protect the pony's future, but so many ponies were called upon to serve the army during the two world wars that the breed was nearly wiped out. It wasn't until the Dales Pony Society was founded in 1963 that numbers began to increase.

The Dales Pony today

Today's Dales Pony is excellent for riding; it has incredible powers of endurance and a steady temperament, so that it can go on day-long treks or long-distance rides. As well as being popular for driving and dressage, Dales Ponies are also good jumpers, with many competing in cross-country trials and eventing. Small herds of Dales Ponies can still be found roaming free in the eastern Pennines.

	1850 Welsh Cobs bred with Dales to improve gait.		1916 Dales Pony Improvement Society founded. Stud book opened.	
1600	1700	1800	1900	
	17th century Galloway Ponies influence Pennine Pony stock, improving speed and sure-footedness.	18th and 19th century Clydesdale, Norfolk, and Yorkshire Roadsters introduced to improve trotting.		1963 Dales Pony Society formed to increase number and quality of ponies bred.

Fell Pony

The beautiful and rugged Fell is an athletic and versatile British native pony. Originally from the moorlands of north-western England, Fells were for generations used both under saddle and as pack animals. Over the years they have been developed into wonderful riding ponies, displaying honesty, intelligence, and friendliness.

imported into Britain by the Romans in the 2nd century. These strong animals could move heavy loads of stone for building roads and walls, whereas the smaller native ponies could not. The black horses were bred with the ponies on the moorlands, to give them greater stature and substance, and so the modern Fell Pony began to take shape.

Breed characteristics

Fells have a free, easy stride and are known for their fast trot, which they can maintain over long distances. Their sturdy legs have good, flat bone, which reaches down to a broad, round hoof noted for its tough blue-coloured horn. Silky feathering covers the lower legs.

History of the Fell Pony

The development of the Fell Pony owes much to the influence of the Friesian, an old Dutch breed – always black –

The Fell Pony today

Fells have their own breed classes at county shows, both in hand and under saddle, but in open competitions they compete successfully alongside larger horses in the working hunter and jumping classes. An even temperament makes the Fell a good child's pony. It also excels in driving competitions.

The predominantly black Fells look magnificent in their harness. Those shown here are being put through their paces before a competition.

MAIN FEATURES
- long, sloping shoulder
- deep chest
- crested neck with full mane
- sturdy, well-muscled legs
- silky feathering
- blue-horned hoof

CHARACTER
- gentle
- tractable
- intelligent
- lively
- kind

COLOURS
Black, brown, or grey.

HEIGHT
135–42cm (13.1–14hh)

COUNTRY OF ORIGIN
Britain (western side of Pennines)

COMPARISON BREED
Dales Pony
A bigger, stronger version of the Fell Pony, from the eastern side of the Pennines, the Dales is renowned for its energetic trot.

	PRE	1700		1800		1900	

2nd century
Friesians imported into Britain breed with native pony stock.

18th century
Clydesdale, Norfolk, and Yorkshire Roadsters introduced to improve trotting.

1912
Fell Pony Society formed.

1945
Breed numbers become alarmingly low, and enthusiasts begin a breeding programme.

RELATED TOPICS
Dales Pony   50
Friesian   96
Driving   194
Pony Club   226
Showing   246

MAIN FEATURES
• small head
• full mane and tail
• alert ears, kind eyes
• free shoulder
• flowing movement

CHARACTER
• kind
• reliable
• gentle
• intelligent

COLOURS
Usually bay, brown, black, or grey; occasionally chestnut.

HEIGHT
118–27cm (11.2–12.2hh)

COUNTRY OF ORIGIN
Britain (Dartmoor)

COMPARISON BREED
Welsh Pony
With its quality, size, and toughness, the Welsh Pony has many traits in common with the Dartmoor; it too, is an ideal mount for children.

Dartmoor Pony

This hardy pony has lived on the southernmost moorlands of Britain for centuries. Because of its size and its wonderfully calm temperament and affable manner, it is an excellent first mount for a child. Although small, it still has the ability to hunt, jump, and be driven, and has great strength and endurance in its compact body.

Breed characteristics

The Dartmoor is known for being sturdily built, but is refined for its small size. It has a small head that reflects its intelligence, with wide-set eyes and alert ears. Most Dartmoors are close coupled with strong hindquarters and loins. Short but proportioned legs have a medium amount of bone, and the feet are tough. The Dartmoor's action comes from a free shoulder, which allows the pony relatively flowing gaits.

History of the Dartmoor Pony

In medieval times, the Dartmoor Pony was noted for its work in the local tin mines, carrying heavy loads across the moor. When the mines closed, most of the ponies were turned out onto the moor, although some were kept for farm work. At the start of the 20th century ponies were bred at the prison on Dartmoor and used by the guards when escorting prisoners to and from outside work. This practice continued until the 1960s.

As for so many native ponies, the two world wars proved devastating to the breed. A breed society had been started in the 1920s, but in World War II only a handful of animals were registered. Local people dedicated to the Dartmoor began to inspect and register as many ponies as they could – and by the 1950s, numbers were safely restored.

Since the late 1980s there has been a scheme to raise the standard of ponies bred on Dartmoor. This involves approved mares belonging to local farmers being turned out for the summer with a pure-bred stallion, and there has been a marked improvement in the quality of the foals born.

The Dartmoor Pony today

Today Dartmoor Ponies are bred all over Britain, as well as in mainland Europe; some have also been exported to North America. The Dartmoor is ideal for children, but its robust nature, combined with its conformation and swinging gaits, makes it quite capable of carrying adult riders; it has also become a favourite as a driving pony.

The Dartmoor is one of Britain's most refined and attractive native pony breeds. It is very popular as an all-round pony for children.

RELATED TOPICS

Welsh Pony and Cob   58
Driving   194
Pony Club   226
Showing   246
Riding holidays   250

1800		1900		
	1898 First attempt to define and register the breed. Dartmoor Ponies entered in the stud book started by the Polo Pony Society.	**1924** Breed society founded, and the first Dartmoor stud book opened.	**1940s** Registration by inspection introduced to help increase numbers.	**1988** Dartmoor Pony Moorland Scheme started to improve the quality of ponies on the moor.

Exmoor Pony

A small, shaggy animal typically bay in colour, the Exmoor is the oldest and most primitive of Britain's native ponies. Although privately owned, some Exmoor Ponies still run freely over the moors in south-west England. Once an invaluable aid to local hill farmers, Exmoors today take part in virtually all forms of equestrian activity, including showing, jumping, driving, and long-distance riding.

Breed characteristics

The Exmoor exemplifies hardiness. A small, sturdy pony with ample bone, it is well proportioned to its size, and can carry heavy burdens in relation to its build. It is a sure-footed animal, with strong legs and feet, and has a long, smooth stride moving freely from the shoulder. The head is large, with small ears, and the dark eyes are surrounded by a ring of light hair, giving the Exmoor its distinctive expression.

To help it survive the cold, wet winters so typical of Exmoor, the pony has a double coat: a soft, woolly undercoat and a longer, oily, water-repellent hair coat. Unique patterns of hair protect vulnerable areas, and the pony also has an 'ice tail' similar to that of Nordic breeds, where the hair splays out in a fan towards the dock, and channels water away from the body.

History of the Exmoor Pony

The Exmoor is believed to be directly descended from ponies that migrated from North America across prehistoric land bridges. Over the centuries, there has been very little cross-breeding, and the Exmoor remains the purest of the British breeds.

Once a Royal Forest or hunting ground, Exmoor – and its ponies – was sold off in 1818. Thirty ponies were taken by the Forest's last warden, Sir Richard Acland, and used to establish the famous Anchor herd, which still exists today. Local farmers, too, bought small numbers at the dispersal sale and began their own herds, keeping the bloodlines pure.

Other owners tried crossing the Exmoor with other breeds, but the offspring weren't hardy enough for the harsh life of the moor; the last of these herds died out early this century.

When the moor became an army training ground in World War II, Exmoor Ponies were nearly killed off; but local people managed to rescue some and used them to re-establish the pony herds. Numbers remained low until the early 1980s, when a publicity campaign drew attention to the rarity and importance of the breed.

The Exmoor Pony today

Today Exmoors are bred throughout Britain, although the total breeding population is less than 500. Some still live free on the moor. Every October, the ponies are rounded up, so that all foals can be inspected by the Exmoor Pony Society before registration.

The mealy markings of the Exmoor Pony make it the most easily distinguishable of all the British pony breeds. It is remarkably pure in type.

	PRE	1850		1900		1950	

1000 BC
Celtic ponies settle on Exmoor and breed with native ponies there. Natural selection ensures only the hardiest animals survive.

1818
The dispersal sale of ponies from Exmoor. The famous Anchor herd of Exmoors founded.

1921
Exmoor Pony Society formed, with the aim of preserving the pure-bred Exmoor.

1940s
Only 50 Exmoors survive World War II. Local people rescue the breed.

1990s
Small, free-living herds established on Exmoor by wildlife trusts.

New Forest Pony

Ponies have roamed free for centuries in the thousands of acres that make up England's New Forest. Like other native ponies, they are now also bred at private studs throughout the world. Enthusiasts refer to these ponies as 'Foresters', and can attest to the generous, talented, and friendly nature of the breed.

Breed characteristics

Anyone looking at a New Forest Pony might be inclined to categorize it as a Welsh Pony, a Connemara, or even a Thoroughbred/pony cross, since many display characteristics of a variety of breeds. Height varies considerably. While the conformation of the smaller ponies reflects a refined quality, the larger ponies have ample bone and substance. However, all New Forest Ponies are agile enough for gymkhana events, and have plenty of jump in them for hunter classes, showjumping, and cross country. They also have plenty of stamina for endurance riding, as well as the movement for driving and dressage competitions.

History of the New Forest Pony

The most notable influence on the ponies living in the New Forest came in 1765. Then, a local farmer brought the Thoroughbred stallion Marske (sire of the famous racehorse Eclipse) to the area to breed with local mares, and the ponies they produced were larger, and more refined. Queen Victoria lent some of her stallions for use in the Forest, sending first an Arabian in the 1850s, then a Barb and another Arabian in 1889. Other members of the nobility offered Dales, Fells, Dartmoors, and Exmoors to enhance the breed. In 1891, the Association for the Improvement of New Forest Ponies was founded, with the aim of finding good stallions that would service the Forest mares.

The New Forest Pony today

Ponies today still travel the Forest freely as they have done through the centuries; all are privately owned by 'commoners' who have Forest grazing rights. Surplus ponies are sold in the annual sales. In recent years, an increasing number of New Forest Ponies have been exported, and the New Forest is now bred throughout Europe, North America, and Australia as an ideal riding pony for children.

On their home range, 'Foresters' find plenty of gorse to pick at, which is rich in iron. They roam in herds in different parts of the New Forest.

1208
Welsh mares added to native stock living in the New Forest.

1852–60
Arabian stallion Zorah lent by Queen Victoria to refine the pony stock.

1891
Founding of the Association for the Improvement of New Forest Ponies.

1890s
Fell, Dales, Dartmoor, and Exmoor stallions used to broaden the mix of blood.

1938
New Forest Pony Breeding and Cattle Society established.

| PRE | 1800 | 1850 | 1900 | 1950 |

1765
Thoroughbred stallion Marske (sire of Eclipse) served New Forest mares.

1850s
New Forest Pony infused with Thoroughbred blood to become a finer pony type.

1889
Arabian and Barb stallions sent to the Forest by Queen Victoria.

1910
New Forest stud book started.

1960
First volume of the stud book published.

1990s
'Foresters' exported as riding ponies for children.

Connemara Pony

Ireland's native pony developed its amazing agility and hardiness over centuries in the desolate, mountainous terrain of the island's western coast. Today's Connemaras reflect that heritage, as they are suitable for all sports that involve speed and nimbleness, such as showjumping, cross country, and endurance.

Breed characteristics

The modern Connemara is a strong, sturdy pony with long, muscular shoulders and powerful hindquarters making it so suitable for competition. The pony is now more refined in appearance, with a fine quality head and neck, which can be attributed to a good dose of Thoroughbred blood.

History of the Connemara Pony

Some believe the Connemara stems from the Scandinavian ponies brought to Ireland by the Vikings. Yet tradition has it that Spanish horses provided the foundation of the breed. According to

legend, when galleons of the Spanish Armada ran aground near the island in 1588, their cargo of Andalusians had to be let loose. These bred with the Irish native ponies, making them more refined. In their isolated habitat, with its scarce grazing, the ponies developed into hardy survivors.

An infusion of Arabian blood in the early 1700s gave strength and stamina to the breed. But over the centuries too much cross-breeding began to dilute the bloodlines and, in the 1920s, the Connemara Pony Breeders' Society was founded to preserve the native type.

The Connemara Pony today

France, Britain, Germany, Denmark, and the USA all boast healthy populations of Connemaras today. This is one of the most popular breeds for children, and larger Connemaras are sought after by adults, since they excel in all competition, from dressage to cross country. They are also becoming more in demand for driving trials.

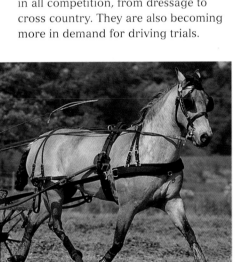

The Connemara Pony is one of the most versatile and highly sought after ponies for children. As a cross-breed it has produced many champion sport horses.

MAIN FEATURES
- well-balanced head and neck
- straight profile
- small ears
- full mane and tail
- short, straight back
- muscular, sloped croup
- short cannon bones
- good, hard feet

CHARACTER
- steadfast
- docile
- gentle, but assertive
- intelligent

COLOURS
Grey, brown, black, bay, dun, and chestnut.

HEIGHT
132–47cm (13–14.2hh), although some are larger.

COUNTRY OF ORIGIN
Britain (Ireland)

COMPARISON BREED
Welsh Pony
This is another native pony of similar origin and size, but the Welsh often bears more Arabian-like characteristics, such as refined bone and a dished profile.

1900s	1990s
Too many crosses with Arabians, Thoroughbreds, and Hackneys dilute Connemara blood.	Connemaras widely exported, both as children's ponies and as competition horses for adults.

	PRE	1600	1700	1800	1900	

1000	1590s	1710s	1923	1926
Scandinavian ponies mix with Irish native stock.	Andalusians add refinement and size to native ponies.	Arabians used to add strength and stamina.	Breed association formed to promote selective breeding, using only the best of the native stock.	Stud book started. Only ponies with pedigree parents on both sides may be registered.

RELATED TOPICS
Welsh Pony and Cob   58
Thoroughbred   70
Andalusian   94
Arabian   128
Driving   194
Pony Club   226
Showing   246

Shetland Pony

With its diminutive stature, kindly nature, and pert expression, the Shetland Pony has always been popular with children, and many top riders tell stories of how a Shetland taught them horsemanship. Level headed and kind generally, the pony can be independent at times, but if it is trained correctly it makes a wonderful mount as well as a good driving pony.

Breed characteristics

Although the Shetland stands at most only 107cm (42in) tall (this breed isn't measured in hands), it is a remarkably strong animal, and one of the world's toughest ponies. It has a compact, thickset body with a broad back; its legs are short, but sturdy; its hooves tough and round; and its stride springy. The pony has an alert look on its petite face, with inquisitive eyes and pricked ears. It has a heavy mane and tail, and during the winter grows a thick, double coat as protection against the elements.

History of the Shetland Pony

The Shetland Pony has lived on the islands that lie off the north-east coast of Scotland for perhaps 10,000 years. Precisely how it came to be there is not clear, but isolated on the islands, with their harsh climate and scarcity of food, the Shetland adapted into a small, extremely hardy creature.

It was first used by crofters, for ploughing and for carrying peat from the hills. However, from the mid 19th century, when laws were passed to stop children working in the coal mines, many thousands of Shetlands travelled south to England to spend their lives as 'pit ponies', hauling coal through the narrow underground tunnels.

The Shetland Pony today

Today, a breed society, formed in 1890, helps to maintain the purity of the Shetland and, in the UK, government subsidies encourage breeders to produce ponies of the highest quality. Now bred in many parts of the world, Shetlands are particularly popular in Europe and in North America. In the USA, they have been bred with Morgans and Hackney Ponies to give larger, finer ponies with much more high-stepping action and agility. Breed enthusiasts are often critical of the American Shetland, because it is so different from the original type.

The Shetland is the strongest pony for its size and easily carries adults. It is a great first pony for children, being kind but quick when required.

MAIN FEATURES
- small
- stocky
- strong profile
- crested neck
- full mane and tail
- thick, double winter coat

CHARACTER
- kind
- tolerant
- inquisitive
- intelligent

COLOURS
All colours are found –
black, chestnut, grey,
bay, dun, roan, piebald,
or skewbald (but
not spotted).

HEIGHT
Maximum 107cm (42in)
(Shetlands aren't measured
in hands.)

COUNTRY OF ORIGIN
Britain (Shetland Islands)

COMPARISON BREED
Exmoor Pony
The oldest of the British
native breeds, this tough,
hardy pony is able to
withstand the worst of
conditions. Like the
Shetland, it has a thick
double coat.

RELATED TOPICS
Exmoor Pony   53
Pony of the Americas   66
Driving   194
Pony Club   226
Showing   246

8000 BC
Scandinavian ponies
arrive in the Shetland
Islands, probably
across land bridge.

1970s
In USA, Hackney and
Morgan blood introduced,
eventually creating a larger,
more refined type known as
the American Shetland.

1983
Shetland Islands
Premium Filly and
Colt Scheme
introduced.

PRE | 1000 | 2000

7500 BC
Scandinavian
ponies crossed
with native
ponies.

9th century
Viking ponies
breed with
native ponies
on Shetland.

1890
Shetland Pony Stud
Book Society formed
to maintain purity and
encourage breeding.

1956
Shetland Islands Premium
Stallion Scheme subsidizes
high-quality registered
stallions to improve
breeding stock.

Highland Pony

The Highland Pony, a true native pony type, is the largest of Britain's nine native breeds. It has a long recorded history and proven pedigrees that date back to the 1880s. Once a universal work horse throughout the Scottish highlands and islands, it is now considered an ideal animal to take its rider trekking over steep hillsides, or over fences in the show ring.

Breed characteristics

Unlike some native breeds, the Highland Pony needs only a pedigree in order to be entered into the stud book; it does not have to pass a physical inspection. As a result, Highland Ponies tend to vary greatly in height, colour, and conformation.

The Highland is a sturdy, strong animal, with a certain elegance; it has sound feet and the ability to handle mountainous countryside with ease.

Nearly all Highlands have markings that link them to a primitive past, such as a stripe along the back and shoulders, and multiple stripes banding the legs. They also have dark points. The Highland is the only British pony breed in which all these markings occur frequently.

History of the Highland Pony

It is said that the ancestors of the Highland Pony inhabited Scotland before the Ice Age, which ended about 10,000 years ago. Like many British ponies, the native stock was influenced by breeding with other horses brought in by invading armies, and by various outcrossings. In the past, there were two distinct types: the small, light pony of the Western Isles, and the larger, more heavily built Garron, which was bred on the mainland.

Highlands were originally bred to work on the crofts or small farms, ploughing and hauling timber and game; and some ponies still work on Scotland's sporting estates, carrying game down from the hills. But today Highlands are known as valuable all-round ponies, good for jumping, and for trekking because of their quiet nature, stamina, and ability to carry weight.

The Highland Pony today

It is estimated that there are 5500 Highland Ponies around the world, most of them in Europe. Highlands are still bred for substance and stamina, but recently the trend has been to produce ponies that are most suited to riding and driving.

Because of its steady nature and good bone, the Highland Pony is increasingly crossed with other breeds such as the Thoroughbred to create talented event horses.

The versatility of the Highland makes it a favourite pony for several different riding activities. It is tough, tolerant, and kind.

1600	1700	1800	1900	

17th century
Arabians influence Scottish native pony, giving it stamina and refinement.

1650s
Percherons and other French breeds add size and strength.

17th–20th century
Highland Pony bred by crofters for farm work and forestry, and as pack horses.

1990s
Highland Ponies crossed with breeds such as the Thoroughbred to produce event horses.

ECTIONS A AND B

AIN FEATURES
dished profile
small ears
large eyes
clean legs
dense bone
sound feet
sure footed
hardy

HARACTER
friendly
intelligent
tractable

OLOURS
ll colours are found
xcept piebald and
kewbald. Grey is most
ommon among Mountain
onies (Section A).

EIGHT
ection A: Not exceeding
22cm (12hh)
ection B: Not exceeding
37cm (13.2hh)

OUNTRY OF ORIGIN
ritain (Wales)

OMPARISON BREED
Dartmoor Pony
his is another ideal
hildren's mount from
ritain, which is full
of quality and it is
sed for all types of
equestrian activities.

RELATED TOPICS
Riding Pony   48
Dartmoor Pony   52
horoughbred   70
ndalusian   94
rabian   128

Welsh Pony and Cob

Among the most beautiful of the native breeds, Welsh Ponies and Cobs are also known for their intelligence, their friendly personalities, and their even temperaments. There are four different types, which vary in both size and substance, but all exhibit grace and spirit, as well as a willingness to work.

Breed characteristics

The Welsh Pony and Cob stud book is divided into four main sections, to help categorize the Welsh types.

Section A ponies, known as Welsh Mountain Ponies, do not exceed 122cm (12 hands). They are tough, thrifty, and adaptable, with a wonderfully steady nature, which makes them ideal first ponies for children.

Section B ponies, known as Welsh Ponies of Riding Type, are taller, with a

maximum height of 137cm (13.2 hands), and slightly lighter in conformation, largely as a result of the infusion of Thoroughbred and Hackney blood. Natural jumpers, like their Mountain Pony ancestors, they are first-class riding ponies for youngsters.

The Section C pony, the Welsh Pony of Cob Type, initially resulted from cross-breeding Section A and Section D ponies, but today is more likely to be the progeny of a Section C mare and stallion. Like the Section B, it is no taller than 137cm (13.2 hands), but it is typically heavier and more compact, reflecting an infusion of Cob and Andalusian blood.

Section D of the stud book is reserved for the Welsh Cobs. These are all over 137cm (13.2 hands), with no upper height limit; most average 152cm (15 hands).

Both types of Cob move with a forceful action from the knees and hocks in comparison to the Section B ponies, which are more sweeping in their movement. Cobs have great stamina and are wonderful in harness, and the larger ponies are excellent mounts for adults.

History of Welsh Ponies and Cobs

All of the Welsh breeds derive to some extent from the Section A or Mountain Pony. Their ancestry is believed to trace back to the prehistoric Celtic pony. In the tough conditions of the Welsh hills, with their sparse vegetation and inhospitable climate, the pony evolved into a small, exceptionally hardy animal, able to survive on the most meagre of rations.

During the Roman occupation of Britain, horses imported from North Africa, presumed to be of Arabian

The Welsh Mountain Pony is unquestionably the prettiest of the British native breeds. Its friendly nature makes it an ideal child's pony.

	PRE	1700	

1st–5th century
Arabian horses
brought by the
Romans breed
with native
Welsh ponies.

12th–15th century
Stallions of mainly
Arabian origin,
imported by returning
Crusaders, influence
Welsh Ponies and Cobs.

origin, mingled with the native ponies, producing offspring with substance and hardiness, yet beautiful in appearance. The physical characteristics of the breed are deemed to have been established by the late 15th century, following a strong infusion of Arabian blood from stallions brought back from the Middle East by the Crusaders.

The Welsh Cobs arose from cross-breeding Welsh Mountain mares with horses of mainly Spanish descent. With their strength, speed, and robust constitution, they would prove invaluable to British armies from the 13th century onwards. In the 1500s, King Henry VIII found these animals so useful that he ordered that all smaller ponies be caught and destroyed. Fortunately, many found refuge in the Welsh mountains, where their persecutors could not follow.

The Welsh breeds found many different callings for their talents. They worked in coal mines, they pulled carts, and they carried the mail on postal routes. They were often the main means of transport on the hill farms of the region; the larger ponies and cobs were used as draught animals, could carry adults with ease, and also handle farm work.

Welsh Ponies and Cobs today

Welsh Ponies and Cobs are known throughout the world for both riding and driving, and all are popular in the show ring, both in hand and under saddle. The smaller types are widely acknowledged as excellent riding ponies for children, and the Cobs compete well in both hunter and competitive driving events.

The Welsh has long been in demand for crossing with other breeds, including Thoroughbreds, Quarter Horses, and Appaloosas, and was used to improve the size and substance of the Pony of the Americas. Today breeders continue to favour Welsh Ponies and Cobs whenever they seek to produce a natural jumper and a horse that can excel at eventing or dressage.

The Welsh Cob is renowned for its extravagant movement, and this is spectacularly displayed in the show ring.

SECTIONS C AND D
MAIN FEATURES
• straight profile
• large, expressive eyes
• clean limbs
• fine mane
• silky feather
• sound feet
• extravagant, high-stepping movement

CHARACTER
• high spirited
• very intelligent
• independent

COLOURS
All colours are found except piebald and skewbald.

HEIGHT
Section C: Not exceeding 137cm (13.2hh)
Section D: Over 137cm (13.2hh)

COUNTRY OF ORIGIN
Britain (Wales)

COMPARISON BREED
Highland Pony
The Highland is tough and intelligent, with plenty of strength, but it lacks the high-stepping movement of the Welsh Cobs.

1800		1900	
18th and 19th centuries Arabian stallions turned out on Welsh hills to refine local stock.	**Late 19th century** Old-style Hackney Roadsters used on Cob mares to produce high-stepping carriage horses.	**1901** Welsh Pony and Cob Society founded. First stud book published the following year.	**1949** Present-day sections of stud book (A,B,C, and D) introduced.

RELATED TOPICS
Eventing   156
Dressage   168
Driving   194
Pony Club   226
Showing   246

Haflinger

The Haflinger is a mountain pony from Austria, but it is popular around the world. Its docile nature, strength, and stamina make it suitable for a range of activities. Both in harness and under saddle, the Haflinger has helped Austria's hill farmers, foresters, and army for hundreds of years.

Breed characteristics

The colour of the Haflinger is one of the breed's most striking characteristics. They are chestnut, varying in shade from blonde to light chocolate, and all have flaxen manes and tails. The pony has an elegant head, associated with more refined breeds, but its back and hindquarters are very strong, equipping it for heavy work. It has a natural sure-footedness, which means it is a valuable pack animal, especially in the mountains.

A wonderfully tractable character is another hallmark of the Haflinger breed, and this, together with its friendly disposition and frugal nature, makes it an excellent family pony.

Haflingers have unusually long lives, and some animals have been known to continue working up to the age of 40.

The people of Austria are very proud of the Haflinger, and each animal born there is branded with an 'H' combined with the national flower, the eidelweiss.

History of the Haflinger

The breed takes its name from the village of Hafling, in the Sarn valley of the South Tyrol mountains. Today's Haflingers trace back to an Arabian stallion, El Bedavi XXII, who from 1868

Austria's eye-catching Haflinger is a versatile pony now seen in all parts of the world. Its distinctive colouring makes it easily recognizable.

1920s
After South Tyrol becomes part of Italy, focus of breeding shifts north, initially based on a very small pool of mares.

1939–45
Bloodlines become blurred as Haflingers are mass produced for military purposes.

1949
Breeding goals established, and a major programme of purifying the breed is begun.

1960s
Haflingers begin to make an international impact, and are increasingly used to strengthen and refine other breeds.

PRE | 1900   1950

c.550
Ostrogoths flee to Tyrol mountains in Austria taking with them their horses, probably of Arabian type, which were crossed with local stock.

1870s–90s
Sons and grandsons of the Arabian El Bedavi XXII used to consolidate features of the Haflinger.

1926
First stud book was published in Austria.

1930s
German army buys Haflingers as pack animals for mountain troops, and spurs interest in the breed.

1958
Stud book closed as post-war breeding programme is deemed a success.

was used to upgrade the local stock. It was one of his sons, Folie, who had the colouring for which the Haflinger was to become famous.

The first attempt to organize Haflinger breeding came in 1897, when the Austrian government hoped the horses would provide additional income for hard-pressed farmers. However, little came of the scheme. After World War I, when the South Tyrol was ceded to Italy, all but four Haflinger stallions were in the North Tyrol, while the vast majority of the broodmares were in the south. There was little choice but for the centre of Haflinger breeding to move north.

In 1921 a breeding co-operative was properly established, and in 1927 the Italian government allowed 100 mares to be imported into the North Tyrol. By the 1930s the breed was thriving on both sides of the border, and the German army was buying Haflingers

Renowned for its kind nature, the Haflinger is extremely popular in many different competitive sports and is the pride of its native land.

for its mountain troops. During World War II, the military's demand for these hardy, dependable animals was enormous, and little care was taken to preserve important bloodlines.

After the war, the Haflinger association in Austria set out the goals for the breed, and for 10 years managed the 2000 or so independent studs as if they were a single farm. A landmark exhibition promoting the Haflinger was held in 1954, and in the 1950s and 1960s Haflingers were exported to Germany, Italy, Yugoslavia, France, Britain, the Netherlands, Turkey, and the USA. Since then, their popularity has gone from strength to strength: Haflingers are now bred in more than 40 different countries.

The Haflinger today

Although used less by farmers and the military, Haflingers still have a role in the mountains, for they can go far beyond the reach of machines. They are attractive driving ponies and have also proved to be top-class trekking animals, for both children and adults.

Norwegian Fjord

The Norwegian Fjord's distinctive markings show that it is closely related to the primeval pony and Przewalski's Horse, the Asiatic wild horse. It is a strong and versatile pony, used for centuries for riding, work in the fields and forests, and pulling the family cart.

Breed characteristics

The Fjord is always dun in colour, with silver mane and tail, and a dark dorsal stripe running from the poll to the tail. The legs are dark and usually have the zebra markings associated with ancient breeds. Traditionally, the coarse mane is cut so that it stands upright.

The Norwegian Fjord's gaits are smooth, it is comfortable to ride, and has terrific powers of endurance.

History of the Norwegian Fjord

The Fjord's strong resemblance to primitive breeds suggests that there has been little cross-breeding for

thousands of years. The Fjord still breeds very true to its type, producing animals remarkably uniform in shape, height, colour, and character.

Ponies depicted in Viking rock drawings in Norway look very similar to the modern Norwegian Fjord. There is evidence that Viking raiders took their ponies with them to other countries, including Iceland, where they formed the foundation stock for the Icelandic Horse.

The Norwegian Fjord today

Still used on farms and for riding in Scandinavia, the Norwegian Fjord is becoming increasingly popular throughout northern Europe, and in the Americas, partly because of its unique appearance. Its gentle nature, strength, and stamina, and its tractable character make it a good driving pony and it is used in several types of competition, including vaulting.

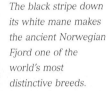

The black stripe down its white mane makes the ancient Norwegian Fjord one of the world's most distinctive breeds.

	PRE	1900		1950

8th–11th century
Vikings take Fjords to mainland Europe, Greenland, and Iceland, influencing local breeds.

pre 1900
In Norway, selective breeding produces a strong, versatile pony suitable for riding and farm and forestry work.

1910
The first Fjord stud book published.

1960s–70s
Fjord becomes very popular for driving and as a child's pony.

Icelandic Horse

The Icelandic Horse has served the people of this remote island for more than a thousand years, carrying them over rough countryside and across lava fields and fast-flowing rivers, as well as pulling their carts, and even providing them with an important source of food. The horse is still very much a part of Icelandic life and there are regular shows and race meetings designed to display the five gaits that are unique to the breed.

Breed characteristics

Small and sturdy, with a deep, compact body and a short, muscular neck, the Icelandic Horse is exceptionally strong, with plenty of stamina. Agile and sure footed, it is prized for its two extra gaits: the *tolt*, a four-beat 'running walk', and the pace, a speedy smooth trot in which the legs move in lateral instead of diagonal pairs. Although good tempered, the Icelandic Horse is very independent and won't necessarily bend to its handler's will.

Icelandic Horses have a remarkably strong homing instinct, and are able to find their own way home if turned loose even hundreds of miles away.

History of the Icelandic Horse

The foundation stock for the Icelandic Horse came with the Vikings, who settled in the country in the late 9th century. These animals are believed to have been Norwegian Fjords and, some sources claim, ancestors of the British Exmoors. Unlike in other European

Another ancient and relatively pure breed, the Icelandic is famed for its smooth, rapid walk, the tolt, *and its pacing gait, used in ridden races.*

countries, the bloodlines of the breed remained pure, thanks to a centuries-old law banning the import of all animals, including horses.

For hundreds of years the Icelandic Horse was the sole means of transport for the Icelandic people, as well as being essential for work on the land. When the first motor vehicles arrived in the early part of the 20th century, they reduced the need for horses, and a society was formed to help ensure the future of the breed.

The Icelandic Horse today

Practical use of the Icelandic Horse today is focused on rounding up sheep from the highlands, but thousands of people take part in sport (trekking, racing, and ice riding) and there is a keen interest in showing. Some herds are still bred for their meat, much of which is exported to Japan.

Because of its special gaits and toughness, the Icelandic Horse is increasingly popular for sport in other countries, especially Germany, but also the USA and Canada.

9th century Fjord and Celtic ponies brought to Iceland by the Vikings.		**19th century** Selective breeding methods introduced, designed to improve speed, gaits, and soundness.	**1904** Breed association founded.	**1960s** Breed becomes increasingly popular for both general riding and competition.

| | PRE | 1700 | | 1800 | 1900 | | |

	12th century Ban on import of animals into Iceland helps to preserve the purity of the Icelandic Horse.	**1783** Many thousands of horses die as a result of a volcanic eruption. Only the very toughest and hardiest animals survive.	**1906** First breed shows held in Iceland.	**1923** Iceland Horse register started.

Basuto Pony

This tough pony from southern Africa is strong and has great powers of endurance. It became famous during the Boer War of the late 19th century, when the British bought more than 30,000 to help them get across the country more easily.

Breed characteristics

Having developed in rough lands, Basuto Ponies are extremely tough and brave, qualities that have made them especially suitable for military use, and for competitive sports such as polo. The influence of Thoroughbred and Arabian horses has given them agility and speed (as well as imparting a particularly fine quality head). Good powers of endurance, which enable them to travel long distances easily, and the ability to carry relatively heavy riders have always made Basutos popular for trekking.

History of the Basuto Pony

The Basuto's homeland is Lesotho (formerly Basutoland) in southern Africa, but it is not an indigenous breed. Allegedly the main foundation stock for the Basuto was acquired in 1828, when Chief Msoshesha of Basutoland raided the South African Cape and captured some of the coveted Cape Horses. Allowed to run free in their new homelands, they interbred freely over the years.

Facing an inhospitable climate, with periods of drought often followed by torrential rain, and with little food readily available, they gradually developed into much smaller but more resilient animals, which became known as Basuto Ponies.

The Basuto Pony today

The Basuto is still popular for trekking, offering visitors an exhilarating way of exploring Lesotho's mountainous scenery. The pony is now also used for leisure riding as well as for challenging sports such as racing and polo.

Tough and tractable, the Basuto has adapted to cope with the rough terrain and conditions found in remote parts of southern Africa.

18th century
Arabian, possibly Barb, and later Thoroughbred blood used to produce one of the best military horses in the world.

1828
Cape Horses captured and taken back to Basutoland (now Lesotho). These were probably only the first of many raids during which such horses were acquired.

1600   1700   1800   1900

17th century
Java Pony and possibly Arabians and Barbs imported by South Africa through the Dutch East India Company.

19th century
Cape Horses breed in the wild in Basutoland. Adapting to cope with the harsh conditions, they became smaller and tougher, and known as Basuto Ponies.

20th century
Popular as polo ponies and for trekking.

Mongolian Pony

The Mongolian is the closest domesticated relative to the Przewalski, the Asiatic horse that is considered to be a direct descendant of the horses that came out of the last Ice Age. With the spartan country of Mongolia for a home, it is frugal, strong, and fast.

Breed characteristics

The Mongolian has many features of prehistoric horses, being compact and stocky with a rather heavy head, and often with zebra stripes on the limbs. It is, however, fine enough in its conformation to be agile and fast when required. The breed is generally extremely tough, with great powers of endurance, and can survive on poor quality food.

Mongolian Ponies are found all over the huge area stretching from Russia and the Mongolian republic to China and Tibet. They have been the working pony for the nomadic tribesmen there for centuries, and vary greatly from region to region, depending on the climate and food, and the availability of other horses for breeding. To a large extent, cross-breeding to make them faster and more manageable has led to a heterogeneous type.

History of the Mongolian Pony

The origins of the Mongolian lie with the Przewalski Horse, which was the last of the Asian wild horses. This takes its name from Colonel Nikolai Przewalski, a Russian explorer who, in 1881, discovered small herds of wild horses on the steppes of north-west Mongolia, at the edge of the Gobi Desert. Today most Przewalskis are bred in captivity, but in recent decades some 60 or so animals have been released into the wild.

Many Russian horses have had an important influence on the Mongolian. The regional variations of the breed – the Hailar, Sanpeitze, Sanho, and Ili,

which is the largest – have all benefited from the infusion of Russian blood.

The Mongolians in their turn have influenced many breeds. Originally Mongol tribesmen used these tough, speedy ponies to help them conquer lands throughout northern Asia and eastern Europe. In many countries the ponies remained after the invaders had left, and were used to develop other breeds, including the Turkoman, Spiti, Bhutia, Manipur, Tibetan, and China Pony, and possibly the Akhal-Teke.

The Mongolian Pony today

In Mongolia, people still depend on their ponies for transport and to work the land, and there are more horses per head of population than in practically any other country. Because of their speed, the ponies are also used for sport (polo and racing, in particular) and, as the country opens up to tourism, they are becoming popular for trekking. The mares are often milked after foaling as their milk can be made into cheese and, when fermented, into a beverage known as *kumiss*.

The Mongolian Pony has been the mainstay of the Mongolian people for centuries and remains crucial to their way of life.

MAIN FEATURES
- largish, heavy head
- small eyes
- short, thick ears
- strong, rather upright shoulders
- broad, deep chest
- short back
- high-set tail
- croup often higher than withers
- short limbs with good bone

CHARACTER
- tough

COLOURS
Black, bay, and dun are the most common.

HEIGHT
127–47cm (12.2–14.2hh) but varies according to region.

COUNTRY OF ORIGIN
Mongolia

COMPARISON BREED
Norwegian Fjord
Similar in type and history, the Norwegian Fjord has the distinguishing mark of a black dorsal stripe, indicating its ancient origins.

	PRE	1800		1900	

prehistory	throughout history	throughout history, but especially 20th century	20th century
Wild horses (now known as Przewalski's Horses) roaming throughout Mongolia provide foundation stock for Mongolian Pony.	Numerous types develop, varying according to local environment and available food.	Russian breeds have a refining influence, especially on the largest local variety the Ili.	Mongolian Pony still prized for its stamina, hardiness, and frugality. Popular for sport and, increasingly, for trekking.

RELATED TOPICS
Norwegian Fjord	62
Polo	220
Hunting	248
Riding holidays	250

Pony of the Americas

The Pony of the Americas, also known as the POA, was developed in the 1950s to provide a mount that was perfect for children. Built like a small horse and with the distinctive markings of an Appaloosa, the POA is versatile enough for gymkhana and attractive enough for halter classes.

Breed characteristics

The Pony of the Americas was produced for young riders who were too big for a small pony, but not ready for a full-sized horse. Originally, the breed standard specified that the pony should stand between 118 and 132cm (11–13 hands) at the withers, but that height limit has since been increased to 142cm (14 hands).

The head of the POA is small and refined, similar to an Arabian's, with a slightly dished profile, convex forehead, and large, expressive eyes. The body of the POA is well muscled, like that of the Quarter Horse, but smaller, with a broad chest, round barrel, sloping shoulders, and powerful hindquarters.

The most important element of the breed is its colouring: the pony should have the markings of an Appaloosa, which must be visible from a distance of 12m (40ft). These characteristics include a spotted coat in any of the classic Appaloosa patterns, as well as the white sclera around the iris of the eye, mottled skin around the eyes, muzzle, and genitals, and vertical stripes on the hooves.

History of the POA

Leslie Boomhower, a lawyer and Shetland Pony breeder in Iowa, founded the breed in 1954, after his Arabian/Appaloosa mare gave birth to a colt foal sired (accidentally) by a Shetland stallion. The foal was pony sized, yet had the stunning markings of the Appaloosa. Boomhower named the colt Black Hand, because of the distinctive pattern formed by the dark spots on its flank, and it became the first official Pony of the Americas and the foundation sire of the breed.

Although the POA is only just over 40 years old, enthusiasts have turned to other breeds – including Welsh Pony, Arabian, Thoroughbred, and Quarter Horse – to help infuse the pony with athleticism, size, and stamina.

The POA today

There are currently more than 40,000 POAs registered in the USA. In recent decades there has been a move to produce POAs that, although still an ideal size for children, have less Shetland blood in their veins. Breeders now strive to achieve a 'little horse' look instead of a pony conformation, which is why the height limit has been raised twice in the past 30 years.

Left: The POA is a great favourite with children, for whom this relatively modern breed was specifically developed.

Right: The POA's attractive markings stem from one of its parent breeds, the Appaloosa. Today the POA is very much a breed in its own right.

1600		1700		1800		1900		2000		2100

17th century
Spanish spotted horses brought to Americas.

1870s
Nez Percé Indians breed distinctive spotted horses that become known as Appaloosas.

1954
Arabian/Appaloosa mare bred to a Shetland produces POA foundation stallion, Black Hand.

1963
Shetland blood begins to be replaced with that of larger breeds, including Welsh Pony, Arabian, Quarter Horse, and Appaloosa.

MAIN FEATURES
- dished face
- stock horse body
- vertically striped hooves
- white sclera readily visible around iris of the eye

CHARACTER
- tractable
- gentle
- willing
- durable

COLOURS
The pony must have Appaloosa patterns and characteristics.

HEIGHT
Maximum 142cm (14hh)

COUNTRY OF ORIGIN
USA

COMPARISON BREED
Appaloosa
The American spotted horse, this is one of the breeds from which the POA is derived.

RELATED TOPICS
Shetland Pony   56
Welsh Pony and Cob   58
Appaloosa   104
Quarter Horse   112
Arabian   128
Pony Club   226
Showing   246

A day at Pony Club camp

Pony Club camp is the highlight of the year as it is a time when everyone gets together to see friends, learn about different aspects of horse and pony care, and practise everything from dressage to gymkhana, polo to showjumping. Louisa Brassey has belonged to the Pony Club for five years and is hoping that she may be considered for one of the teams for dressage, eventing, or showjumping as her pony is an excellent jumper and fairly good at dressage.

Most days are spent practising the different sports in rides during the morning followed by stable management, lectures, or demonstrations before lunch. At the end of the week there are showjumping competitions and the winners win rosettes and a cup each. There is a one-day event over the Pony Club course and there are three classes for different age groups. At the end of all of this there are rosettes and prizes for the best turned out and most improved in each ride.

Being in the Pony Club is a lot of fun and worthwhile at the same time. All the young riders meet lots of new friends and enjoy group lessons, learning new skills from a variety of different teachers.

▲ **12.00pm** 'We practise our balance by going down the jumping lane with our hands on our heads or without stirrups. We all think this exercise is great fun!'

▼ **10.30am** 'Most days we warm up with a group lesson. In our Pony Club there are about seven to nine riders in each group. The rides are sorted out by age and experience.'

▲ **8.30am** 'At many camps the riders stay together in tents, which can be great fun. We travel in daily, bringing our horses in a horsebox. This means we have to get up quite early!'

▲ **1.00pm** 'At lunchtme we sit with all our friends. Our horses also have a rest and are given their own lunch – a haynet – which is their fuel for the busy afternoon ahead.'

▲ **2.30pm** 'Sometimes we have a trainer from outside the Pony Club who helps us with our showjumping, dressage, or cross country and assesses us for the teams. Everyone hopes to be picked, so we all put on our best performances.'

▲ **3.30pm** 'In the afternoon we quite often have a lecture about stable management or we do some team practising over the showjumps or cross-country jumps. Sometimes we practise gymkhana games, which I particularly enjoy.'

◄ **4.30pm** 'Our treat at the end of the day is to have a go around the cross-country course. Sometimes it is quite hot so we have to wash our horses down afterwards and bandage them up for the night. The worst part of the day is having to clean our tack ready for the next day.'

Thoroughbred

Every aspect of the Thoroughbred is built for elegant speed. The world's most distinguished racehorses – Man O' War, Secretariat, Cigar, Mill Reef, Red Rum, Arkle – have all been Thoroughbreds. But the Thoroughbred is capable of being much more than a powerful runner. It is also a tremendous jumper, a steady hunter, and a brilliant dressage horse.

Breed characteristics

There are other breeds of horse that can sprint faster than the Thoroughbred, but none can touch it in a distance race.

Long and lean, the Thoroughbred is sleek as a Greyhound dog and as fit for performance. Thoroughbreds are generally tall horses, with long, slender necks, long, strong backs, and slim legs. They have a refined head, with large eyes, pointed, active ears, wide nostrils, and a delicate profile that tends to belie their power and speed. The withers are often prominent, and powerfully muscled hindquarters with a gradually sloping croup help to propel them over cross-country courses as well as racecourses. A good angle to the shoulders

provides the Thoroughbred with a beautiful, sweeping, long stride.

The breed has three basic body types: the tall, lanky body type of the sprinter; the close-coupled body of the stayer; and the combination type, which amounts to a medium-distance horse.

Right: The Thoroughbred is an outstanding athlete, and reigns supreme in the sport of eventing, as well as on the racecourse.

Below: The speed of the Thoroughbred over a long distance is exceptional, and has given rise to a hugely successful breeding industry worldwide.

1150s
Jennets, Andalusians, Barbs, and Turkmenians bred with native English horses.

1720s
Arabians, Barbs, and Turkmenians imported to increase endurance, stamina, and refinement.

1791
Introduction to a General Stud Book, tracing the pedigrees of English Thoroughbreds, published by James Weatherby.

1873
First volume of American Stud Book published by Col Sanders D Bruce.

1980s
Interest by Middle Eastern nations in racing enables the sport to spread to such places as Dubai.

PRE | 1700   1800   1900   2000

1170s
Galloway horses also used to improve the racing stock.

1690s
Eastern horses begin to be imported, to improve speed and endurance of racehorses.

1808
First volume of General Stud Book, a record of the English Thoroughbred, published by James Weatherby.

1950s
Improved transport allows greater movement of racehorses internationally.

MAIN FEATURES
- athletic
- slender
- long limbed
- long backed
- fast
- hot blooded

CHARACTER
- sensitive
- courageous
- bold
- intelligent
- quick thinking

COLOURS
Bay, dark bay, brown, black, chestnut, and grey.

HEIGHT
152–73cm (15–17hh)

COUNTRY OF ORIGIN
Britain

COMPARISON BREED
Arabian
The Arabian and the Thoroughbred are the only two 'hot-blooded' breeds in the world, and both have influenced speed and quality in numerous breeds.

RELATED TOPICS
Warmbloods   76
Hanoverian   84
Quarter Horse   112
Standardbred   116
Akhal-Teke   122
Arabian   128
Barb   132
Eventing   156
Dressage   168
Showjumping   176
Racing   184
Hunting   248

The sleek slenderness of the Thoroughbred – the quality that makes it a champion – is occasionally the breed's downfall, especially where breeding policies have been geared more to producing speed than to maintaining enough bone. On the racecourse, Thoroughbreds typically reach speeds of 70kmph (45mph), and serious injuries do sometimes befall these delicate powerhouses.

Thoroughbred racehorses often start their careers as two-year-olds, well before their bones have completely developed, which may make them susceptible to injury. However, if left to grow into adulthood before being put under saddle, horses stay very sound into their late teens and even beyond.

The trait for which the Thoroughbred is most famous is courage. It has the heart to meet a challenge, and the guts and determination to continue on bravely, even when injured.

History of the Thoroughbred

The origins of the Thoroughbred lie in the 'running horses' kept by the English kings as far back as the 12th century. Initially, these were mainly of Spanish descent (such as Andalusians, Spanish Jennets, and North African horses). Later, other breeds from Spain and Italy were introduced in order to develop the native stock into faster horses. During the 17th century, when formalized racing had just become established, owners sought to improve the speed and endurance of their racing animals by importing horses of oriental breeding.

The Thoroughbred can trace its lineage back to three stallions brought to England during the late 17th and early 18th centuries: the Byerley Turk (from Turkmenistan, possibly an Akhal-Teke), the Darley Arabian (from Syria), and the Godolphin Barb (from Morocco, via France). From these came three offspring that would forever influence the development of the Thoroughbred: from the Darley Arabian came Eclipse, from the Godolphin Barb came Matchem, and from the Byerley Turk came Herod. The greatest of the three, Eclipse, was foaled in 1764. He was undefeated on the turf, and was an extremely prepotent stallion.

The influence of these desert-bred horses was apparent in their offspring, as the Thoroughbred gained in size and stamina, and developed the ability to run at great speed over long distances.

Breeding records

Few records of breeding practices were kept in the early days, and of these many were incomplete. After diligent research, James Weatherby published his Introduction to a General Stud Book, tracing the pedigrees of English Thoroughbreds, in 1791; the first volume of the stud book itself appeared

Right: The grey Desert Orchid became a legend in the 1980s, winning Britain's prestigious King George IV steeplechase no fewer than five times.

Below: Thoroughbred foals are born early in the year. Weaned together after a few months, they thrive in each other's company.

in 1808 (and Weatherby's still publishes the stud book today). When racing became more popular in the USA, Col Sanders D Bruce of Kentucky started the American Stud Book; this was first published in 1873 and taken over by the American Jockey Club in 1896.

The breeding practices that promoted excellence in the racehorse by matching the best stallions to the best mares also produced a horse with outstanding all-round ability, whose influence has been seen in many different equestrian disciplines. The Thoroughbred became a favourite of fox hunters, since it was such a bold jumper. Before large Warmbloods became the rage in international

dressage competition, Thoroughbreds were often the pure-bred or part-bred choice. The Thoroughbred truly excels in the sport of three day eventing, with nearly every nation competing with one of these courageous horses.

Thoroughbreds have without doubt been the single greatest influence on most modern Warmbloods and have played a large part in the development of numerous other breeds, passing on not only increased size and speed, but also their tremendous staying power.

The Thoroughbred today

Some Thoroughbreds have a reputation for being too hot to handle for many sports, and for lacking the athletic prowess of the European Warmbloods. This has much to do with the racing environment and little to do with the horses themselves. The racehorse is fed a high-energy diet and led out just once a day to its short workout, and any breed forced to endure this regime would also be classified as 'hot'.

There is truth in the claim that Thoroughbreds are often overbred or bred for speed without thought for other qualities. The modern Thoroughbred hoof can be long in the toe with little heel, which is supposed to increase speed, but farriers complain that this eventually leads to a weakness in conformation. Also, many of today's racing Thoroughbreds do not have the substance that racers had 50 years ago, and their legs are often punished on the track. However, breeders are recognizing that substance is vital and are giving this far more serious consideration when choosing mares and stallions for breeding.

After racing, most Thoroughbreds are sold on to become competition horses such as eventers, dressage horses, showjumpers, or hunters. Several go into the showing world and numerous others end up as general riding horses. Because they tend to stop racing at the age of three or four, and because they are so versatile, it is relatively easy for Thoroughbreds to start new careers.

Cleveland Bay

The Cleveland Bay is one of the few bigger horses that breeds true to a colour: all are bay with black points (black legs, mane, and tail). This uniformity of colour has made them popular as carriage horses since it is easy to find matched pairs or teams of four. In their native Britain, they are still used to pull the royal carriages on state occasions.

Breed characteristics

The Cleveland Bay is tough and enormously strong, with great powers of endurance. These features, together with their consistent colouring, and their very amiable temperament, which makes them easy to train, give them the edge over many other breeds, especially for carriage work.

History of the Cleveland Bay

The Cleveland Bay is believed to be the oldest breed in Britain (other than the native ponies). Bred in the Cleveland area of north-eastern England, the foundation stock is said to date back to the Romans, and there are records of a clean-legged bay horse being used in Yorkshire in medieval times. Originally Clevelands were known as Chapman Horses since they were used as pack animals by the travelling salesmen referred to locally as 'chapmen'.

Crosses with other breeds were not unknown: the local racing pony, the now-extinct Galloway, is thought to have been used on the Cleveland Bay to inject some speed and sure-footedness; and the Thoroughbred was introduced to add a touch of refinement. Two Thoroughbreds named as having an influence are Manica, who was a son of the Darley Arabian, and Jalap, a grandson of the Godolphin Barb.

These big, strong horses were used for a range of purposes: for working on the land, for carrying goods, and for hunting, as well as for pulling carriages and carts. As the roads improved, there was a call for lighter, faster carriage horses, and again Thoroughbreds were crossed with Clevelands to meet the demand. Their tall, elegant offspring, known as Yorkshire Coach Horses, became extremely popular and many were exported all over the world.

The coming of the motor car made the Yorkshire Coach Horse redundant, and the breed all but disappeared. Because the pure-bred Cleveland Bays were more versatile, they remained in use as heavyweight hunters and as carriage and farm horses. However, after World War II, with increased mechanization, their numbers, too, went into decline.

There was a revival of interest in the breed in the 1960s, due largely to the intervention of HM Queen Elizabeth II, who bred a number of top-quality Cleveland Bays for use in the royal stables.

The Cleveland Bay today

The purity of the Cleveland makes it invaluable for crossing with other breeds whenever size, substance, and docility need to be injected, and a number of Warmbloods, especially in Germany, have benefited from Cleveland blood. In recent years the Cleveland Bay has been used as a competition horse. The pure-breds have been successful at the lower levels and in the show ring, but it is the part-breds that have excelled. With a little Thoroughbred in their veins they have been successful three day eventers, Olympic showjumpers, and top dressage horses. The Cleveland part-breds might not be as light, elastic, and athletic as some of the modern Warmbloods used for competitions, but they make up for this with their good balance, soundness, and power.

Right: Clevelands are traditionally shown in hand, usually with side reins. Their solid colour and tough 'blue' feet are well-known features.

Below: The Cleveland's proud head carriage and fine movement are already evident in this young foal, indicating a great future ahead.

Timeline

2nd century
The Romans brought in some of the foundation stock.

16th and 17th century
Chapman Horse developed as a pack horse for travelling salesmen ('chapmen').

18th century
Thoroughbred/oriental blood injected into the Chapman Horse to produce the Cleveland Bay.

19th century
Crosses between the Cleveland Bay and Thoroughbred resulted in the Yorkshire Coach Horse.

1883
Cleveland Bay Society formed.

1960s
Mechanization led to drastic reduction of numbers. Interest by British royal family was instrumental in a resurgence of general interest in the breed.

PRE | 1500 | 1600 | 1700 | 1800 | 1900

MAIN FEATURES
- largish head with a fairly straight face
- large eyes
- long ears
- long, lean neck
- sloping, deep shoulder
- long, strong back and hindquarters
- strong limbs with plenty of bone
- bluish black feet

CHARACTER
- kindly
- docile
- can be a little stubborn

COLOUR
Bay with black points. No other colour is allowed apart from a small white star and and some grey in the mane and tail.

HEIGHT
163–5cm (16–16.1hh)

COUNTRY OF ORIGIN
Britain (Cleveland)

COMPARISON BREED
Holstein
Germany's Holstein was influenced by Cleveland blood and has many similar attributes, being tough, strong, and excellent for riding and driving.

RELATED TOPICS
Thoroughbred   76
Hanoverian   84
Holstein   86
Dressage   168
Showjumping   176
Driving   194

Warmbloods

The Warmbloods are *the* 20th-century breed since they meet the growing demand for horses suitable for both sport and general riding. In the Olympic disciplines of dressage and showjumping, for example, most of the successful horses are Warmbloods. By far the vast majority of Warmbloods, however, are used as riding school horses and hacks – and it is in this sphere that, with their generous nature, they truly excel.

Breed characteristics

The aim of Warmblood breeders is to produce not the best possible specimen of a breed, but the best possible horse for riding and sport. The conformation should be balanced and correct, and the paces correct, elastic, and free; the temperament should be such that the horse is easy to train, and the character bold with an air of nobility.

All Warmbloods must go through a grading process before registration for breeding. Specific requirements vary from nation to nation, but generally the horses are assessed for conformation, movement, temperament, aptitude for work, and athletic and jumping ability. Some countries, such as Britain, hold shows for grading, while in others, such as Germany, horses are assessed individually when between two and a half and four and a half years old.

This process is designed to ensure that only the finest animals are used to produce the next generation of Warmbloods. Outside blood is injected whenever a characteristic needs consolidating or strengthening. So an Arabian may be used to improve endurance or the quality of the bone; a Thoroughbred to add refinement, class, and elegance; and another Warmblood if it is from a particularly strong showjumping or dressage line.

Warmbloods are more correctly called breed populations than breeds, since they are defined by the areas in which they are bred. For example, a Dutch Warmblood is one that is born in the Netherlands, but it might easily have a Hanoverian sire and a Holstein dam. The only exception is the Trakehner. These horses were evacuated from Prussia in the 1940s, and are now bred all over the world.

History of Warmbloods

Warmbloods were developed initially to meet the need for cavalry and carriage horses, then, from the early 1950s, to satisfy the demand for riding and sport horses. At all times only the horses most likely to meet a specific goal were used in the breeding. Originally, work horses were refined by crossing them with eastern breeds and Thoroughbreds; these cross-breeds were then refined further by the Thoroughbred, Arabian, and Anglo-Arabian to produce the modern Warmblood. The most successful of these to date are described below.

Australian Warmblood

The foundation sire for the Australian Warmblood was Flaneur, a 180cm (17.3 hands) Holstein who arrived in Australia in 1969. He was followed by more Holsteins, Hanoverians, Trakehners, and Oldenburgs; indeed,

Left: Warmbloods are the modern sport horse, developed especially to excel in competitions. Their movement and athletic jump are renowned.

Right: Most European countries have produced their own Warmblood, crossing their heavier local breeds with the Thoroughbred or Arabian.

1700	1800	1900	
18th century Breeders in Europe begin refining local horses to provide animals suitable for driving and farm work.	**19th century** Coach and lighter work horses infused with mainly Thoroughbred and Arabian blood to produce cavalry and carriage horses.	**20th century** Further refinement by Thoroughbreds, Arabians, and Anglo-Arabians to create the Warmblood.	**1950s–90s** Rigorous selection results in high-quality Warmbloods specifically designed as sport and riding horses.

MAIN FEATURES
- strong and muscular
- good limbs
- elastic movement and big jumps
- great presence

CHARACTER
- tough
- sensible
- easily trained

COLOURS
Bay, chestnut, brown, and grey are most common.

HEIGHT
163–78cm (16 –17.2hh)

COUNTRY OF ORIGIN
Most sporting countries have developed their own breed of Warmblood.

COMPARISON BREED
Riding Pony
This is an elegant, versatile pony which, like the Warmbloods, has been specifically developed to meet modern sporting needs.

RELATED TOPICS
Riding Pony   48
Thoroughbred   70
Selle Français   82
Hanoverian   84
Holstein   86
Oldenburg   88
Westphalian   90
Trakehner   92
Arabian   128
Eventing   156
Dressage   168
Showjumping   176
Hunting   248

for many years the Danish Warmblood was the only non-German Warmblood imported. These stallions were used on some of the high-class Australian Thoroughbred mares of the time, and produced quality offspring, such as Kibah-Tic-Toc (by the Hanoverian Domherr), who won the Olympic gold medal for three day eventing in 1992.

Belgian Warmblood

After World War II a programme to create a Belgian Warmblood was launched by the National Breeding Association of Agricultural Riding Horses. Hanoverians were imported from Germany, and Gelderlanders and Groningens from the Netherlands to cross-breed with Arabian, Anglo-Arabian, and Thoroughbred horses. A stud book was started in 1954. By 1970 there was more of a market for horses suitable for riding and competition than for agriculture, and the organization was renamed the National Breeding Association for Warmbloods. The Belgian Warmblood especially excels at showjumping, with Cyrano being one of its best international stars.

British Warmblood

Hanoverian stallions first stood in Britain in 1960 but no organization provided the opportunities for selective breeding. The British Warmblood Society was started in 1978 and, from then on, increasing numbers of Hanoverian, Dutch, Trakehner, and Danish stallions were brought to Britain. The most important of these include the Dutch Warmblood Dutch Courage, the Selle Français Dallas, and the Danish Warmblood Baron B. Their offspring have already competed for Britain at the Olympics, and with Dutch Gold winning World Cup qualifiers and youngsters winning in all disciplines, the British Warmblood is proving to be a most successful breed.

Danish Warmblood

In Denmark, a breeding programme to produce a national sport horse, known as the *Dansk Varmblood Avisforbund* (DVA), was started in 1962. The stallions imported were mainly Swedish Warmbloods, Trakehners, Hanoverians, and Holsteins, along with some Polish horses, which were bred mainly with local mares.

The Danish Warmbloods have been particularly successful in dressage, with Marzog winning a silver medal at the 1984 Olympics, and in eventing, with Monaco winning the European Championship in 1979.

Dutch Warmblood

The Dutch Warmblood was started in the 1960s. It was developed by crossing the native stocky Groningen and Gelderlander mares with Thoroughbred, Arabian, and Anglo-Arabian stallions.

Dutch Warmbloods are renowned for their superb temperament and their honest nature, which make them extremely easy to train. They are among the most successful of the modern Warmbloods, and they have excelled in all three Olympic disciplines as well as in driving.

The Dutch Warmblood Society divides the breed into five main categories: those suitable for dressage, showjumping, and eventing, which have a strong Thoroughbred influence; the riding horse type, which has more Arabian blood; the carriage horse type, crossed with heavier Dutch blood;

The success of Warmbloods in dressage has been phenomenal, as they have been selectively bred to produce the paces needed for this sport.

and two lighter riding and driving types, one crossed with Lipizzaner.

The registry and stud book is known as KWPN (*Koninklijk Warmbloed Paardenstamboek in Nederland*).

German Warmbloods

The most famous of the German Warmbloods, the Hanoverian, Holstein, Westphalian, Oldenburg, and Trakehner, are described on the following pages, but each region in Germany boasts its own breed of Warmblood. These include the Hesse, in which the Hanoverian and the Trakehner have been the major influences, and which started to develop into an important sport horse in the 1960s; the Bavarian, which has depended largely on Hanoverian bloodlines with some Holstein and Trakehner; and the Rhineland, considered a variation of the Trakehner because so much of this blood has been used in its development.

As a result of reunification in 1990 five further Warmblood breeding associations came under the German umbrella. These were Mecklenburg, Brandenburg, Sachsen-Anhalt, Sachsen, and Thuringen.

German Warmbloods are especially accomplished at dressage and showjumping, but careful selective breeding of the lightest types has also produced good eventers.

New Zealand Warmblood

Warmblood stallions started to be imported to New Zealand in the mid 1970s for breeding with the excellent local Thoroughbred stock, with the aim of producing a horse for showjumping and dressage. The first two stallions to stand in New Zealand were the Hanoverians Winnebago and Witzbold, both of whom produced international stars. Now there are representatives of most European breeds of Warmblood.

Polish Warmblood

The two main Warmbloods in Poland are the Malopolski in the south-east and the Wielkopolski in the north. The Malopolski, used for riding and driving, has been developed from local horses crossed mainly with Arabians and Thoroughbreds and some of the Hungarian breeds. The Wielkopolski has been more successful in sport and

The expressive and intelligent features of this Warmblood reveal a good attitude – always an important aspect to look out for.

has a high proportion of Thoroughbred blood. Trakehners and East Prussian horses have had a major influence.

Swedish Warmblood

The crucial point in developing a Swedish Warmblood came in 1747, when Crown Prince Adolf Fredrik became director of the national stud of Flyinge, and imported Hanoverian, Thoroughbred, Arabian, Oldenburg, and East Prussian horses to use on the small, rather coarse local mares. Over the years, rigorous selective breeding resulted in a very high-class cavalry horse. Today the Swedish Warmblood is most famous for dressage.

Swiss Warmblood

The native mares used to start the Swiss Warmblood in the 1960s were the Einsiedlers, bred at the Benedictine Abbey of Einsiedeln since the 11th century. Top-class stallions were imported – mainly Holsteins, Anglo-Normans, and, later, Selle Français – and rigorous selection methods were imposed, in a planned breeding programme that was led by the national stud at Avenches.

The Swiss Warmblood has a noble bearing and is good at dressage, driving, and showjumping.

The Warmblood today

The future of the Warmblood is bright as, above all others, the breed has been specifically bred for modern-day uses in various different countries, and has been adapted to suit modern trends through selective breeding. It is the ultimate sport horse.

French Trotter

Along with the American Standardbred, the French Trotter is the leading breed in the major industry of harness racing. It is more robust than its American counterpart and is sometimes used for other activities such as jumping and general riding.

Breed characteristics

French Trotters have no standard conformation, but range in type from those that closely resemble the Thoroughbred in appearance to a stronger, sturdier horse with straighter shoulders and more rounded action.

Below: The sensible head of the French Trotter belies the power and speed it displays on the racetrack, both in harness and under saddle.

The latter are particularly valued for ridden trotting races, which are especially popular in France.

Having been bred for nearly 200 years specifically to race at the trot, they are very fast in this gait.

History of the French Trotter

Although officially recognized as a breed only in 1922, the French Trotter was developed during the 19th century. At this time, the sport of harness racing was becoming increasingly popular, and the first dedicated racetrack was opened at Cherbourg in 1836. It was such a success that more tracks were quickly built, mainly in Normandy.

Breeders seeking to produce better trotters went to Britain to buy fast Thoroughbreds, and other English horses with good trotting blood, to put to the local Normandy mares; their offspring became known as Anglo-Normans. The most influential sires were The Norfolk Phenomenon (a Norfolk Trotter) and The Heir of Linne (a Thoroughbred). Breeding of trotters became centred around the two national studs at Le Pin and Saint-Lô in Normandy; important stallions used here included Lavater, James Watt, Phaeton, Cherbourg, and Fuschia, who is considered the patriarch of the breed.

Right: Trotters have great strength, stamina, and movement, and have influenced many breeds in Europe and the USA over the years.

1836
First French harness racing track opened at Cherbourg – a major stimulus to develop a fast trotter.

1864
Société du Demi-Sang ('half-breds') formed, to formalize and encourage selective breeding of the Trotter.

1937
Stud book closed to outside breeds.

1800	1850	1900	1950

1830s–40s
Norfolk Trotters and Thoroughbreds among stallions imported from Britain, resulting in the Anglo-Norman.

1906
Stud book started, leading to recognition of the breed in 1922.

1970s
Trotters used to produce the Selle Français, France's premier sport horse.

MAIN FEATURES
- refined type has similar features to the Thoroughbred; old-fashioned type has straighter shoulders and more rounded action
- strong, short body
- powerful hindquarters
- limbs well formed, hard, and sound

CHARACTER
- courageous
- tough

COLOURS
Most colours are found, but chestnut, bay, and brown are most common. Greys are rare.

HEIGHT
Varies but an average is 165cm (16.1hh).

COUNTRY OF ORIGIN
France

COMPARISON BREED
Orlov/Russian Trotter
Closely related to the French Trotter, this is extremely fast and is generally ridden on the track in France as well as driven.

There were two distinct types of Anglo-Norman: a fairly heavy animal used as a carriage horse by the army, and a lighter, faster harness horse. This lighter type became more and more in demand as harness racing spread across France. In the 1870s, after a track was opened near Paris, breeders sought out ways of producing even faster horses, and imported Standardbreds from the USA to try to inject extra speed. A stud book for the developing French Trotter was opened in 1906 and, to preserve its distinctive characteristics, was closed to outside breeds just over 30 years later.

The French Trotter today
Harness racing is flourishing so there is a great demand for the best of the breed. Many Trotters have been used to produce the Selle Français: Jappeloup, who won the showjumping gold medal at the 1988 Olympics, was sired by a Trotter, and the 1982 World Champion Galoubet was bred from a Trotter mare.

RELATED TOPICS

Thoroughbred	70
Selle Français	82
Orlov Trotter	125
Showjumping	176
Racing	184
Driving	194

Selle Français

The Selle Français was recognized as a breed only in the 1950s, but today it is France's most important sport horse. Strong, agile, and athletic, it is renowned primarily for its outstanding ability as a showjumper, but has also had success in dressage and eventing.

Breed characteristics

This relatively new breed is the French Warmblood. It is tough but active and supple, and is well muscled with strong limbs and good bone. A powerful mover, it is fast and intelligent, making it ideal for most sports.

The Selle Français stud book covers a wide range of types. Those used for competitions, and showjumping in particular, are the most famous. Then there are the racehorses, most of which are used for racing over fences but some are eventers. Almost, but not quite, pure Thoroughbreds, these are called AQPSA (*Autre Que Pur-Sang Anglais*). Lastly, there are the non-specialist horses used for leisure, trekking, and riding schools.

History of the Selle Français

The Selle Français was named as a breed in 1958, and its first stud book was published in 1965 (although it included offspring from 1950 onwards). The Selle Français was produced by crossing regional breeds with Trotters, Thoroughbreds, Arabians, and Anglo-Arabians. All the stock was registered in French stud books, with pedigrees tracing back generations, making

The Selle Français displays its special talent for showjumping as McLain Ward jumps Twist du Balon easily over this big oxer at Calgary.

1958	1980s–90s
Decree creating the Selle Français as a breed.	Selle Français acclaimed as an all-round competition horse, with a particular talent for showjumping.

| PRE | 1900 | | 1950 | |

Early 19th century	1920s–60s	1965
Arabian, Thoroughbred, and Trotter blood used on Normandy mares to found the Anglo-Norman.	Anglo-Normans (and other regional French breeds) crossed with Thoroughbreds to produce a faster, more athletic riding horse.	The first stud book for the Selle Français opened.

the Selle Français one of the few Warmbloods to have received very little foreign blood in the 20th century.

By far the most important of the regional breeds was the Anglo-Norman. This was developed during the 19th century in the heart of Normandy, France's most famous horse-breeding country, by using Norfolk Trotters, Thoroughbreds, and Arabians to refine the local mares (which themselves traced back to the medieval Norman war-horse). About 90 per cent of today's Selle Français trace back to this breed.

The other French regional breeds used to create the Selle Français were the Charolais, Corlay, Vendée, Anjou, Ain, and Ardennes. These were all pedigree half-breds that had been used in their areas as draught animals, and for agriculture, the military, and general riding.

The patriarchs of the Selle Français were a small number of Thoroughbreds. The first was Orange Peel, who stood at the national stud at Saint Lô from 1925 to 1940; his grandson Ibrahim had an enormous influence during the early years of the Selle Français. The next important group of Thoroughbreds were influential from the late 1940s and throughout the l950s and 1960s. First among these was Furioso, a stallion who is probably the most important Thoroughbred in modern Warmblood breeding. Then came Rantzau and Ultimate. The names of these Thoroughbred sires can be found in the pedigrees of virtually every successful modern Selle Français.

The Selle Français today

Although the number of Selle Français mares put to Selle Français stallions is increasing, there is still plenty of cross-breeding, which explains why the breed is suitable for such a wide range of activities. It has produced several international winners in showjumping, including Galoubet (1982 world team gold medallist), I Love You (1983 World Cup winner), Jappeloup (1988 Olympic champion), and Quito de Baussy (1990 World Champion).

The powerful movement and energetic paces, combined with an excellent temperament, make the Selle Français a top showjumper.

MAIN FEATURES
• distinguished head
• long neck
• sloping shoulder
• strong, muscular body
• large, powerful hindquarters
• strong limbs

CHARACTER
• especially trainable
• bold

COLOURS
All colours are found, but chestnut and bay are most common.

HEIGHT
163–8cm (16–16.2hh)

COUNTRY OF ORIGIN
France (mostly in Normandy)

COMPARISON BREED
Warmbloods
These are, in many cases, similar in type to the Selle Français but the French have included more Thoroughbred in their famous sport horse.

RELATED TOPICS
Thoroughbred   70
Warmbloods   76
Arabian   128
Eventing   156
Dressage   168
Showjumping   176
Racing   184

Hanoverian

The Hanoverian is one of the oldest, most numerous, and most successful of the Warmbloods. Hanoverians regularly win the World Breeding Federation of Sport Horses annual championships for showjumping and dressage, and they have won gold medals in all three Olympic disciplines.

Breed characteristics

Hanoverian breeders have long been well organized, and over the years they have assessed and adjusted their breeding programme to produce the kind of horse that is in demand – whether for the cavalry, for drawing carriages, or, as today, for sport. Their current aim is to breed a noble, versatile Warmblood with light and elastic gaits that cover the ground well.

The world-renowned state stud at Celle, which was founded in 1735, is the home of Germany's most successful Warmblood, the Hanoverian.

Whenever necessary, outside blood is brought in to ensure the market is offered the best possible horse. Hanoverians today are elegant, strong, and robust, if a little lighter than they once were. Strict selection ensures that Hanoverians are athletic and good jumpers, and have the gaits needed for dressage. They are bred, too, to be trainable and willing to work.

History of the Hanoverian

The Hanoverian is said to date back to the hefty war-horse of the Middle Ages. In 1735 George II, King of England and Elector of Hanover, founded the state stud at Celle (now in Lower Saxony, north-west Germany), and selective breeding began in earnest to produce horses for agriculture and for work in carriages. Selected stallions, many privately owned, were made available at Celle to the brood mares of local farmers. The bigger local horses were refined with Holsteins and English stallions (Thoroughbreds and Cleveland Bays); later some Neapolitan, Andalusian, Prussian, and Mecklenburg stock was used. By the end of the 18th century the Hanoverian had been turned into a high-class coach horse.

In 1844 the law laid down that only stallions passed by a commission could be used for breeding Hanoverians. In 1867, breeders started a society with the stated aim of producing a coach and military horse, and the first stud book for Hanoverians was published in 1888. The Hanoverian became one of the most popular breeds in Europe for coach and army work. When the demand for these declined after World War I, the breeding aim was adapted to

produce horses that were capable of farm work, yet with enough blood, nerve, and gaits to make a bold riding and carriage horse.

After World War II there was a growing demand for sport and general riding horses, and once again the Hanoverian was adapted. This time, mainly Thoroughbreds were used to refine the breed; occasionally an Arabian, Anglo-Arabian, or Trakehner stallion was used.

The key to the Hanoverian's success has been rigorous selection, a relatively large breed population, and the breeders' willingness to adapt in order to meet the demand of the day.

The Hanoverian today

The Hanoverian breeders' association offers its members many incentives to breed the best – from the famous auctions at Verden to the extensive grading opportunities for stallions, mares, and youngsters. In addition, few breeds have such good records kept about them. These enable breeders to trace bloodlines over many generations, improving their chances of finding the best match between mare and stallion for a given task. It seems likely, therefore, that the Hanoverian will retain its leading position – exemplified by the l997 European showjumping and dressage champions Ratina Z and Gigolo, the l997 World Cup showjumping winner ET FRH, and the 1998 dressage World Cup winner Walk on Top, all being Hanoverian.

Hanoverians have repeatedly excelled in the world of showjumping with their powerful and very athletic jump.

1867	1888	1928
Breeders' association started.	Hanoverian stud book published.	Westercelle centre started, where young stallions could be performance tested and trained in an 11-month programme.

1750	1800	1850	1900	1950

1735	18th century	1844	1920–40	1950
Hanoverian state stud at Celle was founded.	Thoroughbred, Holstein, and Cleveland Bay used to refine local mares, which traced back to the war-horse of the Middle Ages.	Legal requirement that breeding stallions must be approved by a commission.	Some Thoroughbred blood used to refine the Hanoverian to make it more suitable for riding.	Thoroughbreds and Arabians used to produce the world's top sport horse.

MAIN FEATURES
• powerful body
• strong back and feet
• athletic movement
• strong limbs
• tough constitution

CHARACTER
• particularly trainable
• calm
• willing

COLOURS
In the past chestnut was the most common, but today bay, brown, grey, and chestnut, with white markings, are found equally.

HEIGHT
160–78cm (15.3–17.2hh), but usually 163–8cm (16–16.2hh).

COUNTRY OF ORIGIN
Germany

COMPARISON BREED
Holstein
Among the oldest of the German Warmbloods, the modern Holstein has been refined to make it one of the most athletic and elegant of sport horses, excelling in all disciplines.

RELATED TOPICS
Thoroughbred 70
Warmbloods 76
Holstein 86
Trakehner 92
Eventing 156
Dressage 168
Showjumping 176
Driving 194

Holstein

The Holstein is thought to be the oldest of the German Warmblood breeds, and traces its ancestry back to the 13th century. Although Holsteins are relatively few in number, they have excelled in all disciplines.

Since the late 19th century, the Holstein has been supervised by an organization that helps its breeders to adapt to the demands of the market. In the past the Holstein was a top coach horse. Today, partly because of the Thoroughbred blood in its veins, it is a very elegant sport horse.

Breed characteristics

Holsteins are excellent movers, which makes them good at dressage; their powerful quarters make them good jumpers; and their sloping shoulders help to give their strides the freedom that good gallopers need.

History of the Holstein

The grassy marshlands of Schleswig-Holstein in northern Germany are particularly suitable for horses; historical documents show that monks there, close to the River Elbe, were breeding horses as early as 1225.

The area was famous in the Middle Ages for its war-horses. From the 16th to the 18th century they were refined with Spanish, Neapolitan, and Barb blood to become rather heavy but very popular coach horses. In the 19th century, with faster carriages and a continuing demand for light cavalry horses, British stallions were imported to lighten the breed. The most important of these were three Yorkshire Coach Horses, who all traced back to the famous Thoroughbred racehorse Eclipse. They helped to make the Holstein a high-stepping carriage horse that was also strong enough for agricultural work.

British blood was used again in the next major refinement in the 1960s. Holsteins like the famous showjumper Meteor were very powerful but rather hefty for modern requirements. Thoroughbreds were imported from Britain and Ireland – although one, Anblick, was German bred – to make the Holstein more athletic. The most influential were Cottage Son, Ladykiller, and Marlon. Other important outside blood was Ramzes, an Anglo-Arabian from Poland, and Cor de la Bruyère, a Selle Français. The results were very successful: the next generation of stallions were among the most potent in the world of sport horse breeding. These included Landgraf (a great grandson of Anblick) by Ladykiller, and Ramiro (a grandson of Ramzes), out of a Cottage Son mare.

Holstein blood has been very influential in the development of other sport horses, especially the Dutch, Danish, and British Warmbloods.

The Holstein today

The Holstein has many representatives at Olympic and championship level. In dressage, Corlandus was the 1987 European Champion, and Olympic Silvano has won many medals; in eventing there have been horses such

Above: The Holstein's elegance and power is evident as Calvaro and Willi Mellingher soar over one of the fences at Mannheim, Germany.

Right: Finn Hanson and Bergerac demonstrate supreme control and tremendous balance in the dressage arena at the 1996 Olympics.

as the 1976 Olympic medallist Madrigal, and in showjumping the 1994 World Cup winner Libero H.

Demand for this very successful Warmblood for competition and general riding is high and looks likely to continue. It remains very popular in Germany for all types of sport.

1225 First evidence that a horse was being bred by the monks on the banks of the River Elbe in Schleswig-Holstein, northern Germany.	**19th century** Yorkshire Coach Horses from Britain helped to refine the breed, giving it more speed and agility.	**1935** Society of Breeders of Holstein Horses founded, to promote Holsteins for general riding.	**1980s–90s** Holstein acclaimed as one of the most influential breeds of sport horse.

PRE | 1800 | 1850 | 1900 | 1950

Middle Ages Holstein was well-known as a war-horse.	**16th–18th century** Spanish, Neapolitan, and Barb blood introduced to produce high-stepping draught horses that were popular all over Europe.	**1867** State stud founded at Traventhal to breed Holsteins for military purposes.	**1890s** Local breeders form Holstein breeding societies to produce horses suitable for agricultural work.	**1960s** Refined by extensive use of the Thoroughbre

MAIN FEATURES
- tall and elegant with long, crested neck
- sloping shoulders
- strong back and hindquarters
- powerful limbs
- strong feet
- tail carried well (but not high set)
- more powers of endurance than most Warmbloods

CHARACTER
- eminently trainable

COLOURS
Bay, dark bay, and black are most common, but other colours are also sometimes found.

HEIGHT
Wide range but usually 163–73cm (16–17hh).

COUNTRY OF ORIGIN
Germany (Schleswig-Holstein)

COMPARISON BREED
Oldenburg
A robust yet versatile breed, the Oldenburg developed along similar lines to the Holstein, starting as a heavier breed and now excelling as a sport horse.

RELATED TOPICS
Thoroughbred   70
Warmbloods   76
Oldenburg   88
Eventing   156
Dressage   168
Showjumping   176
Driving   194

Oldenburg

The Oldenburg was one of the tallest and strongest of the German regional breeds. In earlier centuries it was much in demand as a strong, elegant, high-stepping coach horse. As the need for such animals declined, the Oldenburg was adapted to become an all-purpose riding horse, and is now one of the leading sport horse breeds.

Breed characteristics

Most Oldenburgs have a fairly international pedigree, which means that there is a good range of types within the breed. But with all breeding stock being chosen because it is strong and athletic with a calm temperament, Oldenburgs today have all the essential qualities of a modern riding horse and outstanding sport horse.

History of the Oldenburg

Bred in Lower Saxony, in north-west Germany, the Oldenburg has much in common with its neighbour, the East Friesian from eastern Germany. Both breeds have been influenced by the Dutch Friesian.

The foundations of the breed were laid by Count Johan von Oldenburg in the late 16th century. He bred his Friesian mares with Danish, Turkish, Neapolitan, and Andalusian stallions, to produce large, strong war-horses. His son, Count Anton, began travelling throughout Europe and brought home the finest Spanish and Italian stallions, to add speed and strength to the local stock. His tenant farmers too were

Versatile and very trainable, the Oldenburg was the tallest and strongest of all the German Warmblood breeds.

Late 16th century
Dutch Friesian mares bred with Turkish, Italian, Spanish, and Danish stallions to produce hefty war-horses.

18th century
The Oldenburg was refined with Thoroughbred blood.

1950s–70s
Cross-breeding with high-class stallions from many European breeds produced a much more refined and successful sport horse.

1500	1600	1700	1800	1900

17th century
Breed named after Count Anton Oldenburg, who helped to refine it with Italian and Spanish horses, and developed a strong, high-stepping coach horse.

19th century
Oldenburg farmers' breeding association brought in more stock from Britain and France to upgrade the breed as an elegant but powerful working horse.

allowed to breed from his stallions, establishing the tradition of small, private studs that still make up the vast bulk of Oldenburg breeders today.

During the 17th century the Oldenburg became famous as a coach horse, renowned for its height, power, and elegance; it was also used as a riding horse. In the 18th century the breed was refined with Thoroughbred blood. During the 19th century, as Oldenburgs served with the army and worked on the land, the breeders moved slowly towards organized management. In 1820, it became illegal to use any but government-approved stallions for breeding. In 1861, the Oldenburg stud book was established, and in 1897 the Oldenburg farmers formed a breeders' association and bought Thoroughbreds, Cleveland Bays, Yorkshire Coach Horses, Normans, and some Hanoverians to further improve the breed.

In the earlier part of the 20th century the Oldenburg was still being used on farms and as a supple, high-stepping carriage horse. As machinery replaced horse power, the stud owners decided to develop an all-round riding horse. In the 1950s, the Thoroughbred Lupus and the Anglo-Norman Condor founded a new Oldenburg stallion line, which produced a series of heavy but elegant mares. From then, and especially since the 1970s, the finest of European stock has contributed to the breed. Thoroughbreds were used first, to refine the Oldenburg, and the resulting mares were then bred to the best available stallions, including Trakehners, Anglo-Normans, Anglo-Arabians, Selle Français, Hanoverians, and Westphalians. The result has been an extremely successful riding horse, smaller and lighter than its forebears and less distinct than before from other Warmbloods, but its great sporting achievements more than compensate for that.

The Oldenburg today

In the 1990s, the Oldenburgs have been especially successful in dressage. Gestion Bonfire has won the World Cup three times; Donnerhall – perhaps the most popular stallion of the decade – has won numerous medals, including ones at both the World and European Championships; and Dondolo has won medals at the World Equestrian Games.

Oldenburgs are particularly successful in the dressage arena, thanks to the rigorous selection process for good paces and temperament.

MAIN FEATURES
- balanced conformation
- often a long neck
- sloping shoulder
- deep, muscular body
- strong hindquarters
- good bone

CHARACTER
- particularly trainable
- bold
- calm temperament

COLOURS
Bay, brown, and black are most common.

HEIGHT
165–78cm (16.1–17.2hh)

COUNTRY OF ORIGIN
Germany (Lower Saxony)

COMPARISON BREED
Westphalian
This is another strong German breed that has excelled as a sport horse in most disciplines.

RELATED TOPICS

Selle Français	82
Westphalian	90
Friesian	96
Eventing	156
Dressage	168
Showjumping	176
Driving	194

Westphalian

Of the German Warmbloods, the Westphalian is second in numbers only to the Hanoverian. It is bred in the heart of Germany's equestrian sports area, Westphalia, and the Westphalian state stud is at Warendorf, some 130km (80 miles) south-west of Hanover. The German Olympic Equestrian Centre is also based at Warendorf, and many of the country's leading competitors have their homes nearby.

Breed characteristics

The Westphalian's major asset is that so many riders are based in its breeding area. They have helped to ensure that the horses bred are suitable for equestrian sport. The result is a tough, sound athlete that has won many major championships in all disciplines. It is often heavier than the Hanoverian but has an attractive and intelligent head, and a strong body with plenty of bone.

History of the Westphalian

The Hanoverian, from the neighbouring breeding area, played a significant part in the Westphalian's development. At first, the latter was simply a heavier version of the Hanoverian with more bone and substance. However, since the 1960s, some Thoroughbred lines have had a major influence, and the breed has become more refined to meet the demands of the market.

One of the greatest Westphalians of all time was Ahlerich who, with Dr Reiner Klimke, won team and individual gold medals for dressage

The state stud at Warendorf has been an important breeding centre for the Westphalian since the early 19th century.

at the 1984 Olympic Games. They also won the World and European Championships in 1982 and 1985. The next great dressage champion was another Westphalian, Rembrandt: outstanding for his personality and presence, he amassed four Olympic gold medals to his credit from the 1988 and 1992 Games. Other successful Westphalians have included Sioux, a member of the eventing team in both the 1972 and 1976 Olympics, and the showjumpers Roman and Fire, who won the World Championships in 1978 and 1982 respectively.

The Westphalian today

The association of Westphalian breeders has led the way in involving sports people in its breeding policy. This has produced excellent results and helped to make the Westphalian one of the most successful Warmbloods.

Left: The Westphalian has perhaps made its name especially through the two great dressage stars Ahlerich and Rembrandt, but it excels in all fields.

Right: A fine example of the breed, Virtual Village Showtime leaps effortlessly over a large oxer to score a clear round at Calgary, Canada, in 1997.

1900		1950	
1904 Westphalian breed register started.	**1920s** Selective breeding of mainly Hanoverian stock produces the stronger, heavier Westphalian.	**1960s** Growing use of the Thoroughbred to lighten the Westphalian.	**1980s–90s** From the late 1970s onwards, the Westphalian is increasingly successful in international competition, especially in dressage and showjumping.

MAIN FEATURES
• athletic, strong
• good gaits
• plenty of substance
  and bone
• balanced conformation

CHARACTER
• trainable
• co-operative
• kind

COLOURS
All solid colours.

HEIGHT
157–78cm (15.2–17.2hh)

COUNTRY OF ORIGIN
Germany (Westphalia)

COMPARISON BREED
Hanoverian
This is another great
German sport horse,
which is bred in the
neighbouring region
and in larger numbers.

RELATED TOPICS
Thoroughbred   70
Hanoverian   84
Eventing   156
Dressage   168
Showjumping   176
Driving   194

Trakehner

The Trakehner is the most pure-bred of all Warmbloods, since in recent times only approved Thoroughbred and Arabian stock has been added to the Trakehner bloodlines. It is also more refined than other Warmbloods, and because of its lighter type has proved to be more successful at sports such as three day eventing.

From its origins as a courageous cavalry and coach horse, the Trakehner, with its celebrated free and easy movement, has become one of the most striking and willing of modern sport horses, with a string of international successes to its name.

Breed characteristics

The Trakehner is an elegant horse with plenty of stamina. It is athletic and spirited, and similar to the stronger type of Thoroughbred. Because of the purity of its bloodlines, it breeds pretty true to type, reliably passing on its characteristics to its offspring – a quality that has made it useful for upgrading other Warmbloods.

History of the Trakehner

The Trakehnen stud was founded in East Prussia (now the border region between Lithuania and Poland) in 1732, by King Frederick William I. Frederick took the best of the local Schweiken ponies and began breeding selectively among them. These tough, versatile ponies had originally been developed as war-horses, from the 13th century on, by the Knights of the Teutonic Order. The new Trakehner line was bred as an attractive, comfortable, and fast cavalry horse; it also served as a popular coaching horse, and a useful light draught animal in farming.

Between 1817 and 1837 the stud introduced Arabian, Thoroughbred, and some Turkoman blood to refine the breed. The results were hugely successful as light cavalry mounts in the 19th century. Although demand for these declined as the 20th century progressed, the Trakehner came to the fore as a performance horse. In the 1920s and 1930s, Trakehners took gold and silver medals in dressage at two Olympics, and won Czechoslovakia's notoriously difficult Velka Pardubicka steeplechase nine times. In the 1930s, there were as many as 10,000 Trakehner breeders and 18,000 registered mares.

With its elegance and proud bearing, this young Trakehner is typical of the breed – a fine example of the success of the German breeding system.

1732
Foundation of the Trakehnen stud in East Prussia by Frederick William I. Selective breeding among local Schweiken ponies produces Trakehner foundation stock.

1945
The flight of 600 Trakehners from East Prussia to western Germany; only a few survive.

1990s
Trakehners bred throughout the world.

1750	1800	1850	1900	1950

1817–37
English Thoroughbred and Arabian stallions purchased and added to the breed. Some Turkoman blood introduced.

1877
First Trakehnen stud book published.

1947
Formation of the Trakehner Association in West Germany to save the breed from extinction.

MAIN FEATURES
- refined head
- broad between eyes
- narrow at muzzle
- face often dished
- good front with crested neck
- sloping shoulder
- strong, medium-length back
- gently rounded quarters

CHARACTER
- trainable, but more spirited than other Warmbloods
- plenty of stamina

COLOURS
Usually chestnut, bay, black, or grey.

HEIGHT
157–73cm (15.2–17hh)

COUNTRY OF ORIGIN
East Prussia

COMPARISON BREED
Thoroughbred
The Thoroughbred is a more refined breed than the Trakehner, since it is bred to race rather than compete, but the two do have many similarities, and the Trakehner has benefited from Thoroughbred blood.

RELATED TOPICS
Thoroughbred 70
Warmbloods 76
Arabian 128
Eventing 156
Dressage 168
Showjumping 176
Driving 194

Towards the end of World War II, when it became obvious that Soviet occupation of East Prussia was imminent, a group of private breeders collected some 600 horses, and made a desperate trek westwards to escape the approaching Red Army. Many more horses were left behind; they were to have a major influence on Russian breeds as well as on the Polish Mazury and Poznan (which developed into the Wielkopolski). The horses that reached safety in Germany were the nucleus from which the Trakehner of today was established. As before, there has been cross-breeding with selected Arabian, Thoroughbred, and Anglo-Arabian lines, but not with other Warmbloods.

Trakehners have, however, been widely used to improve other Warmblood stocks. Influential Trakehner stallions include Abglanz for the Hanoverian, Herbsturm for the Oldenburg, Marco Polo for the Dutch Warmblood, Ibicus and Donauwind for the Danish Warmblood, and Polarstern for the Swedish Warmblood.

In competitions the star is Abdullah by Donauwind, who won the team gold and individual silver medals in showjumping in the 1984 Olympics, then went on to win the World Cup the following year; while Heuringer was the showjumping team silver medallist at the 1994 World Equestrian Games.

The Trakehner today
The Trakehner is produced now all over the world, and there are Trakehner organizations in most countries, reflecting the enormous popularity of the breed. The mother stud book is held by the Trakehner Association, in Neumunster, Germany.

A member of the American dressage team that won the bronze medal at the 1996 Olympics in Atlanta, the Trakehner Peron performs the flying change in perfect balance.

Andalusian

The Andalusian is one of the world's most ancient breeds. Cave drawings found in Spain of horses that seem to be ancestors of the modern Andalusian date back at least 20,000 years. It has certainly retained its characteristic features over the last 1000 years or so, and has been a very popular horse for dressage, for the military, and for improving other breeds.

Breed characteristics

The Andalusian is a strong and compact horse, yet supremely elegant, with an arresting presence. The legs are clean, with plenty of bone, and they have a high, rounded action, which makes the Andalusian particularly suitable for the athletic movements of advanced or High School dressage.

History of the Andalusian

The Andalusian possibly traces back to the ancient steppe horse that some say roamed the area from the Atlas Mountains and Spanish Sierras to Turkmenistan. Others claim that the Andalusian developed from the Przewalski's Horse (the Asiatic wild horse) and that they were refined over the years by breeding with Barbs and Arabians brought by the Moors when they overran the Iberian peninsula in the 8th century.

Spanish horses were known as outstanding cavalry mounts from the time of the ancient Greeks, but they fell from favour in the Middle Ages when, with the use of increasingly heavy armour, they were replaced by stronger breeds. After the invention of firearms in the 15th century, lighter, more agile cavalry horses were once more in demand, and the Andalusian's fortunes rose again.

It was at this time that Andalusians were taken by Columbus and the conquistadores to the New World, where horses had been extinct for thousands of years. The Spanish horses were used as foundation stock for many of the breeds that flourish in the USA today, including the Criollo, Paso Fino, the Mustang, and the Appaloosa.

With the founding of the great classical riding academies across Europe during the Renaissance, the Andalusian really came into its own. Because of its agility and natural balance, it excelled at the gymnastic movements involved in High School dressage, and performed extensively at the royal courts of Europe. The Andalusian was also called on to develop other breeds suitable for High School equitation: the Lipizzaner, Alter Real, Lusitano, Kladruber, and many of the European Warmbloods all used Andalusian blood.

During the 19th century, court life became less ostentatious, and the use of the Andalusian declined. Fortunately, Carthusian monks continued to breed Andalusians, as they had done for centuries, and preserved the purest strain of the breed. Today the Spanish government promotes the Andalusian, and more and more people are appreciating this ancient breed.

The Andalusian today

With a renewed interest in High School dressage, a growing number of schools in Spain are using Andalusians for this spectacular work and giving displays round the world. Their sensible temperament makes them suitable for one of Spain's most famous activities – bullfighting. The *Regjonedores* (mounted bullfighters) use them for High School work in the bullring. Eminently trainable and athletic, Andalusians have recently been used for sport, in showjumping, dressage, driving, and endurance – although often some Thoroughbred blood is added to give the offspring more scope.

Renowned for its calm temperament yet full of presence, the Andalusian breed is the pride of Spain, and a favourite mount at fiestas.

The high-stepping movement, flowing mane, and noble bearing are well demonstrated here as this beautiful Andalusian plays in its paddock.

30,000–20,000 BC
Cave drawings of horses resembling the modern Andalusian made at La Pileta, near Malaga, southern Spain.

16th and 17th centuries
Andalusians used by Spanish colonists in the Americas to found the Criollo, Paso Fino, Mustang, and Appaloosa.

19th century
Carthusian monks' breeding programme preserves the purest strain of Andalusian.

1911
First stud book published.

| PRE | 1600 | 1700 | 1800 | 1900 |

AD 711
Arabians and Barbs brought to Spain by invading Moors.

1580
Andalusians taken to Lipizza (now in Slovenia), where they were used to found the Lipizzaner breed.

17th century
Andalusians used in development of many European Warmbloods, such as the Hanoverian and Holstein. Also infused Lipizzaner, Kladruber, Alter Real, and Lusitano breeds.

20th century
Cross-bred with Thoroughbreds to produce a modern sport horse with plenty of scope.

MAIN FEATURES
- large head
- broad forehead
- convex profile
- muscular, crested neck
- long, sloping shoulder
- deep, close-coupled body
- broad, rounded hindquarters
- quite short cannon bones
- long mane and tail

CHARACTER
- very amenable to discipline
- tremendous presence

COLOURS
Grey is the most common colour, although bay, black, and roan are also found.

HEIGHT
155–60cm (15.1–15.3hh)

COUNTRY OF ORIGIN
Spain

COMPARISON BREED
Lipizzaner
This has the noble bearing and elegant, high-stepping movement of the Andalusian, to which it is related.

RELATED TOPICS
Lipizzaner	100
Dressage	168
Driving	194
Endurance	212

Friesian

An old Dutch breed, which is always black with a long, luxuriant mane and tail, the Friesian has great presence and a spectacular trot. It is most famous as a driving horse, but it is used more and more for displays under saddle.

Breed characteristics

The uniformity of colour has made Friesians very popular in many countries as carriage horses since it is easy to make up matching pairs and teams. Friesians are also a good size for carriage driving competitions because they are not too big and are therefore relatively easy to manoeuvre through the course.

The other major feature of the breed is their fast, high-stepping trot. They flex their legs very high and were used for trotting races before other breeds (such as the French Trotter and the American Standardbred) were selectively bred for this sport.

History of the Friesian

The breed was developed in the northern Netherlands, in the province of Friesland, home of the famous black and white cattle. This is good horse-rearing country with rich grasslands and there is evidence that horses have been here for thousands of years. The Romans are known to have used

Friesland horses, and it is believed that they took some to England where they influenced the development of such native breeds as the Fell, Dales, Shire, and Clydesdale.

Works of art from medieval times show stocky, black horses – looking very much like the modern Friesian – carrying armour-clad knights. As the need for heavy war-horses diminished, Andalusian blood was introduced to lighten the breed, to make it more suitable for carriage work. The

This fine example of the Friesian displays the breed's most prized attributes: active movement, noble manner, and strong conformation.

1000 BC
Fossilized remains of heavy horses in Friesland date back to this time.

18th and 19th centuries
Friesian used to develop other breeds including the Orlov Trotter, Norfolk Trotter, and the Morgan.

1940–4
Resurgence in popularity of Friesian as a means of transport during World War II.

| PRE | 1600 | | 1700 | | 1800 | | 1900 | |

12th and 13th centuries
Eastern horses, brought to the Netherlands by Crusaders from Palestine, mix with native stock. ·

16th and 17th centuries
Andalusians and eastern stock crossed with the heavy native horses to establish the Friesian.

1879
Stud book started, but purity of the Friesian is threatened by cross-breeding to produce a faster trotter.

1990s
Friesians become increasingly popular internationally for showing as well as for driving.

Friesians' heyday came in the 18th and 19th centuries: they were much in demand for agricultural work and for pulling carriages; they excelled in the trotting races so popular at that time; and they were used as the foundation stock for other breeds. Friesians played a part in the development of the Orlov Trotter in Russia, the Norfolk Trotter (ancestor of the Hackney) in Britain, and the Morgan in the USA.

Although a stud book was started in 1879, it was open to cross-bred horses as well as pure-breds. Such was the fashion for using Friesians to inject their spectacular trot, presence, and colour into other breeds that it threatened the purity of Friesians themselves. In 1913 a new association was formed and succeeded in preserving the bloodlines. Despite this the Friesian almost became extinct in the first part of the 20th century, until a shortage of motor vehicles and fuel in World War II led the people of the Netherlands to turn once more to the horse as a means of transport.

The Friesian today

Friesians today are wonderful all-rounders, very popular for showing, driving, and general riding. Crowds love to watch Friesians in action, and they are used internationally in circuses and in demonstrations of High School dressage.

The Friesian is an extremely popular driving horse and, being so easily matched, always looks spectacular in full harness.

MAIN FEATURES
- long, fine head
- arched neck with long mane
- compact, strong body
- sloping quarters
- short, strong limbs

CHARACTER
- willing
- kindly
- active and energetic

COLOUR
Black

HEIGHT
150–60cm (14.3 –15.3hh)

COUNTRY OF ORIGIN
Netherlands (Friesland)

COMPARISON BREED
Fell Pony
This ancient British breed has been influenced by Friesian blood. Fells are usually dark in colour and have energetic paces.

RELATED TOPICS

Fell Pony	51
Andalusian	94
Driving	194
Endurance	212
Ceremonial and working horses	232
Showing	246
Riding holidays	250

97

Irish Draught

The Irish Draught was developed by farmers to be strong enough to pull the plough yet spirited and light enough for riding. Today it is most valued for breeding: when crossed with the Thoroughbred, its offspring are known as Irish Horses, which are ideal for showjumping, eventing, hunting, and general riding.

Breed characteristics

The Irish Draught is a lighter animal than its name suggests, almost light enough to be classified as a Warmblood, and it moves much more freely than the traditional heavy draught horse. It is a very versatile horse, having the strength and stamina to be a good heavyweight hunter, the power through its well-made hindquarters to be a good jumper, and the kindly, bold temperament that makes it popular for riding.

History of the Irish Draught

The early history of the Irish Draught traces back to the 12th century when war-horses taken to Ireland by the Anglo-Normans bred with the native stock. Spanish horses, brought to the island in the 16th century, also had some influence. However, the Irish Draught type really began to emerge in the 18th century when Thoroughbreds were used on native mares to produce light work horses suitable for all aspects of rural life. The breed flourished for a time, but demand fell with the famine of 1847 and the agricultural recessions of the 1870s, and numbers declined. When the

Irish Draughts have influenced the breeding of many Warmbloods and been extremely successful when crossed with Thoroughbreds.

18th century
Irish native mares crossed with Thoroughbreds to produce a light and versatile work horse for farmers.

1970
Irish Horse Board established to help organize breeding of both pure-breds and cross-breds.

PRE | 1800   1850   1900   1950

Late 19th century
Clydesdale and Shire cross-bred with Irish Draught to help meet demand for a work horse in Ireland.

1917
Irish Draught stud book started by the Ministry of Agriculture.

1976
Irish Draught Horse Society established.

MAIN FEATURES
• intelligent head
• straight face
• short, thick, crested neck
• deep body
• powerful, sloping
  hindquarters
• strong limbs
• flat, big bone to limbs
• straight forelimbs
• large feet

CHARACTER
• alert and active
• kind
• sensitive

COLOURS
Bay, brown, chestnut, and
grey are most common.

HEIGHT
152–73cm (15–17hh)

COUNTRY OF ORIGIN
Britain (Ireland)

COMPARISON BREED
Welsh Cob
Although small, the Welsh
Cob is hardy and tough,
and sufficiently versatile to
perform a variety of tasks.

RELATED TOPICS
Welsh Pony and Cob   58
Eventing   156
Showjumping   176
Ceremonial and
working horses   232
Showing   246
Hunting   248

economy improved, the call for such horses again increased, and heavier British breeds, such as the Clydesdale and Shire, had to be imported to meet the demand. Over the years, these were cross-bred with the Irish Draught, producing bigger, coarser animals.

At the beginning of the 20th century the Irish government took steps to help the breed, introducing registration and subsidies for stallions in 1907 and for mares in 1911. Inspections before registration began soon afterwards. A stud book for the breed was opened in 1917, for which 375 mares and 44 stallions were selected, and these animals formed the foundation stock for today's Irish Draught.

As tractors and motor cars took over much of the horse's work, it was for cross-breeding that the Irish Draught became most popular. Recognized as a valuable producer of eventers and showjumpers, it was exported all over the world. Before long, the pure-bred Irish Draught was in danger of dying out and, in the 1970s, the newly formed Irish Horse Board started to give subsidies and organize selective breeding programmes in an attempt to preserve the purity of the breed.

The Irish Draught today
Apart from showing, the main demand for the Irish Draught is for crossing with other breeds to produce sport horses. More and more, it is being called on to give extra bone and substance to the offspring of lighter stock. This means that controls are needed to ensure that the fashion for cross-breeding does not lead to the Irish Draught's extinction. Fortunately in both Britain and Ireland there are societies that are intent on maintaining and promoting the breed.

Irish Draughts are typically active and quick thinking, which helps them to jump fences neatly and with apparent ease.

Lipizzaner

The Lipizzaner is famous as the mount of the Spanish Riding School in Vienna, Austria, where, in a magnificent riding hall, they perform their High School dressage displays. These athletic white horses are so good at this form of dressage that they give performances in many parts of the world; they can also be excellent driving horses.

Breed characteristics

The Lipizzaner is an intelligent and eminently trainable horse. It has a proud carriage, a muscular build, and powerful, elastic movements. The Lipizzaner's compact, harmonious shape helps its balance, and it has a natural ability to collect itself – making it ideally suited to High School work. The Lipizzaners may not be so flamboyant in their paces as some of the Warmbloods, but they do excel at the more difficult dressage movements.

Foals are born black or brown, but most lighten in colour with age, eventually becoming pure white. (Technically, Lipizzaners are greys, as their skin is dark under the white coat.)

History of the Lipizzaner

Although the Austrians made the Lipizzaner famous, the breed is based on Spanish stock; and it is from this that the Spanish Riding School takes its name. During the 16th century the vogue for High School riding swept through the royal courts of Europe. In 1580 Archduke Charles II of Austria imported nine stallions and 24 mares – mainly Andalusians – from Spain and established them in a stud at Lipizza (now in Slovenia) on the Adriatic Sea, to be used for breeding High School horses. Over the ensuing years more Spanish stock was imported, as were Neapolitans from Italy.

The bloodlines of the Lipizzaners were recorded from 1735, when Charles VI founded the Spanish Riding School, building a new winter riding hall in the imperial palace in Vienna. Today's Lipizzaners trace back to six stallions – all with Andalusian blood – imported at the end of the 18th and beginning of the 19th centuries.

The breeding grounds for the Lipizzaner were disrupted during the two major wars of the 20th century. After 1945, Piber in Austria became the main stud for the Lipizzaners used in Vienna, and their breeding became increasingly selective. From then on, stallions would be allowed to breed only after proving themselves at the Spanish School, and mares would have to go through performance tests.

The Lipizzaner today

Although the breed remains relatively rare, with only 3000 animals registered, Lipizzaners are bred increasingly around the world. In Hungary the purebreds, and some cross-breds using the Trotter, have proved to be excellent harness horses. In Slovenia, there is a dressage display unit, and Lipizzaners are crossed with farm mares to make very good horses for agricultural use.

With growing international interest in dressage, the demand for Lipizzaners is increasing all the time.

Left: Probably the most spectacular performance in the world is that given by the Lipizzaners of the Spanish Riding School in Vienna, Austria.

Right: A Lipizzaner skilfully executes the levade, *one of the 'airs above the ground', which requires exceptional balance and power.*

1580
First Spanish horses imported to the stud of Lipizza, now in Slovenia, then in the Austro-Hungarian empire.

Late 18th and early 19th centuries
Imports of the influential stallions Pluto from Denmark, Conversano and Neapolitano from Italy, Maestoso and Favory from the Kladrub stud in Bohemia, and the Arabian Siglavy.

1945
Lipizza becomes part of Yugoslavia. Horses of the Spanish Riding School in Czechoslovakia rescued by US troops. Breed numbers fewer than 250 horses.

1990s
Lipizza becomes part of Slovenia. Breed numbers up to 3000, but survival of horses in former Yugoslavia threatened by civil war.

| PRE | 1800 | | 1850 | | 1900 | | 1950 | |

1735
Spanish Riding School in Vienna built to teach classical horsemanship, train the horses, and preserve the Lipizzaner breed.

1918
Lipizza becomes Italian territory and the Piber stud in Austria becomes the breeding centre for the Lipizzaner of the Spanish Riding School.

MAIN FEATURES
- fairly large head, carried quite high
- often convex face
- compact, muscular body
- powerful hindquarters
- good bone
- short cannon bones

CHARACTER
- intelligent
- extremely willing to learn

COLOURS
Usually grey; very occasionally bay or brown.

HEIGHT
152–63cm (15–16hh)

COUNTRY OF ORIGIN
Austro-Hungarian Empire

COMPARISON BREED
Andalusian
Equally proud and elegant, the Andalusian influenced the early development of the Lipizzaner.

RELATED TOPICS
Andalusian   94
Dressage   168
Driving   194
Ceremonial and
working horses   232

Canadian Horse

Although a relatively unknown breed, the Canadian Horse has influenced a number of other North American horses, including the Standardbred, Morgan, and American Saddlebred. Prized as a trotting horse, the Canadian has been brought back from the brink of extinction more than once. Although there are not many Canadian Horses registered today, they are recognized as good all-rounders.

Breed characteristics

The original old-style Canadian Horse bears a striking resemblance to the Morgan, which the Canadian Horse certainly influenced. It is a stout, compact horse, with a chiselled head and large, wide-set eyes. With its muscular frame and beautiful crested neck, it exudes power and is packed with plenty of stamina.

History of the Canadian Horse

The Canadian Horse is descended from French stock, sent to Canada in the late 17th century by King Louis XIV to develop a breeding programme in what was then a French colony. Only two stallions and 12 mares survived the first journey, made in 1665, but more were sent over in two other shipments.

These horses, more than 40 in total, were of mainly Breton and Norman breeding, but some carried Andalusian blood as well.

The horses remained the property of the king for three years, but were leased to farmers either for money or in exchange for a foal. By 1679 there were 145 horses in the colony. By 1698, that number had more than tripled.

The French-Canadian horses also received an infusion of Friesian blood in the late 17th and early 18th centuries, which improved the horse's trotting ability. Other than this, no other blood was mixed with that of the Canadian. Instead, breeders bred from their own stock, producing a variety of types to meet individual needs.

Despite the harsh conditions, including little food, hard work, rough roads, and poor shelter, this hardy equine actually thrived, and its numbers grew. Many were exported, with some travelling to the West Indies as well as the USA.

In the early years of the 19th century, American interest in French-Canadian horses increased tremendously, because dealers needed to meet the growing demand in the USA for excellent roadster horses. Thousands of horses were exported and, by the late 1870s, numbers in Canada itself had become alarmingly low. In 1886, a stud book was opened to record and preserve the breed, and the Canadian Horse Breeders' Association was formed in 1895.

Dark brown and bay are the predominant colours of the impressive Canadian Horse, which is particularly favoured for driving and riding.

1680s
Friesians used on French-Canadian horses to improve trotting action.

1820s
Canadian Horse used to develop the Morgan, improving its size and speed.

1886
Stud book established.

1980s
After Quebec government herd is dispersed, the Canadian Horse is soon on the verge of extinction.

1600　　　　　1700　　　　　1800　　　　　1900　　　　　2000

1665
Stock from France's royal stables carrying Breton, Norman, and Andalusian blood sent to Canada to develop a breeding programme.

1820s
Cross-breeding with Narragansett Pacer produces Canadian Pacer, giving rise to the American Standardbred.

1895
Canadian Horse Breeders' Association formed.

1990s
Breed numbers restored, with nearly 4000 Canadian Horses registered.

Soon the breed was back on track, and in 1913 the federal government set up a breeding centre at Cap Rouge in Quebec. It was closed in 1940 because of World War II, and the stock was sold. The Quebec government started the stud again several years later, this time at Deschambault, but now began breeding a tall, refined horse, more along the lines of a hunter or jumper. Traditionalists, however, worked on preserving the original type.

In 1979, the Deschambault herd, too, was dispersed at auction, and again the Canadian Horse was in danger of disappearing forever, with fewer than 400 animals entered in the breed register. Dedicated breeders, however, managed to rescue the Canadian from obscurity, and there are now around 4000 Canadian Horses registered with the breed society.

The Canadian Horse today

Most Canadian Horses today are bred for driving. In 1987, a Canadian pair won the North American Pleasure Driving Pairs Championship. The Canadian is also a good all-rounder, being suitable for jumping, dressage, and long-distance riding, as well as for ranch work. It is a sensible animal with a lot of character, and makes a fine general riding horse.

A Canadian shows its paces in the ring. A lively trot and a willingness to work make the Canadian a pleasure to ride in all kinds of competition.

MAIN FEATURES
- close-coupled body
- arched neck
- expressive head
- sound legs and hard feet
- lively trot and animated gaits
- good endurance
- hardy

CHARACTER
- willing
- dependable
- easy keeper

COLOURS
Most are bay or brown, but other colours are accepted by the breed society.

HEIGHT
150–68cm (14.3–16.2hh)

COUNTRY OF ORIGIN
Canada

COMPARISON BREED
The Morgan
This American breed was influenced by the Canadian Horse and is similar in its conformation and stamina. However, the Morgan is smaller and more compact and refined than the Canadian Horse. It also is found in many colours.

RELATED TOPICS
Morgan   106
American Saddlebred   114
Standardbred   116
Driving   194

Appaloosa

The pride of the Nez Percé Indians of the north-western USA over a century ago, today's Appaloosas are known for their endurance and their willingness. They can be found in most equestrian disciplines, from Western sports such as cutting and reining, to racing, hunting, dressage, and eventing or combined training. The breed is strong and athletic, but is gentle enough to be a good mount for children.

Breed characteristics

This colourful horse is most commonly recognized by two coat patterns: the 'blanket', in which a solid coat pattern is interrupted by a splash of white across the hindquarters; and the 'leopard', in which a white coat is spotted like a Dalmatian's. However, there are other Appaloosa coat patterns. A 'few spot' is a leopard with small, or few, markings. A 'spotted blanket' is a solid pattern with dark spots on top of white hindquarters. A 'snowflake' is a solid coat with white flecks. Other distinctive characteristics include vertically striped hooves, mottled skin around the muzzle, eyes, and genitals, and a readily visible white sclera around the iris of the eye.

Occasionally a foal with none of these identifiable traits will be born to Appaloosa parents. The breed association registers these 'solid' Appaloosas but, to be raced or shown, they must undergo parentage verification and inspection.

The conformation of the Appaloosa varies. Many resemble stock horses, which is the result of Quarter Horse blood infusing the breed. These are stocky, close coupled, muscular, and powerful, with a level topline, and well-proportioned neck and head. Other Appaloosas reflect the foundation stock, and they have a more upright build, a small, straight face, short, straight back, slightly arched neck, and sloping croup.

History of the Appaloosa

While spotted horses of various breeding have lived around the world for thousands of years, the Appaloosa was founded by the Nez Percé Indians of Washington, Oregon, and Idaho, in the north-western USA. It is believed that spotted horses first came to the Americas from Spain around 1600, and were captured by the Nez Percé. They became skilful horse breeders, producing fast, sure-footed mounts with great stamina. In 1871, after a war with white settlers over territory, the Nez Percé were forced to relinquish their horses. Many were killed or taken by the US Cavalry, many were gelded, and some wandered free; most that did survive in American hands had their bloodlines diluted through indiscriminate cross-breeding. By the 1930s, the Appaloosa of the Nez Percé had all but disappeared.

It was then that Claude Thompson, a wheat farmer from Moro, Oregon, became interested in preserving the Appaloosa. He began collecting horses from all over the country and started a selective breeding programme, using Arabians to refine the breed. In 1938, he helped to establish the Appaloosa Horse Club – which today is an international breed registry, with over half a million Appaloosas registered.

The breed's name comes from the Palouse region, where many of the horses were raised. White settlers originally called it 'a Palouse horse', which soon became 'Appaloosa'.

The Appaloosa today

In the past, the Appaloosa was mainly known for its ability in Western events such as team penning, cutting, and barrel racing. But today Appaloosas are also being bred for showjumping and dressage; in recent years many have been successful in both endurance and competitive trail riding.

Right: The eye-catching colouring of the Appaloosa is divided into eight different coat patterns, but each horse has unique markings.

Below: Appaloosas are one of the most popular breeds in the world and are ideal mounts for numerous different activities.

1600
Spanish explorers bring spotted horses to the Americas.

19th century
Purity of breed diluted by indiscriminate cross-breeding.

1938
Appaloosa Horse Club established. Arabian blood used to refine the breed.

1983
Appaloosa Horse Club began the Certified Pedigree Option, which allowed breeders to show 'solid' Appaloosas, sometimes resulting from cross-breeding.

PRE	1800	1850	1900	1950	2000

17th and 18th centuries
Nez Percé Indians' selective breeding programme produces fast, athletic, sure-footed horses.

1950s
Quarter Horse blood used to give further refinement and power to the Appaloosa.

1998
Breed society rules changed: in order to be registered, a horse must have two Appaloosa parents.

MAIN FEATURES
- spotted coat
- white sclera readily visible around the iris of the eye
- mottled skin around the muzzle, eyes, and genitals
- vertically striped hooves
- sparse mane and tail
- good stamina
- athletic

CHARACTER
- docile
- even tempered
- tractable

COLOURS
The coat may be variously patterned or coloured, but no greys or Pintos may be registered.

HEIGHT
150–63cm (14.3–16hh)

COUNTRY OF ORIGIN
USA

COMPARISON BREED
Palomino
Like the Appaloosa, the Palomino is chosen particularly because of its distinctive colouring.

RELATED TOPICS
Quarter Horse   112
Arabian   128
Palomino   134
Western riding   202
Rodeo   208
Endurance   212

Morgan

The Morgan is considered to be the USA's first documented native breed, and can be traced back to a stocky little stallion named Figure, who had the strength of a draught horse and the speed of a Thoroughbred. Today's Morgans, like their foundation stallion, have the ability to excel in a number of equestrian disciplines. They have the appeal of both a show horse and a family horse, and a kind temperament to handle both roles with aplomb.

Breed characteristics

The Morgan is a compact horse, with an expressive face, large eyes, and a straight or slightly dished profile. The slightly crested neck blends into well-

All Morgans have developed from one prepotent stallion named Figure, born in the late 18th century. His characteristics continue in the breed.

defined withers. The Morgan is known for being a sound horse with flat bone and good substance to its limbs, yet it is refined in build.

Morgans have developed into two basic types: the old-style Morgan, which is stout and powerful; and the elegant, refined park horse. Both are known for having excellent stamina and vitality as well as a good nature.

History of the Morgan

The Morgan of today can trace its lineage to one stallion. Born in West Springfield, Massachusetts in 1789, Figure, a small dark colt, had unknown parentage. While some historians name True Briton, an English Thoroughbred, as the colt's sire, others point to Canadian Horse, Welsh Cob, Friesian, or even Norfolk Trotter within his genetic mix. When Figure was a yearling, he was given to a Vermont schoolteacher named Justin Morgan as payment for a debt. Figure was lent out to neighbouring farms, where he toiled as a plough and logging horse. When Figure matured, it was soon discovered that he was a multi-talented stallion – one that could outrun the fastest Thoroughbreds in match races, haul heavier loads than massive draught horses, and trot faster than most harness racers.

His reputation spread quickly, and soon New Englanders brought their mares to breed with Figure, who then became known by his owner's name. The stallion put his stamp on future generations, passing on his traits to progeny with amazing success.

The breed's famous trotting ability made it a favourite harness racing

horse during the 1840s. Morgans served as cavalry mounts during the American Civil War – on both sides. They also helped deliver mail via the Pony Express in the late 1800s. In 1894,

1789	1820s	1840s–50s	1894	1948
Figure, the foundation sire, born. Believed to be of Canadian, Friesian, Welsh, or Thoroughbred stock.	Canadian Horses used to give Morgans greater size and speed.	Morgans used to improve speed of the Standardbred.	American Morgan Horse Register started.	Stud book closed to outside breeds.

| 1750 | | 1800 | | 1850 | | 1900 | | 1950 | | 2000 |

1790s	1870s	1990s
Foundation sire and progeny bred with local mares of various breeding, including English Thoroughbred and Norfolk Trotter.	Morgans influence the American Saddlebred and Tennessee Walking Horse.	Successful as a sport horse, especially in driving, dressage, and Western riding.

MAIN FEATURES
• close-coupled body
• arched neck and
  expressive head
• sound legs and feet
• flashy trot and
  animated gaits
• good endurance

CHARACTER
• energetic
• co-operative nature
• versatile

COLOURS
Bay, black, and brown are
most common. Chestnut,
grey, Palomino, cream,
dun, and buckskin are
also found.

HEIGHT
142–57cm (14–15.2hh)

COUNTRY OF ORIGIN
USA (Vermont)

COMPARISON BREED
American Saddlebred
A flashy park horse that
is known for its animated,
high-stepping trot, the
American Saddlebred is
taller and has lankier
conformation than the
Morgan. Nine out of
10 Saddlebreds carry
Morgan blood.

the first volume of the American
Morgan Horse Register was opened.
More than 132,000 animals have since
been registered. In 1948, in an effort
to preserve the characteristics of the
breed, the stud book was closed to all
horses that did not have registered
Morgan parentage.

The Morgan has also influenced
several other American breeds,
including the Standardbred, Tennessee
Walking Horse, and Quarter Horse.
Nearly 90 per cent of today's American
Saddlebreds have Morgan blood.

The Morgan today
Enthusiasts disagree over the two types
of Morgan. Some believe that all
Morgans should reflect the foundation

sire – as the powerful, old-style Morgan
does. Others prefer to see the breed
excel as a showy, high-stepping park
horse, with the refinement and carriage
seen in breeds such as Arabians and
American Saddlebreds.

With versatility and performance
continuing to define the breed, the
Morgan's reputation is growing in
sports such as driving and dressage.
It was the first American breed to
represent the USA in the World Pairs
Driving competition. More Western
riding enthusiasts are discovering the
breed's talents, as Morgans delve into
athletic events such as cutting and
reining. Since many are small enough
to be eligible for pony classes, they
also make ideal mounts for children.

*In the show ring
the Morgan looks
magnificent with
its tremendous
presence, spectacular
movement, and
animated gaits.
It is a great
American favourite.*

RELATED TOPICS
Quarter Horse   112
American Saddlebred   114
Standardbred   116
Dressage   168
Driving   194
Western riding   202
Showing   246

Missouri Fox Trotter

In the USA in the 19th century, a horse with a peculiar lateral gait was developed in the rough terrain of the Ozark Mountain foothills. Settlers who were in need of a gentle, easy-to-ride mount began selectively breeding for what is now known as the Missouri Fox Trotter – a horse that has the stamina to travel long distances with its ground-covering, pleasurable gait.

Breed characteristics

The lateral gait known as the fox trot is unique to the breed. At this gait, the horse walks with its front legs, and trots with its hind legs. The horse is easily able to maintain the fox trot for great stretches of time. It is not a high-stepping animal as many gaited horses are, but rather one that offers a smooth, comfortable ride. Because the back feet have a sliding action rather than a two-beat trot, the rider experiences little jarring in the saddle. The Fox Trotter also performs a flat-footed walk and a regular canter.

The breed is known for its stamina and soundness, but is also recognized for its willing disposition. A medium-sized light horse, the Fox Trotter has an intelligent head sporting a neat profile and large, alert eyes. It has an elevated neck, sloping shoulders, slender body, short back, and rounded croup.

History of the Missouri Fox Trotter

In the early 19th century, pioneers from Tennessee, Kentucky, and Virginia were settling the rugged foothills of the

The smooth natural lateral gaits of the Missouri Fox Trotter make it the ideal mount for those who have to be in the saddle for long periods of time.

1850s
Arabians, Morgans, and Plantation Walkers brought to the Ozark Mountains of Missouri, bred for easy-to-ride gaits.

1880s
Thoroughbred, Standardbred, and Morgan blood added to the Missouri Fox Trotter to improve speed and movement.

1982
Registration limited to horses with at least one parent registered with the MFTHBA.

1850 — **1900** — **1950**

1870s
Saddlebred and Tennessee Walker blood added to give the horse a pleasing appearance and disposition.

1948
Breed association formed for the Fox Trotter. In 1958 this was reorganized under the name the Missouri Fox Trotting Horse Breeders' Association (MFTHBA).

1983
Registration criterion again changed. All horses now required to have both parents registered with the MFTHBA, thereby closing the stud book.

Ozark Mountains in Missouri. They had brought horses with them, but it quickly became apparent that, in this rocky and forested terrain, a horse with natural lateral gaits would be most ideal. The settlers turned to farmers who were selectively breeding horses that could perform the gliding fox trot. These breeders were to blend American Saddle Horses, Standardbreds, and Tennessee Walking Horses with the good trotters of the day such as Morgans, Thoroughbreds, and Arabians, to produce what became known as the Missouri Fox Trotter.

Soon the settlers were using these unique Ozark horses to help work cattle ranches and to serve as transportation for local officials, from the sheriff to the doctor and the tax assessor. In the early 20th century, the townspeople and farmers took to car and tractor, but the Fox Trotter survived because so many of the cattle ranchers in the region found the horses to be irreplaceable.

The Missouri Fox Trotter today

Today the Fox Trotter is still most popular in its home state, but there are more than 52,000 registered horses in the USA, Canada, Austria, and Germany. They have come to be a favourite mount of US Forest Rangers.

Fox Trotters are typically shown under Western saddle, as well as in halter classes. Nine out of 10 registered Missouri Fox Trotting Horses are used for family pleasure riding. Their excellent stamina is becoming better known, and those involved with long-distance competitive trail riding are also being drawn to the breed.

Although a relatively new breed, the Fox Trotter is becoming extremely popular for a number of sports including driving and endurance riding.

MAIN FEATURES
- low, sweeping gaits
- elevated head and tail carriage
- unique fox trot
- sure footed

CHARACTER
- docile
- reliable
- gentle

COLOURS
All colours are found, including Pinto markings, roan, and buckskin.

HEIGHT
142–63cm (14–16hh)

COUNTRY OF ORIGIN
USA (Missouri)

COMPARISON BREED
Tennessee Walking Horse
This is another gaited horse that has its origins in the southern states. It is larger, and performs the running walk and rack, instead of the fox trot.

RELATED TOPICS

Thoroughbred	70
Morgan	106
American Saddlebred	114
Tennessee Walking Horse	118
Arabian	128
Driving	194
Western riding	202
Showing	246

Mustang

There are wild horses throughout the world, but few conjure up romance as does the Mustang of the American West. Many think of the Mustang as an elegant, Arabian-like animal, but in reality it is a diminutive, wiry horse with keen senses and the ability to survive much hardship.

Breed characteristics

The Mustang is small, incredibly hardy, and able to withstand the elements. Occasionally there will be a Mustang born that is a 'throwback' to its

The Mustang is famous as the American wild horse, romantically linked to the great Western films depicting cowboys and indians.

Spanish or Barb heritage, and it will display the size, substance, and carriage of its forebears. But most Mustangs are stocky and sure footed, with good feet, strong constitutions, and excellent stamina. Type and conformation vary considerably and depend on the herd.

It is a myth that Mustangs cannot be tamed, and that they are rebellious and mean-spirited. Mustangs are usually quite tractable, and many develop deep bonds with their owners; but it is important for more than one individual to work with the horse so that it becomes socialized to people, and not to one particular person.

History of the Mustang

The Spanish brought beautiful Andalusians and Barbs with them to the Americas when they first settled in the new land in the 16th century. Some of their horses escaped and banded together into their own herds, developing into what is now known as the Mustang.

Over the years, escaped domestic horses joined the herds, and some wild stallions 'stole' tame mares out of their pastures, so later generations of Mustang lacked the quality and substance of their ancestors.

Native Americans were the first to tame these wild horses; white settlers too caught some of them and, for a time, found the Mustang's innate 'cow sense' invaluable. However, as ranchers began to use the land to raise and graze cattle, the wild Mustangs were looked upon more as a liability than an asset. Many Mustangs were shot to save the grazing for other animals, and

horses that were once broken to saddle were now sent to meatpacking plants.

By 1926, the number of Mustangs in the USA had declined from two million horses to one million. Within 10 years,

1550s
Spanish horses brought to the Americas by the conquistadores.

1988
Kiger Mesteno Association founded, dedicated to preserving the virtually pure-bred Spanish-type mustang found in an isolated area of Oregon in 1977.

PRE | 1800   1900

17th century
French horses bred with the American horses in the southern states.

1880s
East Friesian coach horses imported from Germany also added to the mix of the American feral horse.

1957
Spanish Mustang Registry founded, to preserve the last remnants of the old Spanish imports and to form a breeding herd with a large gene pool.

1971
Wild Free-Roaming Horse and Burro Act passed to protect and control the Mustang.

MAIN FEATURES
• small
• hardy
• short neck
• dense bone
• hard feet

CHARACTER
• intelligent
• can be gentled

COLOURS
All colours, including Pinto
and Appaloosa markings,
are found.

HEIGHT
137–52cm (13.2–15hh)

COUNTRY OF ORIGIN
USA

COMPARISON BREED
Basuto Pony
The Basuto developed in a
similar way to the Mustang
and is extremely tough,
agile, and fast.

the population stood at 150,000.
Extermination of the Mustang
continued until 1971, when the Wild
Free-Roaming Horse and Burro Act
was passed, to protect and control wild
equines. Even under protection, with
rangeland dwindling and populations
of humans and cattle increasing, the
Mustang's numbers still needed to be
reduced. In 1973 the government
started an adoption scheme – and it still
exists today. For a small fee, members
of the public can buy a Mustang, but it
remains government property for one
year, to be sure that the adopter can
adequately meet the horse's needs.

There are several strains of Mustang
with their own breed associations,
including that for the Spanish Mustang,
founded to preserve the Barb-type
horse, and for the Kiger Mustang,
promoting a strain founded in Oregon.

The Mustang today

As civilization continues to encroach
on the American wilderness, the plight
of the Mustang remains a serious
concern. The Bureau of Land
Management, which is currently in
charge of the horses' welfare, has been
accused of mismanaging the Mustangs.
However, the adoption scheme has
introduced riders to some very talented
horses, excelling particularly in
endurance riding. Some of these
mustangs compete in dressage and
showjumping – two very unlikely sports
for Western-type horses.

*Today there is concern
about the future of
Mustangs in the wild,
but those that have
been tamed are tough
and trainable, and
have adapted well
to domesticated life.*

RELATED TOPICS
Basuto Pony   64
Andalusian   94
Barb   132
Dressage   168
Showjumping   176
Western riding   202
Rodeo   208
Endurance   212

Quarter Horse

Known as 'America's Horse', the Quarter Horse is bred to 'do it all', from racing to taking children to their first ribbon. With the largest breed society in the world backing up this wonder horse, the Quarter Horse is one of the most successful breeds in history.

Breed characteristics

There are two basic body types for the Quarter Horse: the stock horse type, and the running Quarter Horse type. The stock horse is shorter, well muscled, and stocky, yet agile and swift enough to perform its ranch duties. The running Quarter Horse is a lighter horse, like a Thoroughbred, and is built to sprint.

Quarter Horses shown in hand, in halter classes, are often referred to as 'bulldog' type, because of their bulky, muscular build and their jowly appearance. Reining and cutting horses are bred smaller, but have powerful haunches and a cat-like movement. The Western pleasure horse has a level topline and natural, easy gaits. Running Quarter Horses have long legs and lean physiques. But with all Quarter Horses, no matter what the type, their power, their stamina, and their willingness to please are a solid testament to their ability and versatility.

History of the Quarter Horse

In the 1690s American colonists began crossing imported English horses with the Chickasaw Pony – which originated from Spanish and Barb stock brought over by Spanish settlers and later adopted by Chickasaw Indians. The

Quarter Horses excel in Western sports as well as numerous other activities. The breed is willing, agile, and extremely versatile.

1560s
Spanish horses including Andalusians and Barbs bred by Chickasaw Indians.

1752
Thoroughbred used to give speed and refinement.

1800s
Various draught horses used to give strength to the Quarter Horse.

1990s
Growing European interest in the breed, especially in Germany.

PRE | 1600 | 1700 | 1800 | 1900

1690s
Indian Chickasaw horses crossed with English horses by colonists.

1700s
Spanish blood crossed back into Anglo-American horses to result in the Quarter Horse.

1870s
Morgans used to further refine the breed.

1940
American Quarter Horse Association founded.

1940s
Thoroughbreds give added speed to the racing stock, and enlarge the gene pool.

result was a small, hardy, and quick animal who was a willing work horse during the week and a competitive match racehorse at weekends.

Flat racing over short distances became popular in the colonies and, over the decades, this 'short-horse' gained a reputation as the fastest sprinter around. Even when matched against the long, lean Thoroughbred, the smaller horse was the one to finish ahead in half-kilometre (quarter-mile) races. So it became known as the 'Quarter Horse'.

The Quarter Horse found another calling in the 1800s. Pioneers heading West needed a hardy, willing horse to haul their wagons and carry cattlemen in the saddle. They discovered that the breed had 'cow sense', and the Quarter Horse soon became an asset on cattle ranches. Cattlemen continued to breed this horse long after the arrival of the automobile.

In 1940, a group of horsemen came together to preserve the Quarter Horse breed and founded the American Quarter Horse Association (AQHA). In the late 1940s, there was an infusion of Thoroughbred blood, but then the stud book closed. Today, crosses between the Quarter Horse and Thoroughbred are registered as Appendix horses.

The Quarter Horse today

There are now more than 3.5 million Quarter Horses throughout the world. Europe has been importing Quarter Horses at nearly the same rate that North America imports Warmbloods. Germany in particular has become fascinated with the many talents of the breed.

Because there are many bloodlines producing specialist athletes, Quarter Horses perform in nearly every riding discipline. They are not only ideal for ranch work and Western classes; many have been trained for international level dressage. The Quarter Horse's speed and agility allow it to excel in barrel racing and other gymkhana events, but it is also a powerful jumper. And while the Quarter Horse still competes as a racehorse, the breed is a solid all-round family horse.

The Quarter Horse is reputedly the fastest horse over 500m (quarter of a mile) and is spectacular in the breed's many sprint races.

MAIN FEATURES
• powerful hindquarters
• small, intelligent head
• muscular, rounded croup
• short back
• small feet

CHARACTER
• willing
• versatile
• good natured
• tractable

COLOURS
All colours are found, but sorrel is most common. Appaloosa patterns or Pintos are not allowed by the breed society.

HEIGHT
142–63cm (14–16hh)

COUNTRY OF ORIGIN
USA

COMPARISON BREED
Thoroughbred
This is another horse built for speed, although the Thoroughbred is a distance racer and the Quarter Horse a sprinter. The Thoroughbred has been used to refine and improve the Quarter Horse.

RELATED TOPICS

Thoroughbred   70
Andalusian   94
Morgan   106
Dressage   168
Showjumping   176
Racing   184
Western riding   202
Pony Club   226
Riding holidays   250

American Saddlebred

The American Saddlebred is the 'peacock' of the show ring – all fire and flash, with an exaggerated, high-stepping action. The breed originated in the southern USA, where plantation owners needed a horse to carry them comfortably across the fields. Today the Saddlebred is seen in every major equestrian sport.

Breed characteristics

The Saddlebred has a long and lean appearance, with a refined head, and an upright, swan-like neck. Most are narrow through the chest and have clean legs and flexible, long pasterns. The croup of the Saddlebred is level with the tail; for the gaited classes in the show ring, the tail is set artificially high, usually by means of surgery.

The Saddlebred is shown in either three- or five-gaited classes under saddle, and in fine-harness classes. Three-gaited horses are judged at the walk, trot, and canter, where the horse's conformation, behaviour, and action are paramount. It executes its gaits in a collected, yet animated manner, with high elevation. The five-gaited Saddlebred is shown in the same three natural gaits, but also has two man-made gaits, the 'slow gait' and the 'rack'. Both are four-beat gaits with the slow gait performed by moving in almost a prancing motion, lifting the legs very high and elevating the forehand. When the Saddlebred racks, it moves faster in a ground-covering

This herd of young Saddlebreds is destined for the show ring following some intensive training to develop their natural high-stepping movement.

17th century
European colonists bring Galloway and Hobby horses to North America and, through selective breeding, develop the Narragansett Pacer.

1776
The Thoroughbred/ Narragansett Pacer cross recognized as a fixed type known as the American Horse, an all-purpose riding horse.

1830s
Morgan and Thoroughbred blood used to give more substance and action.

| PRE | 1700 | | 1750 | | 1800 | | 1850 | | 1900 | |

1706
Thoroughbreds imported to cross-breed with the Narragansett Pacer.

1800–10
Breeding centred in Kentucky, and the horse became known as the Kentucky Saddler.

1840s
American Saddlebred is now a well-established breed.

1891
Breed association and register formally established – the first in the USA.

20th century
Widely used in the show ring and for driving and hunting.

It takes a considerable amount of time and patience to train the American Saddlebred to perform in the accepted manner in the show ring.

MAIN FEATURES
- long, arched, swan-like neck
- long, straight profile
- narrow chest
- long, sloping pasterns
- large eyes, curved ears
- level croup and back

CHARACTER
- alert
- quick
- animated
- sensitive

COLOURS
Chestnut, bay, brown, and black are most often found, although some are grey, roan, Palomino, or Pinto.

HEIGHT
152–63cm (15–16hh)

COUNTRY OF ORIGIN
USA

COMPARISON BREED
Tennessee Walking Horse
Another gaited show horse that developed in the southern USA.

stride, snapping its knees and hocks up quickly. Fine-harness horses are shown in an animated walk and a park trot, in which the horse snaps the front legs up and extends them outwards.

History of the Saddlebred

In the 18th century, American colonists began crossing the small, sturdy Narragansett Pacer with the large, refined Thoroughbred. Known simply as the American Horse, this new cross was to be influential in American history, serving in the Revolutionary War, accompanying pioneers following Daniel Boone through the Cumberland Gap into Kentucky, and helping Kentuckians fight the British and their Indian allies during the war of 1812.

Breeding good American saddle horses became a priority in Kentucky, and in the early 1800s the breed came to be known as the Kentucky Saddler. Used mainly on plantations because of their comfortable, ground-covering gaits and their sure-footed manner, they were also bred to satisfy something else: man's vanity. The Kentucky Saddler was developed into a stylish, fancy horse, beautiful in harness, yet strong enough for farm work, and fast enough to win match

races against another farmer's horse. In the 1830s, additional Morgan and Thoroughbred blood was used to give greater substance and action – and the American Saddlebred was born, becoming well established as a breed by the mid 1840s. A stallion named Denmark, who was born in 1839, was designated the foundation sire; over 60 per cent of Saddlebreds trace their pedigrees back to him.

Saddlebreds were reportedly the chosen mounts of famous cavalrymen during the Civil War, including General Robert E Lee, Ulysses S Grant, and Stonewall Jackson. When the war was over, breeders began to promote the Saddlebred as a show horse, and breeding for flash and animation became the rage.

The Saddlebred today

Saddlebreds are far more than just flashy park horses. With their friendly, responsive nature, they are popular as parade horses and as police mounts. Some are successful hunters and jumpers; others have been known to barrel race. The Saddlebred's newest calling, however, is in dressage because of its animation and its naturally elevated forehand.

RELATED TOPICS
Thoroughbred   70
Morgan   106
Tennessee Walking
Horse   118
Dressage   168
Driving   194
Showing   246
Hunting   248

Standardbred

The fastest trotting horse in the world, the American Standardbred is known mostly as a harness racing animal, and it is used to upgrade other breeds of harness racers around the globe. However, many are finding careers away from the racecourses.

The name Standardbred was first used in 1879: in order to be registered, harness racers had to prove they could run a mile (1.6km) within the standard time of two minutes 30 seconds. Standardbreds often race faster than this today, with several running the mile in under one minute 50 seconds.

Breed characteristics

The Standardbred is both like and unlike the American Thoroughbred. Although typically a bit shorter and stockier than the Thoroughbred, the horse has refined legs, powerful shoulders and hindquarters, and a well-proportioned back. It has a unique, squarish profile, which is not as refined as the Thoroughbred's. Standardbreds are built sound and sturdy, and – unlike some Thoroughbreds, which have large feet – their feet are in proportion to their bodies.

The horse has two racing gaits: trotting and pacing. The pace is a lateral gait, in which both legs on one side of the body move together. In the trot, the legs move in diagonal pairs. Because pacers usually trot when not racing, they are trained and raced with 'hobbles', straps linking the front and back legs on each side to keep them moving together.

Standardbreds begin their racing careers at two years old, and many breeders and trainers believe that trotters take more time to develop. This is why there are more racing pacers than trotters – by a margin of four to one. Whether trotting or pacing, Standardbreds can reach speeds of up to 55kmph (35mph), and tend to reserve their greatest burst of speed for the final quarter of the race.

History of the Standardbred

The earliest harness racers in the Americas were the Narragansett Pacer and the Canadian Pacer, which raced in

The poise and proud manner of the Standardbred give it a similar look to the Thoroughbred, to which it is closely related.

1630s
Dutch horses (Friesians) and English horses crossed in New England to produce the Narragansett Pacer.

1788
Messenger, a stallion who traces back to all three foundation Thoroughbreds, imported into USA. Improves trotting speed and size of Standardbred.

1980s
Standardbred Pleasure Horse Organization founded to find new careers for retired racing horses, and encourage use of Standardbred as a riding and driving horse.

1600　　　1700　　　1800　　　1900

1720s
English Thoroughbreds crossed with Narragansett Pacer and Canadian Pacer to create faster trotting and pacing horses.

1740s
Hackney and Morgan blood added to increase trotting ability.

1879
Breed name established.

1939
United States Trotting Horse Association founded and Standardbred stud book established.

New England in the 17th century. When English Thoroughbreds were crossed with several other breeds, including the Norfolk Trotter, the Hackney, the Morgan, and the Canadian Pacer, it resulted in a horse that became known for its two distinctive racing gaits.

The original trotting races in the 17th century were held in fields on ridden horses. However, farmers and breeders began to take their match races more seriously, and by the middle of the 18th century trotting races were held on official courses, this time with the horses in harness. Breeders quickly moved to improve their trotters, and selected bloodlines that could produce faster horses. In 1788, Messenger, a grey Thoroughbred stallion, was brought to the USA from England and became one of the most influential sires in the breed; he produced both runners and trotters, with the trotters possessing great action, speed, and heart. In 1849, Hambletonian, a descendant of Messenger, was born of a crippled bay mare who was bred to

the ungainly, belligerent Abdullah. Sold as a cast-off, Hambletonian proved to be a prolific sire, and his offspring, too, were natural trotting athletes. Today nearly every trotter and pacer can trace its lineage back to this great horse.

The Standardbred today

Many think of the Standardbred only as a harness racer, but it takes part in a host of other riding and driving events. The Standardbred Pleasure Horse Organization, founded in the USA in the 1980s, helps to promote the breed in other riding and driving disciplines.

The breed has the usual natural gaits, and even pacers can be retrained to trot. Cantering and jumping comes naturally to Standardbreds, and they can be seen on cross-country courses, and in the showjumping and dressage arena (where some are mistaken for Thoroughbreds). Because harness racers travel around the country during the racing season, they can handle a busy schedule without getting ruffled. Their even tempers also make them good ranch horses and trail mounts.

The world's fastest trotter, the Standardbred is exceptionally fast in harness, with a top speed of 55kmph (35mph).

MAIN FEATURES
- sturdy build
- flat back
- slightly rounded croup
- powerful hindquarters
- large head

CHARACTER
- steady temperament
- easy to train
- people oriented

COLOURS
Usually bay or brown, but other coat colours are seen.

HEIGHT
145–73cm (14.1–17hh)

COUNTRY OF ORIGIN
USA

COMPARISON BREED
Thoroughbred
This is the ultimate racehorse, and has had a considerable influence on the Standardbred's breeding. It is similar in conformation to the Standardbred, but more elegant, with a longer neck.

RELATED TOPICS
Thoroughbred   70
Morgan   106
Dressage   168
Showjumping   176
Racing   184
Western riding   202
Showing   246

Tennessee Walking Horse

The Tennessee Walking Horse is known for its gentle disposition and its kind manner towards its rider. It is often thought of as a show horse because of its elevated, exaggerated gait, but Tennessee Walkers are versatile animals suitable for many riding disciplines. Originally the mount chosen by plantation owners in the American South, its smooth and easy 'running walk' makes it sought after as a pleasure horse today.

Breed characteristics

The Tennessee Walker's natural gaits are the flat walk, the smooth and easy running walk, and the 'rocking horse' canter. In both types of walk, the head nods in rhythm with the movement. Along with its unique gliding gaits, the Tennessee Walker is also known for its great endurance and hardiness. Bred for generations in an area noted for its rich, grassy hillsides, it is sure footed and solidly built, but it is not a coarse breed. It does have a flashy way of going, which is evident in breed shows, where it performs its high-action paces.

History of the Tennessee Walker

The origin of the Tennessee Walking Horse can be found in Narragansett and Canadian Pacers. These horses were blended in the early 1800s by Tennessee farmers who were striving to develop a saddle horse that could manage the mountainous terrain. During the Civil War, Confederate Pacer and Union Trotter blood was infused, resulting in a sturdier horse called the Southern Plantation Walking Horse or Tennessee Pacer. Breeders continued to refine and add stamina, mixing Thoroughbreds, Standardbreds, Morgans, and American Saddlebreds with their new gaited horse.

In 1885 a cross between the stallion Allendorf, from the Hambletonian family of trotters, and Maggie Marshall, a Morgan mare, produced Black Allan, who became the foundation sire of the Tennessee Walking Horse breed.

The Tennessee Walker quickly gained popularity because it had easy-to-ride gaits and never seemed to tire. During the late 1800s, it was common for farmers to hold match races with their nimble Walkers – many of which had just finished ploughing in the fields.

Even when the automobile was introduced in the area during the early 1900s, many Tennessee communities kept their Walking Horses because they could manage the poor roads with ease. In the early 1950s, the Tennessee Walker began to gain a reputation as a showy gaited animal, and breeders sought bloodlines that emphasized presence, refinement, and intelligence.

The Tennessee Walking Horse today

Tennessee Walkers are better suited to pleasure riding than to the Olympic disciplines, although many can take low jumps with ease. They are excellent for long-distance riding because of their stamina and even temper. At the annual Tennessee Walking Horse Celebration, the horse displays its versatility in a range of classes, including halter, harness, and Western pleasure.

Left: Today the Tennessee Walker is highly prized as a show horse. Few breeds look as specactular as these eye-catching animals in the ring.

Right: This striking American breed was originally bred to 'walk' the plantations in comfort. It is now a very versatile all-rounder.

1780s
Canadian and Narragansett Pacers were brought to Tennessee counties.

1830s
Canadian and Narragansetts crossed to make a new Pacer.

1939
Annual breed show first held in Shelby, Tennessee.

1950s
Popular as a sport horse and for pleasure riding.

PRE | 1850   1900   1950

1860s
Confederate Pacers and Union Trotters used to produce a sturdier breed of horse.

1870s
Thoroughbreds, Standardbreds, Morgans, and American Saddlebreds bred with the Tennessee Walking Horse to give refinement and stamina.

1935
Tennessee Walking Horse Breeders' Association of America founded.

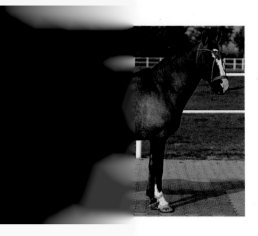

Criollo

The Criollo, Argentina's native horse, is probably the horse with the best endurance in the world. Today's Criollos reflect the hardiness and stamina of their forebears, and the breed is the most popular in Argentina.

Breed characteristics

This hardy little horse, with its brawny body and strong, sturdy legs, is famous for its stamina and ability to exist in harsh conditions with scant supplies of food and water. The Criollo has traditionally been small, with some actually qualifying to be pony height. Recently, however, the horse has been bred a bit larger.

History of the Criollo

The Criollo is the pride of Argentina and has been very influential in the development of the polo pony. It is tough, agile, and willing.

While many believe that the Criollo's ancestors were from a shipment of the finest Andalusian stallions and mares brought to Argentina in 1535 by Pedro de Mendoza, founder of Buenos Aires, it is now thought that the early Spanish horses were not only Andalusians, but also hardy Garranos and Sorraias.

When Buenos Aires was destroyed by Indians a decade or so later, many horses were left to wander the wild windswept plains, where little grows and water is scarce. Many perished, but those that survived actually flourished. Later settlers captured the tough little horses and trained them as pack animals and for riding.

In the late 19th century, the Criollo was crossed with imported European and American stallions in order to produce a faster, larger, and more refined horse, but the experiment nearly ruined the breed. Nature, however, took its course, for these cross-bred animals could not survive in the difficult conditions. In the early 1900s, Argentine breeders decided to re-establish the true Criollo by breeding only from the remaining pure-bred horses.

The Criollo is known best for its incredible endurance. In 1925, Swiss Professor Aimé Tschiffely took two Criollos, Mancha and Gato, on a trek of 21,500km (13,350 miles) from Buenos Aires to New York, crossing mountains and deserts, in all types of weather, riding and packing alternately on the pair. Both horses made it wonderfully through the three-year ordeal, and lived until they were well into their 30s.

The Criollo today

The Criollo is mainly a working cow horse, but it is also a pleasure horse. Because of its agility, quickness, and temperament, it is also ideal for rodeo events. However, endurance rides are where this small horse really shines.

1493
Columbus brings first Spanish horses to Central America.

1960s
Criollos crossed with Thoroughbreds to develop good polo ponies – fast and agile, but also very sound.

PRE	1700	1800	1900

16th century
Andalusians, Garranos, and Sorraias brought from Spain to the Americas, cross-breeding to produce the Criollo.

1880s
Criollos cross-bred with European and American stallions to produce faster, larger horses, but nearly ruining the breed's hardiness.

1918
Official breed society formed to promote the Criollo, which now figures in the Argentine government stud book

Paso Fino

The graceful Spanish Paso Fino is aptly described by its name, which means 'fine gait'. The horse is known for its *brio condido*, or hidden fire, which means that it has energy and spirit, but also a steady temperament to hold that energy in check. Enthusiasts enjoy the horse for its intelligence, brilliant movement, and beauty.

Breed characteristics

Like many Spanish breeds, the Paso Fino has a lovely upright carriage and is very alert and active when under saddle. Intelligent and willing, the Paso is attentive to its owner.

The Paso Fino has a natural four-beat lateral gait, which gives a wonderfully smooth ride at three primary speeds going from slow to fast: *paso fino, paso corto,* and *paso largo.*

History of the Paso Fino

The Paso Fino is derived from three breeds – the Andalusian, the Barb, and the now-extinct Spanish Jennet, which was known to be a pacer. Spanish explorers brought their horses to the New World in the late 15th century, and cross-breeding produced the foundation stock for what would become *Los caballos de paso fino,* or 'the horse with the fine step'.

The Spaniards dispersed these cross-breeds into Central and South America (especially Peru and Colombia). Soon they were also found in the Dominican Republic, Cuba, Jamaica, and Puerto Rico. It was here that breeders took

This small proud horse has a natural four-beat gait, which is wonderfully comfortable, making it popular for parades as well as the show ring.

the horse a step further and gave it refinement and style, infusing the breed with more Spanish Jennet.

The Paso Fino today

Many Paso Finos are now used as pleasure horses, and are moving into competitive trail and endurance classes as well. They have their own breed shows and are lovely parade horses.

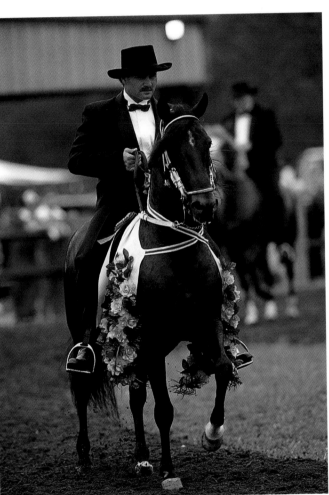

MAIN FEATURES

- elegant
- close-coupled body
- short legs
- active lateral four-beat gait
- comfortable ride
- flowing mane

CHARACTER

- exhibits *brio* (controlled spirit and energy)
- proud
- willing
- alert
- active

COLOURS

All colours are found.

HEIGHT

132–57cm (13–15.2hh)

COUNTRIES OF ORIGIN

USA, Peru, Colombia, Caribbean

COMPARISON BREED

Andalusian
Although bigger than the Paso Fino, this horse has the same proud, high-stepping movement, and flowing mane.

1493
Columbus brings Spanish horses to the Americas.

1990s
Confepaso (Confederation of Paso Fino) formed to promote international competition. Its members are Europe, the USA, Puerto Rico, Colombia, Venezuela, Dominican Republic, Panama, and Aruba.

PRE | 1900

1950

1550s
Breeding farms on the Caribbean Islands use the Spanish Jennet to enhance the Paso Fino's unique gait.

1972
Paso Fino Horse Association founded in the USA to protect and improve the breed.

RELATED TOPICS

Andalusian   94
Barb   132
Endurance   212
Showing   246
Riding holidays   250

Akhal-Teke

Bred by Turkmen tribesmen as war-horses and racehorses for thousands of years, Akhal-Tekes are tough, athletic horses that have adapted well to a variety of modern sports.

Breed characteristics

Native to the barren lands of Turkmenistan, the Akhal-Teke can withstand considerable changes in temperature and a life without much food and water. Its toughness and resilience have also made it a good horse for sport. It is raced locally and has great powers of endurance. In 1935 Turkmenian horsemen, wanting to prove the stamina of their Akhal-Tekes, rode from Ashgabat to Moscow – an extraordinary journey of 4000km (2500 miles), which lasted 84 days.

History of the Akhal-Teke

According to some sources, the Turkmen tribesmen guarded the purity of their Akhal-Tekes for thousands of years. They were certainly bred in an area where this might have been feasible, since it is surrounded by mountains and desert. However, others contest this claim, insisting that the Akhal-Teke is descended from horses left behind by Mongol raiders in the 13th and 14th centuries.

It is unquestionably very similar to the Turkoman horse, which has been bred in neighbouring Iran for many centuries. Some say the Turkoman and the Akhal-Teke are different strains of the same breed, and that it is from them that the influential Arabian horse was developed.

The Akhal-Teke in its turn has had an influence on a number of breeds. The Byerley Turk, one of the foundation sires for the Thoroughbred, is said to have carried Akhal-Teke blood. The Trakehner has been influenced by the Akhal-Teke, as have Russian breeds such as the Don, Karabair, and Karabakh. There was some cross-breeding with the Thoroughbred in the early 20th century, with the aim of producing faster long-distance racehorses. But the resulting product did not have so much of the Akhal-Teke's natural resilience.

The Akhal-Teke today

The Akhal-Teke's blood is ancient and much valued for use in developing new breeds. It is also popular as a riding horse, and has proved good at dressage, eventing, and showjumping as well as for racing and endurance. An Akhal-Teke stallion, Absent, won the individual gold medal in dressage at the l960 Olympic Games.

Today, large numbers of Akhal-Tekes are found at the Tersk stud, in the northern Caucasus mountains.

Right: Although rather shallow in the body, this ancient breed is extremely tough and resilient, and performs successfully in many sports.

Below: Most Akhal-Tekes have a beautiful golden sheen to the coat and this is evident among the herd seen here drinking at a lakeside.

PRE	1800		1850		1900		1950	

2000–1000 BC
Akhal-Teke bred in Turkmenistan and used by the Turkmen tribesmen.

13th–14th century
Possible influence by Mongol ponies.

1935
Trek from Ashgabat to Moscow to demonstrate the Akhal-Teke's extraordinary powers of endurance.

20th century
Thoroughbred blood introduced, to make a faster racehorse especially over long distances.

Kabardin

The Kabardin has been bred in the northern Caucasus mountains since the 16th century. Sure footed, tough, docile, and intelligent, it is good for riding and driving, as well as capable of carrying heavy loads as a pack horse.

Breed characteristics

The Kabardin is a strong horse for its size, with great powers of endurance. It has a long, thin head, rather short neck, and straight shoulders. The back is short and straight, with a broad, sloping croup. The limbs are clean and powerful, with good bone and strong feet, and the horse is remarkably agile and sure footed – essential features for a good mountain horse.

History of the Kabardin

The Kabardin has been used by the nomadic peoples of the northern Caucasus mountains for centuries. It was developed by crossing local stock with neighbouring breeds such as the Karabakh, Turkmenian, and Persian (Iranian) horses.

The earlier Kabardins were quite small, but from the 1920s they were crossed with larger horses such as the Thoroughbred to make them better mounts for the military and more suitable for agricultural work. More recently so much Thoroughbred blood has been used that a separate type, the Anglo-Kabardin, has been recognized, with lighter and more refined characteristics, added height, and even greater powers of endurance.

The Kabardin today

Today the main breeding centres for both the Kabardin and the Anglo-Kabardin are in the Kabardino-Balkar and Stavropol regions of Russia, where they spend summers grazing in mountain pastures, moving down to the foothills for winter.

This tough and remarkably fine breed is hardy and has great stamina. It is used for a wide range of activities in the remote Caucasian region.

1500		1600		1700		1800		1900	

16th–17th century
Local stock, likely to have had Mongolian origins, was upgraded and refined with Turkmen and Arabian blood to produce the Kabardin.

17th–20th century
Used by tribesmen in the mountains; highly prized for its agility and staying power.

20th century
Refined and made larger by the use of outside blood, mainly Thoroughbred.

Orlov Trotter

The Orlov was the first breed in the world produced specifically for harness racing. Its development began in the 1780s, and by the end of the 19th century there were more than 3000 stud farms in Russia specializing in its breeding. The Orlov has been used to improve many other Russian breeds, such as the Kladruber, Tersk, and Don.

and Dutch origin, they produced Bars I, who became the foundation stallion for the breed. He was bred to Arabian, Dutch (including some Friesians), Danish, Mecklenburg, and British mares. Through considerable in-breeding, the type was consolidated, and by the 19th century the Orlov had become the world's fastest trotter.

Breed characteristics

The Orlov is a strong, elegant horse, with very athletic movement and a tough constitution. Handsome and tall with good bone, it is light and well proportioned, with powerful quarters.

When American Standardbreds took supremacy in trotting at the end of the century, the Russians started importing the faster horses, and used them to give the Orlov greater speed. In 1949 the faster breed was recognized, and called the Russian Trotter.

History of the Orlov Trotter

It was Count Alexius Grigorievich Orlov who, in the early 1780s, took to Russia a mixture of horses that created this speedy breed. Of Arabian, Danish,

The Orlov Trotter today

The breed has to some extent been overtaken by the Russian Trotter, but is still used for riding and driving, and as an improver of other breeds.

Originally bred for harness racing, the Orlov had a big influence on the trotters of the 19th century. It is now virtually synonymous with the Russian Trotter.

MAIN FEATURES
• small head
• long neck
• tall and light in build
• muscular, powerful
• fine, hard limbs

CHARACTER
• courageous
• tough

COLOURS
Most are grey or bay, but some are black or chestnut.

HEIGHT
160–3cm (15.3–16hh)

COUNTRY OF ORIGIN
Russia

COMPARISON BREED
Standardbred
This is the American equivalent of the Orlov, and was developed as a trotter specifically for racing.

1780s	1949
Russian Count Orlov imported a mixture of breeds, which were selectively bred to produce the Orlov Trotter.	Russian Trotter recognized as a breed. In the ensuing years more American Standardbreds imported to give the Russian Trotter greater speed.

1750	1800	1850	1900

1784	1830–90	1890–1917
Birth of Bars I, the foundation sire in the development of the Orlov Trotter.	The Orlov generally considered the fastest breed of trotter in the world of harness racing.	American Standardbred reaching higher speeds: over 250 Standardbred mares and stallions imported into Russia to breed with the Orlov.

RELATED TOPICS

French Trotter	80
Standardbred	116
Racing	184
Driving	194

Australian Stock Horse

Australia has long depended on horses for work with the cattle and sheep on its huge stations. Today this role is fulfilled by the Australian Stock Horse, a smaller and more robust version of the Thoroughbred. Stock Horses are also in demand for the rodeos that are a popular feature of Australian life, and they are used for jumping, eventing, polo, endurance, and various forms of racing. Some have become successful in international competitions, most notably the 1982 World Three Day Event Champion, Regal Realm.

Breed characteristics

The Australian Stock Horse needs to be agile and quick thinking, for herding animals, as well as able to tolerate a fairly frugal life. Because of this they tend to be tough, wiry, compact horses that are fast and able to turn quickly, with a sensible, generous nature that makes them particularly amenable to training and hard work.

History of the Australian Stock Horse

The foundation stock for the Australian Stock Horse was the Waler, the famous cavalry horse of the 19th century, which was bred in the excellent horse-rearing lands of New South Wales. The Waler's ancestors were imported from South Africa and Chile at the end of the 18th century. These horses were said to have Dutch, Spanish, Arabian, and Barb blood and, as with so many of the breeds around the world,

Regal Realm with Lucinda Green became World Event Champions in 1982, putting the Australian Stock Horse firmly on the map as a sport horse.

1790s
First shipment of horses to Australia from the South African Cape (these were the foundation stock for what eventually became the Australian Stock Horse).

20th century
Walers infused with Thoroughbred, Arabian, Percheron, Quarter Horse, and some pony blood to develop the Australian Stock Horse.

1971
Formation of the Australian Stock Horse Society and opening of the stud book.

1800	1850	1900	1950

19th century
Mainly Thoroughbreds and Arabians used to develop the Waler, which was considered the finest cavalry mount in the world.

1914–18
Allied forces made extensive use of Walers. These horses were dispersed around the world when the war was over, since quarantine laws prohibited their return to Australia.

1988
Stud book closed.

they were then crossed with the Thoroughbred to produce the Waler.

Walers were used initially for herding cattle and sheep, then as a mount for the Australian cavalry. They were such a success that, during the 19th century, they were imported by other countries, especially India, where they were used by the British army.

During World War I more than 150,000 Walers were exported as mounts for the Allied armies in India, Africa, Palestine, and Europe. Those used by the Australian cavalry were not allowed to return home because of the quarantine laws there. A bronze memorial to them in Sydney bears the inscription: 'They suffered wounds, thirst, hunger and weariness almost beyond endurance, but never failed. They did not come home.'

In the 20th century further changes were made to the Waler: some Arabian and Thoroughbred blood was added as a refining influence, some Percheron to lend substance, and Quarter Horse to give more agility and the qualities needed for herding stock. The result was the Australian Stock Horse.

It was not until 1971 that a breed association was formed, but branches were quickly set up throughout Australia. By 1979, the society had 12,000 members, and more than 40,000 horses had been registered. Today, the Australian Stock Horse Society is working to promote the breed and to make it more uniform in appearance.

The Australian Stock Horse today

Although the Australian Stock Horse is the most numerous breed in Australia today, it faces two rather different rivals. More and more Warmbloods are being bred for sport, and the motorbike is used increasingly for herding sheep and cattle. Nevertheless, the Australian Stock Horse is so versatile, tough, and athletic that it is likely to survive the competition.

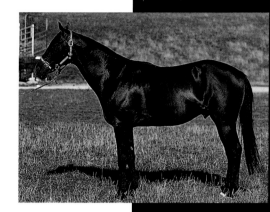

Still used extensively on the ranch as a work horse, the Australian Stock Horse is a great athlete able to fulfil many roles.

MAIN FEATURES
- fine features but vary in type
- light forehand
- strong back and quarters
- good limbs
- great endurance

CHARACTER
- sensible
- tough
- brave and quick

COLOURS
Most commonly bay.

HEIGHT
147–65cm (14.2–16.1hh)

COUNTRY OF ORIGIN
Australia

COMPARISON BREED
Warmbloods
Extremely versatile and widely used, the Warmblood is specifically bred for the competitive sports of today.

RELATED TOPICS

Thoroughbred	70
Warmbloods	76
Arabian	128
Barb	132
Eventing	156
Western riding	202
Rodeo	208
Riding holidays	250

Arabian

The Arabian is the oldest pure-bred horse in existence. It has been renowned for over 3000 years, and its blood has influenced more breeds than any other horse. The Arabian is known mostly for its beauty and incredible stamina, but the breed has a great deal of versatility. Arabians make superb racehorses, flashy park horses, and fine dressage horses, but where they truly excel is in endurance events and long-distance competitive trail rides.

Breed characteristics

The Arabian is one of the most distinctive horses in the world. It has a beautiful, dished profile, large, wide-set eyes, and curved, pricked ears. Its small head is set on an arched, refined neck with a clean throat. Legs are clean and delicate looking, but have substantial bone and hard, sound feet. The horse has a short back and a flat croup, with a long, flowing tail set very high. Its coat is fine and silky. It has strong lungs and large nostrils, which contribute to its ability to work unstintingly for long periods.

Very intelligent and quick thinking, Arabians are willing, tractable animals when trained properly.

Most Arabians are grey, chestnut, or bay. Black Arabians are uncommon, but are not as rare as they once were.

Black absorbs heat, and a desert horse would not be efficient with such a coat, so diligent breeders used to eliminate the colour from their bloodlines. Today most Arabians do not live in the desert, and breeders are beginning to meet a demand for black horses.

Early history of the Arabian

Because the Arabian breed is older than any other horse, and because it flourished and was nurtured in the Arabian peninsula for so long, it was once believed that the horses must have originated there also. However, the fossils discovered in the Arabian peninsula have since been identified as those of the onager. In fact the first horses appeared, not in the Middle East, but on the North American continent. Numerous prehistoric horses migrated over the land bridge that existed at what is now the Bering Strait into Siberia, continuing west and spreading south into countries today known as Turkey, Syria, Iraq, and Iran.

By about 2500 BC the nomadic Bedouin people of the Arabian peninsula had mastered the region's fiery horses. They had an almost fanatical devotion to maintaining the purity of their stock, and a desert sheikh could recite the entire ancestry of his animals from memory. These were the forerunners of today's

Left: The most influential breed of all, the Arabian is especially renowned for its speed and stamina, and is an outstanding endurance horse.

Right: The Arabian's intelligent head, with flared nostrils, tapered muzzle, and wide-set eyes, along with flowing mane, are well demonstrated here.

PRE	1800		1900	

2500 BC
Wild horses domesticated by Bedouin nomads in Arabia.

1099–1249
Crusaders returning from Palestine bring Arabian horses to northern and eastern Europe.

1570
Polish Arabian strain founded.

1836
Shagya Arabian strain founded in Hungary.

1893
Turkish exhibition at the Chicago's World Fair features 45 Arabians and awakens interest in the breed in the USA.

1990s
Enthusiasm in the Gulf States for racing Arabians leads breeders to produce animals specially for the racetrack.

1500 BC
Use of Arab horses widespread in trade and warfare in Middle East.

711 AD
Muslim armies conquer Spain and introduce Arabian horses to western Europe.

16th century
Light cavalry horse developed by European armies, using Arabian blood.

1878
Influential Crabbet Stud founded in England, using Arabians of desert and Egyptian stock.

1908
American stud book started.

1980s
Arabian's popularity soars, especially in the USA where it is seen as a symbol of status and wealth.

MAIN FEATURES
- tapered muzzle
- dished profile
- wide-set eyes
- high-set tail
- long, flowing mane
- fine, arched neck
- flared nostrils
- hot blooded

CHARACTER
- affectionate
- quick
- intelligent
- versatile

COLOURS
Chestnut and grey
predominate, but
all colours are now found.

HEIGHT
147–55cm (14.2–15.1hh)

COUNTRY OF ORIGIN
Arabian peninsula

COMPARISON BREED
Thoroughbred
The only other 'hot-
blooded' horse in
existence, the
Thoroughbred owes its
origins to the Arabian.

RELATED TOPICS
Thoroughbred   70
Barb   132
Eventing   156
Racing   184
Endurance   212
Showing   246

An Arabian racehorse showing its paces in training. Racing of Arabians is becoming increasingly popular internationally.

Arabians. They were bred for their stamina for everyday survival in the harsh desert conditions, and for their courage and speed in the constant raids and skirmishes between tribes.

Over the centuries the Bedouin in what is now Syria gained the reputation of breeding the finest Arabian horses, and stallions and brood mares were traded freely. By 1500 BC, the horse had become the backbone of trade, communications, and warfare in the Middle East, and was to remain crucial to civilization for many centuries afterwards.

A growing influence

In about AD 630, Islamic warriors began to fight their way north from the Arabian peninsula, and then battled west across North Africa. By 711 they had conquered Spain. Their mounts were largely Turks and Barbs, but among them were many Arabians. From these developed the Andalusians that Columbus took to the New World; they in turn helped to found the many breeds thriving in the Americas today. Meanwhile, other European horses were infused with Arabian blood as knights who had joined the medieval crusades to Palestine returned with eastern horses.

From the 15th century on, as firearms made massive war-horses and their heavily armoured riders obsolete, the Arabian contributed to the emergence of the fast, agile cavalry horse, which dominated European battlefields well into the 20th century.

Arabian horses had also been brought into the studs of the ruler of the Turkish Ottoman empire, and from there, during the 18th century, they were introduced into the world of European horse racing. The Darley Arabian, one of the foundation sires of the Throughbred breed, arrived in England in 1703.

International fame

The royal houses of Europe took a particular interest in Arabians, and in the 19th century they were established in a number of royal studs. But perhaps the most famous stud of the time was Crabbet Park, in England. In 1878, Wilfrid Scawen Blunt and his wife Lady Anne found a source of pure-bred Arabian horses and began to import them to Crabbet. For nearly a century the Blunt family dedicated themselves to conserving the purity of the breed, and in turn provided foundation stock for breeders in many other countries, including Russia, Poland, Australia, and North and South America. The stud was dispersed in 1971, but its influence on the breeding of the Arabian horse is still felt today.

In the USA, interest in the breed leaped beyond a handful of devotees after Turkey exhibited 45 Arabians at the 1893 World Fair in Chicago. The US stud book was established in 1908, with 71 animals registered. In 1994, the 500,000th horse was registered. There are now more Arabians in North America than in the rest of the world put together.

Status symbols

In the 1980s, the Arabian's popularity soared to unbelievable heights. Many individuals who were not experienced with horses were captivated by the image of the Arabian: long mane and tail fluttering around a wild-eyed, prancing, snorting animal. Celebrities found a new way to demonstrate wealth and status with the splendour of the Arabian. Prices soared, particularly in the USA – $150,000 (£100,000) or even $1 million (£650,000) was paid for these showpieces. New breeders sprang up to meet the demand and began overbreeding, particularly the ultra-refined, fiery horses. Inbreeding to exaggerate type was also common.

When tax laws concerning horses were changed, the market for Arabians collapsed. The horses were suddenly worth much less, and there were far too many of them. However, the recent interest of the Gulf States in racing Arabians has brought a new outlet for these fine animals, and many are now being specifically bred for racetrack and endurance events.

The Arabian today

There are many different types of Arabians in existence today. The Persian and Egyptian types, which are thought to be the oldest, have beautiful refined conformation. Polish Arabians, introduced in Poland at about 1570, are not as refined as their Middle Eastern counterparts, while the Shagya Arabians, a strain founded in Hungary around 1836, are larger and more substantial animals.

Whatever their type, Arabians are currently being bred away from the wild-eyed, temperamental halter horse of the 1980s. Breeders are meeting the demand for quiet, athletic horses to perform in a myriad disciplines, including reining, cutting, dressage, jumping, and saddleseat. At breed shows Arabians demonstrate their versatility under many different saddles. In dressage shows, the Arabian is quickly gaining popularity for its expressive movement and its self-carriage. The Arabian's true calling, however, is endurance. It is unmatched by any other breed in long-distance riding, and holds world records in 160km (100 mile) endurance races. It is not only consistently among the first to finish, it also has a reputation of winning the coveted 'best conditioned' horse in the race because of its extraordinary stamina and fitness.

An Arabian prancing loose in the paddock, clearly displaying its proud bearing, graceful movement, and natural beauty.

Barb

The Barb is a true desert horse, with incredible stamina and hardiness borne out of harsh living conditions. It originated along the infamous Barbary Coast of North Africa, principally in Morocco, but because of rampant cross-breeding it is uncommon to find a pure-bred Barb today. Many horse enthusiasts are critical of the Barb's conformation, its fiery temperament, and its athletic ability. Even so, it has had an important role in the foundation of many breeds, and perhaps only the Arabian has had a greater influence on the modern horse.

Breed characteristics

The Barb is a light riding horse known for its stamina and its prepotency. Although spirited, it can be very reliable with a skilled rider. It has a powerful front end, high withers, a short back, and a sloping, narrow croup. It carries its tail low.

The legs are clean and defined, and the hooves are hard, sound, and small. Its gaits are not spectacular, but workmanlike; it has a nice, even trot with some knee action, and gallops like a sprinter – indeed, its speed has influenced racing breeds such as the Thoroughbred, the Quarter Horse, and the Standardbred.

The term 'Barb' is often applied in a general sense to the horses of Morocco, Algeria, Tunisia, and Libya, but not all North African horses are Barbs, since there are numerous horses of oriental blood throughout this region.

History of the Barb

The Barb's origins are obscure, and many historians have speculated on its true beginnings. Although it is possible

The small, wiry Barb, seen here in its simple traditional dress, has influenced the development of many breeds, most notably the Thoroughbred.

500	1000	1500	2000

600
Arabian blood infuses Barb (Turkmenian/Caspian) for greater refinement and added tractability.

750s
Andalusian infused with Barb blood during the Moorish invasion.

1800s to present
Barbs increasingly cross-bred with Arabians; now, few pure-bred Barbs exist.

1987
The World Organization of the Barb Horse founded in Algeria to preserve the breed.

that the Barb and Arabian are related, it is most likely that they are descended from two different primitive horses.

We do know that the Barb originated in northern Africa during the 8th century. There is some evidence that it arose from crossbreeding between the Turkmenian (which produced the Akhal-Teke) and the Caspian (closely related to the Arabian) and descendants of Iberian horses along the coast of North Africa. There are several varieties of Barb, including Algerian, Moroccan, and Tunisian.

When Barbs were imported to Europe, they were often mistaken for Arabians simply because their handlers were northern African Muslims who spoke Arabic. The celebrated Godolphin 'Arabian', one of the three founding sires of the Thoroughbred, was in fact a Barb stallion. He was given as a gift to the French king by the Moroccan sultan, but his worth was not fully appreciated. It has been said that he was working as a cart horse in the streets of Paris when in about 1730 an Englishman named Edward Coke bought him and took him to England. After the death of Coke, the horse was

acquired by the renowned breeder Lord Godolphin, who used him for breeding with native English mares. In more up-to-date literature, the stallion is correctly referred to as the Godolphin Barb.

The Barb's influence on other breeds has been enormous: it has passed on its athleticism and power, swiftness, and endurance – as well as its spirit and fiery nature – to the Spanish Barb, the Quarter Horse, the Mustang, and the Appaloosa, as well as to the Lusitano, the Andalusian, and many others.

The Barb today

The Barb is now bred primarily in Algeria, Morocco, Spain, and throughout southern France although, because of difficult economic conditions in its homeland, the number of pure-bred animals is decreasing. The World Organization of the Barb Horse was founded in Algeria in 1987 to promote and preserve the breed. However, with the political turmoil that has affected Algeria throughout the 1990s, it is difficult to say whether the breed will continue to grow – either in numbers or in purity.

Today's Barb has been crossed with so many other breeds that it is in danger of losing its true identity.

MAIN FEATURES
- long, narrow profile
- distinctly sloping croup
- flat shoulder
- bushy mane
- low-set, bushy tail
- almond-shaped, 'hooded' eyes
- hardy
- good endurance

CHARACTER
- spirited
- intelligent

COLOURS
Most are grey, but bay, chestnut, black, and brown are also found.

HEIGHT
142–52cm (14–15hh)

COUNTRY OF ORIGIN
North Africa

COMPARISON BREED
Arabian
This is another desert-bred horse that has had an enormous influence on other breeds.

RELATED TOPICS

Thoroughbred	70
Andalusian	94
Appaloosa	104
Mustang	110
Quarter Horse	112
Standardbred	116
Arabian	128

MAIN FEATURES
• golden coat
• light mane and tail

CHARACTER
• unique to each breed

COLOURS
Three shades of a newly minted gold coin, with white mane and tail.

HEIGHT
Typically 145–73cm (14.1–17hh), but can be any size.

COUNTRY OF ORIGIN
The majority of breeding takes place in the USA.

COMPARISON BREED
Pinto
Like the Palomino, the Pinto is a colour type not a breed.

Palomino

Known as the horse touched by Midas, the golden Palomino has a universal appeal. The Palomino is actually a colour of horse, not a breed, and there has been a recent rise of interest in breeding horses of all types to produce a gold-coated horse.

Breed characteristics

The Palomino colour is seen in many breeds worldwide: there are miniature Palomino horses just a few hands high, as well as large horses. The common denominator is the body colour, described as that of a newly minted gold coin, with variations from light to dark, together with a flaxen mane and tail. The Palomino should have dark skin beneath its golden coat, except under any white markings.

Palominos are of many different breeds, so vary hugely in conformation and temperament. In North America, where the Palomino is bred more widely than anywhere else, over 50 per cent of Palominos are stock horses, most of Quarter Horse breeding. The rest are pleasure and park horses represented by hunters, American Saddlebreds, Arabians, Morgans, and Tennessee Walking Horses.

History of the Palomino

Horses with coats of gold and flaxen manes and tails have been around for centuries all over the world: the ancient Greek warrior Achilles rode one, and they served Chinese emperors as well as at the court of the Spanish queen, Isabella. The cowboys of the American West favoured the Palomino and other coloured horses when choosing mounts to work their ranches.

The source of the Palomino's name is unknown, but it is believed to have Spanish origins.

The Palomino today

Palominos are competitive in many sports and Western events, and they are also very flashy halter horses. Perhaps the world recognizes the Palomino best when it is dressed for the parade route, for matched Palominos always catch the eye in festive processions.

The beautiful colouring of the Palomino has made it a favourite worldwide, nowhere more so than in the USA for Western work.

RELATED TOPICS

Morgan	106
Quarter Horse	112
American Saddlebred	114
Pinto	135
Western riding	202
Showing	246

1550s
Spanish stock including Palomino horses brought to Americas.

1980s
More than 90 per cent of Palominos registered with the PHBA are Quarter Horses.

PRE	1850		1900		1950	

1800s
American cowboys begin to favour horses with striking coat colours and patterns, including the Palomino, Pinto, and, later, the Appaloosa.

1936
The first registry, the Palomino Horse Association, founded in the USA.

1941
Founding of Palomino Horse Breeders of America (PHBA). This association now has some 69,000 Palominos in its register.

Pinto

Like the Palomino, the Pinto is not a breed, but a coat pattern found in a number of different breeds. However, because the Pinto colouring tends to reproduce itself, there are several registries for Pinto horses (particularly in the USA), and many pure-bred horses are able to obtain dual registration. Today there are coloured horses in almost all riding and driving disciplines, in various bloodlines throughout the world.

Breed characteristics

Four types of Pinto are registered. The stock type is a Western riding horse, usually of Quarter Horse breeding. The hunter type is a spotted English horse of mainly Thoroughbred breeding. Saddle-type Pintos have Saddlebred, Tennessee Walker, Hackney, or gaited horse breeding; and the pleasure type has the conformation or blood of the Arabian, Morgan, or Welsh Pony.

Two main types of coat pattern are recognized: the tobiano (large, bold patches of colour) and the overo (irregular, lacy, white markings, which rarely cross the spine), although there are several intermediate patterns.

History of the Pinto

There were Pintos among the horses taken to the New World by Hernando Cortez of Spain in 1519. The American Indian was drawn to these beautiful 'painted' horses, and trained them for use in battle. The American cowboy, too, loved the flashy appearance of the

Pinto and, along with the Palomino and Appaloosa, it became a favourite for exhibitions, rodeos, and parades.

The Pinto today

Western enthusiasts have always been drawn to the Pinto, but now there is growing interest in the 'coloured sport horse'. Some Warmblood breeders are known for producing Pintos; they are also sought after by dressage riders.

The spectacular markings of Pintos are generally known as piebald (black and white) or skewbald (other colours and white) in Britain.

MAIN FEATURES
- distinctive coat, with either the bold tobiano pattern or the lacy, irregular overo pattern

CHARACTER
- varies according to breed

COLOURS
All colours with white markings, but no Appaloosa patterns.

HEIGHT
All sizes – from miniature horses to large Warmbloods.

COUNTRY OF ORIGIN
Worldwide, but known mostly in the USA.

COMPARISON BREED
Palomino
Like the Pinto, the Palomino is a colour type rather than a breed.

1519
Spanish stock, including coloured horses, turned loose in the Americas.

1800s
American cowboys use Pintos with Mustang blood because of their stamina and hardiness.

1980s
Warmblood breeders produce coloured sport horses.

| PRE | 1700 | | 1800 | | 1900 | |

17th century
American Indians use and breed coloured horses.

1947
The Pinto Horse Association of America founded.

RELATED TOPICS
Mustang 110
Palomino 134
Driving 194
Western riding 202
Pony Club 226
Showing 246
Riding holidays 250

A day in the life of a physiotherapist

An equine physiotherapist requires veterinary permission and referral before they can offer an opinion on a patient. This enables them to be more effective in their treatment and gives them the opportunity to work very closely with the veterinary profession.

Amanda Sutton is responsible for the treatment and management of acute and chronic musculoskeletal injuries in horses. She assesses and treats them using her hands and electrotherapy. She also exercises the horses and stretches their bodies to improve strength and flexibility. She teaches these procedures, where appropriate, to the groom and owner, so that they can be carried out regularly.

Amanda likes to see the injury immediately it has been sustained or within 48 hours. However, she often sees horses that have shown a loss of performance over several years.

She works as part of a team, liaising with the farrier, saddler, trainer, and veterinary surgeon. Her practice has been built up over 10 years and employs and trains other physiotherapists. She is often asked by the chief veterinary officer involved to cover and provide physiotherapy at many of the major three day events in England.

▲ **10.00am** 'I observe the standing posture and symmetry of the horse. This gives me clues as to exactly what problem there may be with the horse's back. I have to be careful when doing this procedure.'

▼ **9.30am** 'It is important that I check over the tack and its possible implication in areas of bruising or hypersensitivity. This is the routine starting approach to assessing back and performance problems.'

▲ **9.00am** 'My day starts at 8am at the clinic when I talk directly with owners and vets and write up case notes. After that, I assess any inpatient with the rest of my colleagues. Watching a horse during exercise allows me to identify loss of power or decreased flexibility and to identify any mechanical problems. Exercise in a sand school is used to develop strength and to progress rehabilitation.'

▶ **11.00am** 'A horses's recovery from lower limb injuries is often hampered by poor circulation and scar tissue. Physiotherapy aims to maximize the tissue's ability to heal and to provide the ideal conditions for this. Here I am using laser therapy to help the resolution of shin soreness.'

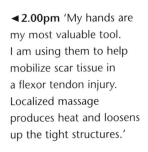

◀ **2.00pm** 'My hands are my most valuable tool. I am using them to help mobilize scar tissue in a flexor tendon injury. Localized massage produces heat and loosens up the tight structures.'

▲ **10.30am** 'It is very important to analyze functional movement in order to decide the significance and nature of a problem. This exercise helps to maintain suppleness and prevent stiffness. It mobilizes the soft tissues and improves joint flexibility. I have to be extremely careful though, because it is very easy for the horse to develop trick movements.'

▲ **3.00pm** 'A lot of my patients have been involved in a fall or traumatic incident such as pulling back violently when secured. This results in soft tissue overstretching and the jamming up of movement of the underlying structures. Mobilization techniques help to restore full function and pain-free movement.'

◀ **4.30pm** 'My last patient of the day is in the pool as swimming can be incorporated into a rehabilitation programme. It is useful as a non-weight bearing exercise in situations where we want to reduce the effects of concussive exercise on joints or limbs.'

Clydesdale

One of the best known of all draught horses, the Clydesdale is a handsome, powerful animal, and has a quiet, friendly disposition. It was once strictly known as a Scottish work horse, but now enjoys an international reputation as a show and exhibition horse.

Breed characteristics

The Clydesdale is a beautiful, well-put-together draught horse with imposing presence. Although large, it is not

There are few more impressive sights than a team of Clydesdales on parade in full harness with traditional brasses.

heavily muscled, and a perfect specimen of the breed should convey an impression not of sheer bulk, but of great strength and activity.

Its movement is distinctive, with the horse raising each hard, rounded hoof clear off the ground so that someone standing behind would be able to see a flash of horseshoe. The legs are straight and well placed underneath the massive body, adding to the high-stepping action the horse displays while moving forwards.

History of the Clydesdale

Native horses in Scotland centuries ago were originally bred to carry knights into battle. In the early 18th century, descendants of these small, sturdy war-horses were crossed with imported Flemish stallions, in order to produce a bigger, heavier horse suitable for hauling coal and other loads, as well as working the fields.

It was not until the 19th century that the Clydesdale began to develop the conformation it displays today, taking its name from the area in which it was bred (now known as Lanarkshire). The system of hiring stallions, in which a number of owners shared the cost of using a particular sire to put with local mares, helped to fix the features of the breed. It quickly gained popularity, replacing the Shire as Scotland's favourite draught horse.

The Clydesdale Horse Society was founded in 1877, and helped to encourage breeding from the best possible heavy horses in the district.

Before World War II, Clydesdales were widely exported for heavy haulage work until mechanization

gradually took over. Large numbers were shipped to the USA and Canada, as well as to Australia, New Zealand, and other Commonwealth countries. The Clydesdale's exceptional temperament and willingness to work have made it a favourite in all parts of the world.

The Clydesdale today

There are still farmers in many countries who use the Clydesdale for traditional farm work, especially in less accessible areas where mechanical equipment would make too much mess. Ploughing matches using Clydesdales are a great tourist attraction, as well as proving how adept the horse is in difficult terrain.

At breed shows, teams of up to six horses are harnessed to display their beauty and action, and in-hand classes are popular, too. Their use is also expanding for parades and exhibitions: Anheuser-Busch, the company that brews Budweiser beer, owns a herd of more than 250 Clydesdales, which are used for promotional work all over North America, as well as featuring in television commercials.

A growing number of people are discovering the pleasure of riding Clydesdales, and some enthusiasts have trained them for dressage. However, the breed is perhaps best suited to crossing with other horses, such as the Thoroughbred, to produce an athletic performance horse capable of showjumping and eventing.

A pair of Clydesdales takes part in a ploughing match, showing their skill in an art still practised by work horses in many parts of the world.

1715–20
Flemish stallions imported to breed with native mares in the Clydesdale region, to produce bigger, heavier horses.

1877
Clydesdale Horse Society formed to promote breeding.

1700

1800

1900

1830s
Stallions in Clydesdale mated with local stock as well as northern England mares to produce large, strong horses that would form the foundation stock for the breed.

1850s
Black Horses (Shires) brought north from the Midlands and used by Scottish breeders to consolidate the strength and size of the Clydesdale.

1980s
Crosses with lighter horses, such as the Thoroughbred and Arabian, to develop a modern sport horse.

MAIN FEATURES
- short back
- well-sprung ribs
- powerful hindquarters
- muscular
- straight, feathered legs
- sound feet
- convex facial features

CHARACTER
- docile
- eager to please
- willing

COLOURS
Most commonly bay or brown, with white stockings and a blaze, but black and chestnut are also seen, as well as roan. There may be occasional splashes of white on the belly.

HEIGHT
165–83cm (16.1–18hh)

COUNTRY OF ORIGIN
Britain (Scotland)

COMPARISON BREED
Shire
This British breed is closely related to the Clydesdale, and similar to it, but bigger and more powerful. It is predominantly black with plenty of white feather.

RELATED TOPICS

Shire	140
Driving	194
Ceremonial and working horses	232
Showing	246

Shire

Known to many as the 'Gentle Giant', the Shire is the world's largest horse but, despite its massive size, it is a kind, willing, docile creature. It has a long history of serving as a draught horse extraordinaire, and can still be seen working today in Britain on farms or pulling brewery wagons.

Breed characteristics

The Shire is one of the most powerful horses ever bred. What it lacks in speed, it certainly makes up for with its great strength and stamina. Its large, compact body has deep, powerful shoulders and forearms. The chest is wide and hindquarters are well muscled. Its head sports a Roman profile and a large jowl. Most Shires have white legs, feathered with long, silky hair that covers their strong, rounded hooves.

History of the Shire

At the beginning of the 14th century, 100 horses from Lombardy were imported into England to cross with the native mares, in order to produce a horse that could carry the weight of a knight in full armour. It is thought that the Shire is directly descended from this medieval Great Horse. But it is unlikely that the Shire itself was a war-horse, since even the smallest modern Shire could not fit into the armour worn by the horses of that time.

Instead, the Shire developed because farmers wanted a horse that could help them cultivate the land quickly, as well as move heavy loads and pull their carts and coaches through rough countryside with bad roads. The Shire takes its name from the Midland shires, or counties, of England, where the horse was raised.

The Shire crossed with the Thoroughbred has produced many useful sport horses in its native Britain, and is widely exported.

	PRE	1700		1800		1900	

14th century
One hundred stallions imported into England from northern Europe to produce the Great Horse.

16th century
Friesian horses, hired to help drain the Fens in eastern England, breed with descendants of the Great Horse, resulting in the creation of Lincolnshire Blacks.

18th century
Black Horses of the Midlands and Fens crossed with Thoroughbreds, to create a sizeable horse.

1870s
Cart Horse Society (later Shire Horse Society) founded.

1950s
Breed revived after almost becoming extinct.

Throughout the 1800s, the Shire was an essential feature in England's commercial life. Besides its major role in agriculture and forestry, it also worked in towns and cities, transporting goods from the docks and railways. To help ensure breeding from the best possible bloodlines, a breed association was formed in the mid 1870s. Originally called the Cart Horse Society, it changed its name to the Shire Horse Society in 1878, and the first stud book to record the pedigrees of the breed was published in 1882.

The Shire, like so many of the heavy breeds, was brought almost to the point of extinction after World War II, as mechanization took jobs away from draught horses. In Britain in 1947 and 1948, as many as 100,000 Shires were reputedly killed every year, and the number of foals registered annually dwindled to a mere 80. But gradually, thanks to the efforts of breeders dedicated to preserving this dying line, the Shire population recovered

to such a point that today in Europe, as many as 500 pure-bred foals are registered each year.

The Shire today

Oddly enough the Shire's popularity seems to be growing in a time when heavy horses are outnumbered in mechanical horsepower by hundreds to one. Even today, some farmer use them to turn over their fields, they are still active in the forestry industry, and they do promotional work for organizations such as brewery companies.

Shires are now found in other parts of Europe, as well as the USA, Canada, Australia, and New Zealand. While by no means common, because their size makes them impractical for most equine pursuits, they are always popular at shows and exhibitions. Breeders are also now crossing shires with lighter horses such as Thoroughbreds and Warmbloods to produce substantial, level-headed performance horses.

This traditional turnout is being driven as a unicorn (a pair led by a single). Shires have an abundance of feather on their legs, with strong feet.

MAIN FEATURES
- well-muscled, rounded body
- massive head, with a Roman profile
- powerful legs
- lots of feather
- sound feet

CHARACTER
- strong
- willing
- even tempered

COLOURS
Mostly black, bay, or brown, although some are chestnut or grey.

HEIGHT
165–91cm (16.1–18.3hh)

COUNTRY OF ORIGIN
Britain (England, Midlands)

COMPARISON BREED
Clydesdale
A Scottish draught horse that was influenced by the Shire, the Clydesdale is not quite as powerful, and matures more slowly.

RELATED TOPICS

Clydesdale	138
Suffolk	142
Percheron	148
Driving	194
Ceremonial and working horses	232
Showing	246

Suffolk

The Suffolk is regarded as the purest draught breed in Britain. There has been very little to interfere with the horse's development through the centuries, mainly because its homeland was fairly isolated from the rest of the country. Also called the Suffolk Punch, it is known for its compactness, its power, and its hardy constitution.

Breed characteristics

The Suffolk is one of the shorter draught breeds, usually standing around 163cm (16 hands) high, because it has short legs in comparison to its massive body. However, it is still a very large horse, often weighing over one tonne. It is well muscled, with a crested neck, and a noble profile. Because of its conformation, with the short but substantial bone in its legs, it has a lower centre of gravity, which is why it is such a powerful pulling animal.

The Suffolk is known for its sound feet, and the legs are clean with no feather, so they do not become caked with mud when working in the fields. Despite its great size, the Suffolk does not need large amounts of food, and it has a pleasant, willing personality, making it sought after as a farm horse.

History of the Suffolk

The Suffolk horse dates back to the early 1500s, but there are few records of how the breed originated. It takes its name from the county in south-east England where it was bred, an area separated from the rest of the country by the North Sea and marshlands. The farmers of the region produced the Suffolk to meet their need for a horse that had the stamina and strength to turn over the heavy clay soil, but would also thrive on small rations. They bred horses only for their own use, and rarely had any to sell; because Suffolks stayed largely confined to their birthplace, the breed was kept free from outside influences and significant cross-breeding.

All Suffolk horses can trace their male lineage to the foundation stallion, Crisp's Horse of Ufford, born in 1760. Within just a few years the Suffolk became well known for its ability to win pulling matches throughout the county. Its popularity increased, and some Suffolks were even exported to Europe and parts of North America.

Mechanization had a severe impact on the Suffolk, and its numbers fell even further than those of other working breeds. After reaching its lowest point in the 1950s, the Suffolk has bounced back in recent years, and its population is now steadily growing.

The Suffolk today

The breed has now been exported to many other countries, including Italy, Russia, Africa, and Australia; in Pakistan, Suffolk stallions are used to produce horses for the army. East Anglia, the breed's homeland, is still where the largest number of Suffolks can be found. They are currently being bred with lighter horses, such as Thoroughbreds and Warmbloods, to produce hunters and jumpers with excellent bone and hardy constitutions.

Left: The chestnut colouring is a particular feature of the Suffolk. It is the only British work horse to be clean legged (no feathering).

Right: The docile and gentle nature of the breed is well demonstrated in the head and expression of this Suffolk, shown in full harness.

1877
Suffolk Horse Society founded.

1990s
Renewed interest in the breed as Suffolks crossed with Thoroughbreds and lighter Warmbloods to produce hunters and jumpers.

PRE	1700		1800		1900		2000

1500s
Horses from East Anglia bred to develop Suffolk.

18th century
Norfolk Trotter, Cob, and Thoroughbred blood used in an attempt to refine conformation and movement.

1880
First stud book published.

1950s
Breed numbers decline sharply as a result of mechanization, but gradually improve as Suffolk exported.

MAIN FEATURES
- massive body
- muscular shoulders
- thick, crested neck
- short, straight legs, with short cannon bones
- hardy
- powerful puller

CHARACTER
- willing worker
- docile
- gentle

COLOURS
Chestnut (seven different shades), with no white other than a star on the forehead.

HEIGHT
163cm (16hh)

COUNTRY OF ORIGIN
Britain (Suffolk)

COMPARISON BREED
Percheron
This is another heavy draught horse, originating in France, and the only other one that is clean legged.

RELATED TOPICS
Percheron 148
Driving 194
Ceremonial and working horses 232
Showing 246

Brabant

Also known as the Belgian Draught and the Brabançon, the Brabant has been called the most powerful living tractor in the world. Many Brabants weigh in at more than one tonne, and their tremendous strength and size have been in demand by farmers for centuries. The horse has also been used to improve many other European breeds, with Brabant stallions

The great strength and muscle power of such breeds as the Brabant make moving through snow, mud, or heavy soil an easy task.

contributing to the bloodlines of French, German, and British heavy horses. It takes its name from the province of Brabant in central Belgium, its principal breeding area.

Breed characteristics

Because Belgian breeders have been careful not to cross-breed with other horses, the Brabant is very pure in type. It is an extraordinarily powerful horse, with a willing nature and a good attitude towards work. It has been used for ploughing, logging, harvesting, and

all other types of work on the land. Despite being incredibly large, it is a gentle horse that is easy to train.

Two of the Brabant's most distinctive features are its massive muscles and its thick, crested neck. It also has a wide chest, short legs, a stout, close-coupled body, and rounded croup. Brabants mature at a young age, and are useful for hard work even into their 20s.

In the USA, the breed is known as the American Belgian, and it is a lighter, more refined horse. While European Brabants are typically

16th–18th century
Selective breeding of large, black Flanders or Flemish horses produces foundation stock for the Brabant.

1870s
Three regional groups of Brabant firmly established, differing only in minor points of conformation.

PRE	1800	1850	1900	1950

1878
Brabant stallion Brilliant wins the International Championship at Paris, increasing demand for the breed.

1885
Stud book opened, published by the *Société Royale de Cheval de Trait Belge.*

20th century
In the USA, Thoroughbreds and Quarter Horses used on the American Belgian to produce riding horses.

MAIN FEATURES
• powerful hindquarters
• crested neck
• massive muscling
• straight profile with
  broad facial features

CHARACTER
• willing
• docile
• even tempered
• gentle

COLOURS
Most European Brabants
are chestnut or red roan
with black points. The
American Belgian is often
sorrel with light points.

HEIGHT
160–70cm (15.3 –16.3hh)

COUNTRY OF ORIGIN
Belgium

COMPARISON BREED
Ardennes
This is another uncommon
draught breed, found
in France and Belgium,
which has benefited from
Brabant blood.

chestnut or red roan, and usually have dark points, with a medium amount of feather on the legs, the American Belgian is generally sorrel with a flaxen mane and tail, and has only a little feather on its legs.

History of the Brabant
The Brabant is the direct descendant of the Flanders, or Flemish, Horse, the great war-horse of the Middle Ages. Down the centuries, selective breeding fixed the characteristics of the horse. Until the 1900s, there were three types of Brabant, each having a different bloodline, and being bred in a different region. These were the Big Horse of the Dendre, the Grey Horse of the Nivelles, and the Colossal Horse of Mehaigne. Today they all share one stud book, because they are so similar in colour, height, and conformation.

At one time, the majority of horses in Belgium were Brabants. But numbers sharply decreased after World War II,

and the breed had to be saved from the brink of extinction. In the past 40 years the Brabant has been exported all over the world.

The European Brabant has been used effectively to improve other European horses, adding size and substance to such breeds as the Rhineland, the Ardennes, and the Dutch Draught.

The Brabant today
The future for the European Brabant is uncertain: like many of the draught horses, it is typically being bred for meat. The American Belgian horse is bred for show and harness. Its numbers have begun to increase in North America, as equine enthusiasts become more aware of draught breeds as a result of seeing them in action at exhibitions and fairs. The American Belgian is also being crossed with lighter breeds such as the Thoroughbred and Quarter Horse to produce a substantial riding horse.

A pair of Brabants, Belgium's heavy draught horse, makes light work of drawing a tram around the streets. Brabants are very broad and strong, and have great pulling power.

RELATED TOPICS
Ardennes   146
Dutch Draught   150
Ceremonial and
working horses   232
Showing   246

Ardennes

The Ardennes is one of the oldest of the European draught horses. Bred in both Belgium and France, it was originally relatively small and energetic, but was developed into a massive, immensely powerful animal ideally suited to pulling heavy loads and equipment.

Breed characteristics

The Ardennes is very similar to the Brabant or Belgian Draught, except that it has a slightly lighter, smaller build. A medium-heavy work horse, it is a robust animal, sturdy, and able to survive on relatively little food for its great size. It also has a willing, tolerant nature and a steady temperament.

Generally, the Ardennes features an angular, expressive head, and a thick, crested neck. It is extremely well muscled, with a broad chest, stout body, and a short, strong back, which leads to a rather steep, short croup. The breed is relatively short, at only 152–63cm (15–16 hands) high, but has strong bone in its legs and supports its massive weight with sound, rounded hooves. For its size, the Ardennes has an energetic way of going, and is quite springy when trotting.

History of the Ardennes

The breed has been living in the Ardennes region of Belgium and France for 2000 years, roaming the

This excellent example of the Ardennes is shown outside the splendid stables, hundreds of years old, seen at many of the great European studs.

PRE	1700		1800		1900	

8th century
Arabian blood infuses Ardennes.

18th century
Arabians again introduced to improve endurance.

19th century
Belgian Brabant used to give Ardennes more size and power.

20th century
Numbers declining but still used locally for farm work and in vineyards, and it is a crowd pleaser at shows and fairs.

plateau that spans the border between the two countries. The Belgian version of the breed originated in the mountains. It is thought to be descended from the heavy draught horses described by Julius Caesar, in his account of the conquest of Gaul in the 1st century, as hardy, tireless working horses owned by a German tribe living along the Rhine River.

The Ardennes has not been without some outside influence. Like many horses in the region, it was probably infused with Arabian blood as a result of the Islamic invasion of Europe, which ended in the 8th century, and Arabian blood was introduced again in the 18th century, to lighten the breed and improve its staying power.

Such was its incredible strength and hardiness, that the French emperor Napoleon Bonaparte was said to have chosen the Ardennes to pull heavy artillery and supplies for his campaign against Russia in 1812 – over a distance of more than 2000km (1300 miles).

In the late 19th century, cross-breeding with the Brabant produced an even stronger, bigger horse, one that was better suited to the demands of farm and forestry work; as a result, the modern version of the Ardennes is much like the Brabant.

The Ardennes today

Although the Ardennes is bred mainly in the Belgian and French mountains, it is also found in several areas of Sweden, which now has its own version of the breed, with its own stud book. While the Ardennes itself has benefited from the blood of other breeds, it has in turn been used to improve other cold-blooded horses, increasing both their size and their strength, especially in Sweden, Germany, and the USA.

The Ardennes is still used occasionally as a work horse on small farms and in vineyards and forestry, as well as serving as a draught animal in towns and cities; it is also raised specifically for the meat market. Although the numbers of this breed are not as strong as they once were, the Ardennes is still a popular attraction at breed and draught horse shows throughout northern Europe.

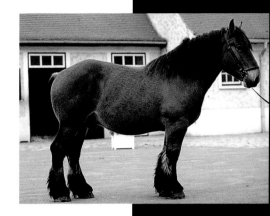

The fine head of the Ardennes, with its expressive eyes and ears, slightly concave profile, and large jaw, suggests a probable infusion of Arabian blood.

MAIN FEATURES
- short and stocky
- crested neck
- thick body
- powerful hindquarters
- little feather on feet
- large, rectangular head
- large eyes, pricked ears

CHARACTER
- willing
- strong
- tough

COLOURS
Bay, roan, chestnut, grey, and Palomino.

HEIGHT
152–63cm (15–16hh)

COUNTRY OF ORIGIN
Belgium and France (Ardennes region); a version is also bred in Sweden.

COMPARISON BREED
Brabant
The Brabant, which is also bred in Belgium, is closely related to the Ardennes, having been used to give it added size, strength, and power.

RELATED TOPICS
Brabant   144
Ceremonial and
working horses   232
Showing   246

Percheron

With substance, beauty, and style, the Percheron is a powerful and striking draught horse. It is different from many other 'cold bloods' because of the significant Arabian influence, which has added spirit to its strength. While most are found in harness as well-matched teams of blacks or dapple greys, Percherons are also being used more frequently as riding horses, displaying versatility in disciplines such as dressage and jumping.

Breed characteristics

Several types of Percheron exist, from lightweight to heavyweight. The larger ones may be rather uncomfortable to ride because of their broad girths and backs – most stand about 173cm (17 hands) high and weigh about 800kg (1800lb); but those that range from 157 to 170cm (15.2–16.3 hands) are found to give a pleasant, lively ride. The almost featherless legs have ample bone, helping to support a solid, well-proportioned body. The influence of Arabian blood has given the Percheron unusually fluid action for a heavy horse. The breed is known to be gentle, and is intelligent and easy to train.

History of the Percheron

Breed historians claim that the ancestors of the Percheron were small, stocky, but powerful animals, developed in the province of Le Perche, northern France, to provide mounts for knights going into battle. It is likely that these horses received an infusion of Arabian blood from stallions left behind by Islamic invaders after they were defeated at the battle of Poitiers in AD 732.

Eastern blood was introduced again in the 18th century, when Arabian stallions at the royal stud at Le Pin were made available to breeders in the Perche region, who at that time provided mounts for the military as well as draught animals. The Arabian Gallipoli is believed to have sired the legendary Jean le Blanc, born in 1823, who was designated the foundation stallion of the Percheron breed.

From 1839, there was a growing market for Percherons in other countries, especially North America; thousands were exported there during the last half of the 19th century, and up until World War II. Farmers and teamsters alike found that the Percheron's gifts were many and, by 1930, there were more Percherons in the USA than four other major draught breeds combined.

The Percheron today

Although mechanization largely ended the Percheron's role as a work horse, the breed has found a new function as a city carriage horse and parade horse. It is also a popular mount for medieval jousting tournaments and renaissance fairs. As show horses, Percherons participate in competition hitching, driving, in-hand, and riding classes in both Europe and the Americas.

Percherons can perform well under saddle, and some have been known to make good jumpers, but there is a growing recognition of the value of cross-breeding the Percheron with Thoroughbreds or Warmbloods to get the size, substance, and disposition of a cold-blooded horse mixed with a lighter type. Because of the breed's gentle nature and its beauty, many horse owners are turning to the full-blooded Percheron as a pleasure horse.

Left: A pair of Percherons working the land. They are generally grey or black and, for a heavy breed, display relatively little feather on the legs.

Right: A team of six Percherons on parade, in a fine turnout with traditional brass and black leather harness.

	PRE	1700		1800		1900	

8th century
Stocky French war-horses infused with Arabian blood.

12th century
Eastern horses, returning with crusading knights from the Middle East, influence the war-horse that is to become the Percheron.

1760
Arabians at the royal stud in Le Pin add brilliance and flash to the developing Percheron.

1883
Percheron Horse Society founded, and stud book started.

1980s
Percherons crossed with Thoroughbreds and Warmbloods to produce performance horses.

MAIN FEATURES
- wide, deep chest
- long, level croup
- short back and loins
- well-muscled haunches and thighs
- animated gaits
- clean legs (very little or no feathering)

CHARACTER
- gentle disposition
- alert
- intelligent and tractable
- willing worker

COLOURS
Only black or grey Percherons may be registered in Europe, although the USA will also register sorrels.

HEIGHT
157–80cm (15.2–17.3hh)

COUNTRY OF ORIGIN
France (Normandy)

COMPARISON BREED
Brabant
This is another European draught breed that is experiencing a resurgence in popularity because of its tractable nature and its strength.

RELATED TOPICS
Arabian   128
Brabant   144
Driving   194
Ceremonial and
working horses   232
Showing   246

Dutch Draught

The Dutch Draught horse, thought to be the largest of all the European draught horses, originated in the Netherlands about 100 years ago. Breeders there were looking to develop a powerful horse that was a willing worker with a quiet temperament, but that could also move quickly and steadily. Although not a common breed today, the Dutch Draught is still occasionally found doing heavy draught and farm work.

Breed characteristics

The Dutch Draught is a massive horse, and extremely solidly built. It has a wide and strongly muscled chest, with an exceptionally wide barrel, and heavily muscled loins and hindquarters. The legs and feet have developed as a result of years of breeding for solid, sound bone, and they display silky feather to their hooves.

The head has a straight profile, with a kind eye, small ears, and a wide muzzle, and it is set upon a thick, relatively short neck.

The horse moves with a free, swinging gait, and although it is a quiet draught horse, it can step out easily when asked to do so. It matures at an early age, and most are reported to live well into their 20s and 30s. Its great

An enchanting Dutch Draught foal enjoying a rest in the paddock. Even at such a young age it is easy to see the size and strength developing.

PRE	1900			1950

| **1890s** Zeeland horses crossed with the Brabant and the Ardennes. | **1900–10** New cross-bred horses used to add strength to other native horses to produce the Dutch Draught. | **1914** Royal Netherlands Draught Horse Society founded. | **1924** First stud book opened, with entry restricted to horses with known pedigrees. | **1950s** Breed numbers decline as demand for heavy horses falls, but before long the Dutch Draught begins a new career as a show horse. |

MAIN FEATURES
• massive neck
• powerfully muscled
  forearms, chest,
  and hindquarters
• short legs
• kind eye
• small ears
• wide muzzle

CHARACTER
• quiet
• docile
• willing
• active

COLOURS
Chestnut, grey, and bay
are most common;
occasionally black.

HEIGHT
168cm (16.2hh)

COUNTRY OF ORIGIN
Netherlands

COMPARISON BREED
Brabant
Also known as the Belgian
Draught, this closely
resembles the Dutch
Draught, and has similar
origins to it. The Brabant
is the older breed, and is a
little smaller, yet it matures
at a slightly slower rate.

*The short, strong legs, with big knees and hocks,
and the powerful back give the Dutch Draught
the strength to pull heavy loads.*

stamina and strength have made it
an ideal horse for farmers, working
a range of difficult soils.

History of the Dutch Draught

The Dutch Draught, which resembles
the Belgian Brabant, is a relatively new
breed of heavy horse, with records
dating from only this century. It was
produced originally by crossing
Zeeland mares with the Brabant
and the Ardennes.

Its ancestry can be traced through
the national stud books of the Royal
Netherlands Draught Horse Society,

which were first opened in 1924.
Only the offspring of registered stock
was eligible for entry into the stud
book, which makes the Dutch Draught
the purest of the Dutch breeds.

The Dutch Draught today

This is the heaviest of all Dutch horses
and is ideal for hauling heavy loads or
ploughing fields. With the advent of
tractors and other motorized farm
equipment, there has been a decline in
the Dutch Draught's numbers, but there
are still prime examples of the breed
seen at shows all over the Netherlands.
Nowadays Dutch Draughts are mostly
used as show and exhibition horses,
and their massive build is certain to
draw an enthusiastic crowd.

RELATED TOPICS
Brabant   144
Ardennes   146
Ceremonial and
working horses   232
Showing   246

A day in the life of a draught horse

Horses have been used to deliver beer to public houses since commercial brewing took off in the 16th and 17th centuries. A handful of British breweries still use horses to deliver beer to their pubs because they are economical over short distances and because they promote their products in a bright, cheerful, and traditional way. Horses have been setting out from Young's Ram Brewery in Wandsworth, south London, every weekday for more than 400 years, pulling up to three tons of beer on flat carts called drays. Young's horses, which are housed in stables at the back of the brewery, are mainly black and white Shires but also include chestnut Suffolk Punches and grey Percherons. Their day begins with breakfast at 5.00am, followed by a couple of hours' rest before they are groomed, ready to work.

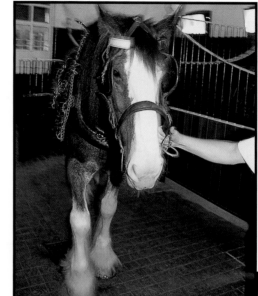

◄ **7.40am** Wandle Tom is now ready for action. He is led out of the stables, where he has spent the night with a dozen other horses, to meet up with his partner, Wandle Harry.

Harry and Tom are both magnificent Shires; the white feathers on their legs require careful brushing to keep them looking clean at all times.

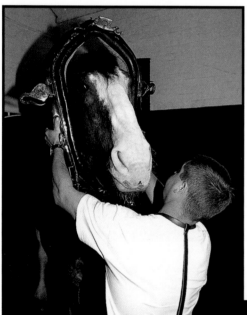

▲ **7.30am** The horses get dressed. Here, drayman Gary McHale slips a leather and chromium collar over the head of Wandle Tom.

► The reins are fitted through the hames, metal rings on the collar. The ends of the reins are made of chain to prevent Wandle Tom biting through them while he is waiting outside each of the pubs.

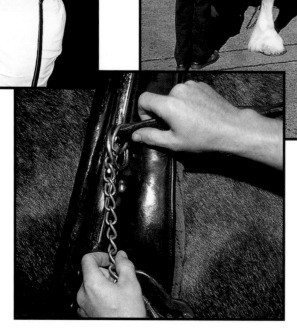

▲ **7.41am** Two horses are needed to pull a dray that may carry as much as three tons of beer. Gary McHale and Henry Coward go through their daily routine of securing Wandle Tom and Wandle Harry to a long pole protruding from the front of the dray.

▼ **7.45am** The horses have now pulled the empty dray to a loading bay next to the brewery cellars, where beer is kept before it goes off to the pubs. Gary and Henry load up the dray.

▲ **7.55am** Wandle Tom and Wandle Harry are now on their way to their first port of call, staying calm in the heavy traffic building up in Wandsworth town centre. All the horses know the route well and some even stop of their own accord at red traffic lights.

▲ **8.05am** Wherever possible, the horses are guided along back streets and side roads to avoid the worst of the rush-hour traffic. People along the route love the sound of horses' hooves going past and often stop to admire the horses.

◄ **8.30am** Wandle Tom and Wandle Harry enjoy a well-earned snack as beer is unloaded at the Spotted Horse in busy Putney High Street. The horses deliver drays to two pubs most days, finishing work around noon.

EVENTING

Eventing is a true test of versatility for both horse and rider, since it encompasses the three disciplines of dressage, cross country, and showjumping. Competitions take place at all levels – from local beginner events to World Championships and the Olympic Games.

Over the years the cross-country course has become the heart of the competition. For the spectator, there is nothing more exciting than watching horses and riders tackling the seemingly daunting obstacles with disdain, as they plunge into water and out, spring up and off banks, or skilfully negotiate complex combinations of fences.

History of eventing

Eventing (also known as horse trials or combined training) started at the beginning of the century with what was in essence an endurance competition to test the stamina of cavalry horses. The soldiers, too, had to prove themselves in these so-called *chausée* races by jogging for several miles alongside their horses. The aim was to deliver important messages over a long distance in the shortest possible time. Until shortly after World War II, the competition was mostly reserved for cavalry riders called 'The Military'.

In 1882 Lieutenant Roeder of Austria-Hungary completed the first known endurance ride, travelling with two

mares from Strasbourg in France to Granada in Spain, a distance of 2100km (1300 miles) in 53 days. Ten years later, 115 German cavalry riders and their horses travelled 600km (375 miles) from Berlin to Vienna, while 93 Austro-Hungarian cavalry riders made the same journey in the opposite direction. Only 66 of the Germans and 36 of the Austro-Hungarian riders completed the distance, with the winner finishing in a time of 71 hours 26 minutes. However, the winning horse died of a heart attack just after the ride, as did the horse that was placed second.

Within a few years, public pressure forced the competition to change, to put much stronger emphasis on the welfare of the horse. A Frenchman, Captain Paul Bausil, who was the greatest expert in endurance riding at this time, instigated a training programme that would help to ensure the horses were fit enough to survive the rigours of the test.

The first complete event, called the *Championnat du cheval d'armes*, took place in Paris in 1902. At this stage the dressage test was considered the most important aspect of the competition. This entailed a freestyle dressage with *piaffe, passage*, and Spanish walk, and flying changes of leg at canter, every two strides. This was followed by 4km (2½ miles) of steeplechase over 14 fences in a time of nine minutes, and a group ride over 60km (37 miles) in three hours 45 minutes, with a showjumping class the next day. However, from 1903 onwards the emphasis changed and the dressage stage became less important than the cross country and showjumping.

In 1905, Bausil and a colleague named Graf d'Ideville helped to organize the first races over natural fences, to test not only the horse's stamina but also its ability to go across country. Most of the so-called 'raids' lasted three days, with the horses having to cover 50–80km (30–50 miles) a day. Veterinary surgeons tested

the animals throughout the competition to ensure that they were not being pushed beyond their limits; meanwhile judges marked style and behaviour on the cross-country course.

Eventing at the Olympics

In the early 1900s the influential Italian showjumper Federico Caprilli, who founded the two-point or forward seat style of riding most commonly used today, became interested in eventing. With his help, the first international competition (without dressage) took place in 1911, with 124 entrants. This was so successful that eventing was featured in the Stockholm Olympics in 1912. The competition began with a 50km (30 mile) endurance ride in a maximum of four hours, with 5km (3 miles) in the second half being completed in 15 minutes. After a rest day, contestants took part in a 3.5km (2 mile) steeplechase, with 10 fences, in a maximum of five minutes 50 seconds. Showjumping of 16 fences up to 1.3m (4ft 4in) high and a dressage test completed the event.

At the 1920 Olympics in Antwerp a second endurance test was substituted for the dressage. This was the first time that civilians (but only men) were allowed to compete. In 1924 the Olympics were held in Paris and the competition was, in principle, of much the same format as today. Dressage took place on day one. Day two began with a 7km (4½ mile) ride on roads and tracks, then came a 4km (2½ mile) steeplechase, followed by a further 15km (9 mile) stretch on roads and tracks, and an 8km (5 mile) ride across country, with a 2km (1.2 mile) final gallop. Optimum speeds were set for each of these phases, with bonus points being awarded for faster riding. The competition ended with a showjumping class, which took place after a compulsory rest day.

There have been many changes since, the more important of which are given here. The rest day was abolished in

Frenchman Paul Bausil takes a breather during the 1904 Paris–Rouen–Deauville race. He helped to bring new rules on welfare to horse trials.

British national champion Owen Moore, on Lightfoot, plunges into the famous lake fence at Badminton during the cross-country test in 1998.

1928. Shorter roads and tracks were introduced in 1960, as was the '10-minute box'. This is a compulsory halt before the cross-country phase, during which the horses are examined by officials and veterinary surgeons to make sure they are fit enough to continue; riders and grooms can also attend to the horses in this time to prepare them for the next stage of the competition. 1967 saw the abolition of the final gallop. The dressage test has varied over the years, but is now generally at 'medium' level. Since 1968 it has been permissible to use either a snaffle or a double bridle.

Top nations and riders

In the early modern Olympics, Sweden was definitely the leading country, winning a total of seven gold medals. The vast improvement in transportation of horses around the world in the 1950s and 1960s enabled riders and horses from the southern hemisphere to compete internationally and, over the last decade, Australia has been the most successful country at the Olympics. At World and Open European Championships, Britain has been the most successful nation, and – without doubt – the hub of eventing today is in Britain. Other countries that

The Australian team stands on the gold medal rostrum at the Barcelona Olympics in 1992 – a proud moment and every event rider's dream.

have been a strong force in the sport over the years are Germany, France, and the USA.

Although New Zealand riders have yet to win an Olympic team gold, they have enjoyed great individual success. Mark Todd is considered by many to be the master of eventing of the last decade and is famous within the sport for winning two consecutive Olympic gold medals – in 1984 at Los Angeles and in 1988 at Seoul – on his diminutive Thoroughbred Charisma. Todd's countryman Blyth Tait was an individual gold medallist at the 1996 Atlanta Olympics, and went on to become the 1998 World Champion (a title he first won in 1990).

Matthew Ryan of Australia and the American Bruce Davidson have both had considerable success at the Olympics, and Bettina Overesch

TOP EVENTING NATIONS	
Country	Main venue
Britain	Badminton/Burghley
Ireland	Punchestown
USA	Lexington
Germany	Luhmuhlen Rodenberg
France	Compeigne/Chantilly
Australia	Sydney
New Zealand	Taupo
Sweden	Falsterbo

became the first German to win an individual gold at the Open European Championship in 1997. Although Britain's Mark Phillips and Lucinda Green are not competing today, they are two riders who made a huge impact on the world of eventing, winning the prestigious Badminton horse trials on 10 occasions between them in the late 1970s and early 1980s. Other influential British riders of the time include Princess Anne, Virginia Leng, and Mary Gordon Watson.

The sport today

All international eventing runs under the rules and regulations of the International Equestrian Federation (FEI), whose headquarters are in Lausanne, Switzerland. There are regulations regarding the height, width, and number of fences, distances, and speed. National equestrian federations have their own rules based on those of the FEI, although these may be adapted to suit local conditions.

The sport really starts at the Pony Club level, and this is where most international riders begin their careers. In some countries, there are also adult Riding Club events for those who do not wish to go on and compete at national level.

At national and international level, there are four age groups, each having their own championships: Pony Riders, Juniors, Young Riders, and Seniors. For each of these there are four or five different grades of competition. These are much the same in most countries, although they may be given different names. In English-speaking countries these levels are generally known as Pre-Novice or Training (the beginner class), going on to Novice, Intermediate, and Advanced. Consistent success at one level results in the horse and rider being upgraded to the next.

One day events, which are sometimes held over two days because of the sheer numbers of competitors involved, serve as training and qualifying competitions for horses and riders before they can take part in a three day event. These may be national competitions or CICs (*Concours Internationaux Combinés*), which are the international equivalent, open to riders from abroad.

There is a star rating for the premier one day events (CICs) and three day events (CCIs or *Concours Complets Internationaux*), ranging from one star, which is for novice horses, to four star, which represents the highest standard, for championship or Olympic Games level. In most of these events the championship or major class will attract television coverage.

The horses in these classes will normally have been on the competition circuit for three to four years, and are 10–16 years old; the age range of riders at top level is early 20s to mid 40s.

Elements of eventing

Of the three phases that make up eventing, the cross country is considered the most important, and is said to have a relative influence of 12, compared with 4 for showjumping, and 3 for dressage. However, the scoring system is currently under review for the millennium, and if changes are implemented, they may alter the relative influence of the three phases.

Each phase is scored separately and, at the end of the competition, the penalties incurred are added together. The winner of the event is the rider with the fewest penalties overall.

In a team competition, there are generally four riders in a team, with the three lowest scores being added together; again, the team with the lowest score is declared the winner.

Above: One of the sport's greatest riders – double Olympic gold medallist Mark Todd rides through the water complex at Britain's Gatcombe course.

Left: Pony Club eventing is the ideal training ground for more advanced events. Many an Olympic champion has started here.

DRESSAGE This is the most formal phase of the competition, and riders at the higher levels usually dress in a top hat and tail coat. The dressage test always opens the event, and demonstrates the degree of training achieved by horse and rider; their performance in this

	MODERN FORMAT OF A TYPICAL THREE OR FOUR STAR THREE DAY EVENT		
Day	**Description**	**Distance**	**Optimum time**
Day 1	Horse inspection		
	Dressage		
Day 2	**Cross country** (speed and endurance)		
	Phase A Roads and Tracks	4840m/3 miles	22 min
	Phase B Steeplechase	2760m/1¾ miles	4 min
	Phase C Roads and Tracks	9900m/6 miles	45 min
	Horse inspection (10-minute break)		
	Phase D Cross-country course	6506m/4 miles	11.25 min
Day 3	Horse inspection		
	Showjumping		

With bigger international three day events, dressage is sometimes held over two days to accommodate the large number of competitors.

Above: The elegance and precision required to score good marks in the dressage phase is well demonstrated by the USA's Kerry Millikin.

Below: The new scoring system should make it easier to evaluate performance.

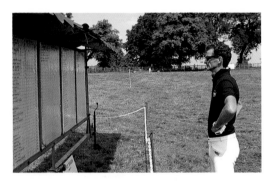

phase will often give a good indication of their performance in the cross country and showjumping.

The test takes place in an enclosed arena, which measures 20 x 40m (about 66 x 131ft) for novice competitions, and 20 x 60m (approximately 66 x 197ft) for advanced and international events.

The horse and rider have to perform a set series of movements, according to the layout of the test. Each level has a different test: at a four star event, for example, the horse needs to be able to perform not only the basic walk, trot, and canter movements but also the demanding lateral movements of shoulder-in and half pass at trot, and flying change at canter.

The test can take up to six and a half minutes to perform approximately 20 movements, each of which attracts a maximum of 10 points. Four 'collective' marks (again with a maximum of 10) are also given, reflecting the overall impression of the test: one set of marks relates to the position and seat of the rider; the other three are for the paces, submission, and impulsion shown by the horse. As many as three judges assess the correctness, quality, regularity, and expressiveness of the performance as a whole.

At the end of the test, the total number of points awarded to each individual is deducted from the maximum possible score, to give the number of penalty points. This score is then taken through to the next phase of the competition.

CROSS COUNTRY The cross-country phase is the most demanding part of the competition. It is designed to test the horses' jumping ability over a wide variety of fences, at speed and over natural terrain. In a three day event an endurance element is added, which includes two sections covering several miles of roads and tracks as well as a steeplechase course to be tackled at near-racing speed. These different phases make the event a virtual equestrian triathlon, requiring more versatility than any other equine sport. The 10-minute compulsory break before the cross country ensures that horse and rider are sufficiently refreshed and fit to tackle this exciting stage of the competition.

In this phase, various penalty points are given for refusals or falls at fences, for example, and some errors, such as taking the jumps in the wrong order, result in elimination. The penalties incurred, including those for exceeding the optimum time for completing the course, are added together, and the lower the final score, the better.

Today's courses are beautifully built and increasingly 'horse friendly'. This is a result of co-operation between the national federations and the FEI who have run seminars throughout the world over the last 10 years with the aim of improving all aspects of course design and building. Strict rules governing the height, width, and

The roads and tracks phases serve as a warm up before the steeplechase, and a cool down period prior to the cross country.

materials used have made a big difference to the safety of the fences.

Many of the fences look enormous, but they are designed to challenge the riders without frightening the horses. By using ingenious designs that make the riders think, it is possible to create a demanding cross-country course without overfacing young or inexperienced horses. Such fences include ditches, banks, and steps, combinations of fences with different strides between them, those going uphill and downhill, and jumps into and out of water, to name only a few.

It takes many months of patient training to build up the trust and confidence between horse and rider that are required to tackle the demanding courses met at the highest level of the sport. A horse may need around three or four years' training to progress from novice to the top level; and not all will have a suitable

RULES

Among the most significant rule changes for many years are the 1996 abandonment of the zones at obstacles within which penalties could be incurred, and the abolition of the minimum weight of 75kg (165lb) for rider and tack in the cross-country phase.

There is a minimum age at which horses can start competitions: this is five years for a horse at novice level, and seven years for horses competing at international and four star levels. Rider safety has also become a major issue. All must wear safety hats. In all but a few countries (where temperatures are uncomfortably high during the summer) it is also compulsory to wear body protectors. There are very strict rules regarding clothing and equipment, and failure to comply with these can result in disqualification.

CROSS-COUNTRY PENALTIES

Fault	Penalties
First refusal, run-out, circle of horse at obstacle	20
Second refusal, run-out, circle of horse at same obstacle	40
Third refusal, run-out, circle of horse at same obstacle	Elimination
Fifth cumulative refusal	Elimination
Fall of horse and/or rider at obstacle	60
Second penalized fall of horse and/or rider on the course	Elimination
Error of course not rectified	Elimination
Omission of obstacle or boundary flag	Elimination
Retaking an obstacle already jumped	Elimination
Jumping obstacle in wrong order	Elimination
For every commenced period of 3 seconds in excess of optimum time	1
For every commenced period of 3 seconds in excess of 15 seconds under the optimum time	1
Exceeding the time limit (which is twice the optimum time)	Elimination

Left: Dual World Champion Bruce Davidson of the USA takes Broadstone Harvest Moon over an innovative fence at Bramham's three star event.

Right: Sweden's Paula Tornquist on SAS Monaghan shows determination and style during the showjumping phase at Badminton in 1998.

temperament or be sufficiently bold to compete to this standard. Because of the undulating nature of the cross-country course in particular, tendon injuries do occur, so it is essential to follow a systematic training programme that carefully conditions the horse over several months to prepare it for the competitive season.

SHOWJUMPING The showjumping phase is not a test of how high or far a horse and rider can jump. Instead, it is designed to test their ability to produce a good performance after a strenuous cross-country round. The course usually consists of 12 knockdown fences, no higher than 1.2m (4ft) or wider than 1.4m (4½ft), which may include a water jump at advanced standard three day events.

In a three day event the showjumping is on the last day, and so takes place after the cross country. There is always a vet check beforehand, to ensure that the horse is sufficiently fit to continue. A tired horse will not jump as cleanly and carefully as a fitter, better trained horse. This phase can be the final decider between victory and defeat,

SHOWJUMPING PENALTIES	
Fault	**Penalties**
Knockdown	5
Foot on lath (edge), tape, or strip in water	5
First disobedience	10
Second disobedience in whole test	20
Third disobedience in whole test	Elimination
Fall of horse and/or rider	30
Second fall of horse and/or rider	Elimination
Error of course not rectified	Elimination
Omission of obstacle or boundary flag	Elimination
Retaking an obstacle already jumped	Elimination
Jumping an obstacle in wrong order	Elimination

and always produces a huge surge of adrenalin for the riders and their supporters alike.

In a one day event the showjumping often takes place *before* the cross country which, as the horses are fresh, gives a completely different emphasis to this phase of the competition.

The scoring system is essentially the same as for ordinary showjumping, but the number of penalty points incurred for each fault is different. As with the cross country, the lower the score at the end of the round, the better.

Animal welfare

Increasingly, the focus on animal welfare is becoming stronger and this, in turn, is putting pressure on organizers and cross-country course designers, as well as the competitors themselves, to ensure that at no stage is there any kind of abuse such as over-riding a tired horse. Officials have the power to disqualify a rider from the competition and subsequent events, as well as imposing a fine. No competition, regardless of level, is able to take place without a veterinary surgeon and doctor being present.

Event sponsorship

Organizing and conducting an event involves a huge number of people, many of whom are volunteers. Even so, overheads are extremely high. Most riders do not have sufficient capital to own and compete a major competition horse. The most successful riders attract owners who not only provide the horse but also fund the day-to-day running and competition costs.

Increasingly, sponsorship is discussed and, with the obvious advantages to both organizers and riders, everyone in the sport would like to see this develop further. Currently there are stringent rules governing the carrying of advertising material by horse and rider, and this influences the investment that sponsors are prepared to make. If the sport is to expand, it is essential that sponsors feel they will get good value for their money.

The Professional Event Riders' Association (PERA) was launched in 1997, with the specific aim of giving the world's key riders a higher, and therefore more marketable, profile, in order to gain greater sponsorship for the sport as a whole.

In some countries, notably the USA and Britain but increasingly elsewhere, a few events today do carry major sponsorship or are given media coverage, and these also attract large numbers of trade stands selling or promoting products such as horse transporters, clothing, horse feed, saddlery, and other equine requisites.

The event horse

Not every horse is right for every rider, and in order to achieve success it is essential that horse and rider establish a rapport and are able to work together

The inspection panel checks a horse's heart rate during the 10-minute compulsory break to ensure it is fit to proceed to the cross-country phase.

well as a team. Whatever the natural ability of the horse, it must have the right spirit, attitude, and real desire to work with the rider, both in training and competition.

Although there is no set formula for the appearance of the successful event horse, the leading animals tend to be of a similar type; they may differ in size, but they have one common factor – they are all true athletes.

Of all breeds, the Thoroughbred undoubtedly gives the best performance in eventing – and therefore is the most popular. However there have been some excellent performances from Thoroughbreds crossed with Warmbloods such as Holsteins and Hanoverians. These cross-bred horses tend to perform more flamboyantly in the dressage test, while maintaining the typical athleticism of the Thoroughbred on the cross-country course and its enormous stamina and resilience in the showjumping phase.

Key eventing people

Eventing demands a complete partnership between horse and rider, and the trainer plays a large part in encouraging this to develop. Groom, farrier, and vet are often the unsung heroes of an eventing team, all having an important influence on how the horse performs, and on its well-being. Competition officials are crucial to the event as a whole, ensuring that it is run smoothly and safely.

THE RIDER The event rider must not only be thoroughly familiar with the exact criteria of each competition, but also have an understanding of the individual horse and how it behaves in a host of different circumstances. There are many people who are good at training a horse but it takes special talents to be a successful competition rider. For example, he or she must be able to remain cool in difficult situations and, most importantly, be able to communicate to the horse clearly and simply what it is required to do.

Riders must be concerned about their own physical fitness, as well as that of the horse. It is widely recognized that exercise such as running, swimming, and weight training, together with riding itself, gives the best results.

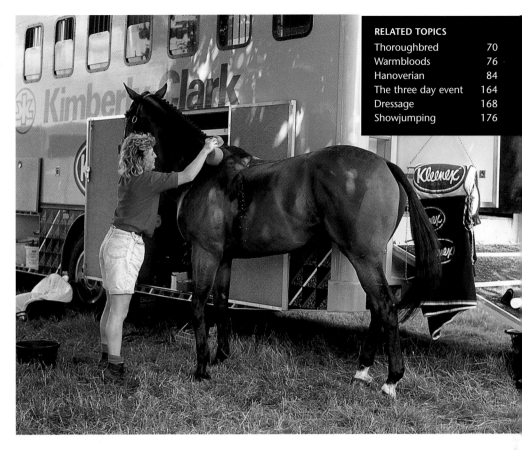

RELATED TOPICS	
Thoroughbred	70
Warmbloods	76
Hanoverian	84
The three day event	164
Dressage	168
Showjumping	176

THE OWNER Owners do not necessarily come from the equestrian industry or have extensive knowledge of it, but they do undoubtedly have a great and genuine love for horses. They are an essential link in the chain to success since it is primarily their financial support that makes it possible for horse and rider to compete.

THE TRAINER Few riders succeed without a trainer's help. This may take the form of day-to-day general advice on riding technique and horse management, or specialized coaching in dressage or showjumping in preparation for a major competition. The trainer needs to be able to make an accurate assessment of the rider's ability and, in many cases, will recommend a competition programme to suit.

THE PHYSIOTHERAPIST Physiotherapy is relatively new to equestrian sport, but is steadily becoming more important for both horse and rider.

Like any athlete, a horse can become tight and sore in the muscles, and an appropriate physiotherapy programme can be of enormous benefit. It is essential that the physiotherapist works

A wash down to remove sweat and grime after the cross country is welcomed by most horses. In hot conditions it is vital to cool the horse quickly.

closely with the rider, groom, and vet to develop the best programme for each individual horse.

OFFICIALS There are many other people who have key roles at competitions. At international events, the dressage judges (the ground jury) have the highest profile since they are in charge of the competition as a whole. Members of the ground jury inspect and approve the cross-country course before the event starts. They also conduct the 'horse inspections', in which they evaluate the horses' soundness at the start of the competition, during the compulsory 10-minute halt, and before the final showjumping phase.

Working with the ground jury is the technical delegate, who acts as the official controller of the competition. Doctors and veterinary surgeons are also present throughout the competition, and numerous other officials are required, all responsible for different aspects of the event.

The three day event

Three day eventing is the most versatile, and often most exciting, of all the Olympic equestrian sports. It combines dressage, cross country, and showjumping and a mistake during any of these stages can cost a rider crucial points in the championship.

The sport requires both riders and horses to be very fit and well prepared as they must tackle three very different and demanding disciplines. Most eventers will have had a thorough all-round background in riding, starting in Pony Clubs or other riding clubs before deciding to specialize. They will then go on to work very closely with a top team of trainers, grooms, vets, and farriers throughout their career to ensure that they and their horse perform to the best of their ability.

Bettina Overesch is Germany's top three day event rider and was European Champion in 1997. Here we see her riding her own horse Watermill Stream.

▲ **3** 'As Watermill Stream is checked over in the 10-minute box, I concentrate on the course plan, studying the fences coming up on the cross-country course.'

◄ **4** 'A positive start to the cross-country phase will set us up for a perfect round.'

◄ **1 Day one** 'Dressage must be met with my full concentration, as well as Watermill Stream's, as it is a precise sport. It is also very important to do well at this stage to get into a good position for the second day.'

► **2 Day two** 'During roads and tracks I regularly check the time to ensure that we will not incur penalties. Allowing four minutes per kilometre generally works out right.'

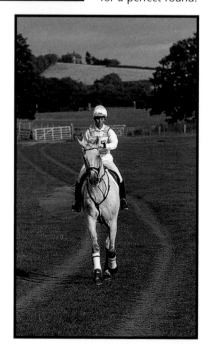

▲ **5** 'As we approach the next fence on the cross-country course we are both working hard. It is vital to know exactly what to do at each fence–such as the speed and angle of approach to take, as it makes a difference to the time we take to complete the course.'

► **6** 'The power and speed of my horse is best seen during one of his perfect jumps.'

▲ **7 Day three** 'Walking the showjumping course with our trainer allows me time to memorize the whole route and pick up any tips for the course.'

► **8** 'Showjumping on the final day decides the overall winner. This part of the event is done in reverse order of merit, so, as I am going last, it means that a clear round will ensure that I am the winner.'

DRESSAGE

Dressage in its most basic form is simply the schooling groundwork that makes any horse a safe and pleasurable ride. At its highest level, it is a demonstration of elegance and athleticism, with complete harmony between horse and rider. Dressage developed as a sport during the last century, and today is popular on every continent, particularly in Europe.

Classical beginnings

Dressage has its origins in the classical training methods taught at the great riding schools of Europe in the 16th and 17th centuries, which themselves were derived from the techniques laid down by the Greek historian Xenophon, in the 4th century BC.

The word dressage derives from the French verb *dresser*, meaning simply 'to train'. Taking the form of a series of progressively difficult gymnastic exercises, the training is designed to develop the horse's strength and athletic ability, and improve the quality of its natural gaits. The result is a willing and obedient horse, responsive to the subtlest of commands from the rider. This basic training is invaluable for every horse, regardless of the discipline in which it may specialize later on.

Basic dressage (or 'flatwork' as it is known colloquially) also forms the foundation of training for any rider, whatever the discipline, encouraging a supple and independent seat through which to communicate with the horse.

The first competitions

The first dressage competition that was recorded was held on 25 April 1873 in Pressburg (then part of the Austrian Empire, now Bratislava in Slovakia). Dressage was part of the programme of the first international horse show, held in Turin, Italy, in 1902. Ten years later, in 1912, dressage as an individual competition was among the equestrian sports included in the Olympic Games for the first time; and the first Olympic team competitions took place in 1928.

It was not until 1952 that non-commissioned officers and women were allowed to compete in Olympic dressage, and not until 1965 that the present-day structure of European and World Championships was introduced. Since then the sport of dressage has enjoyed burgeoning popularity. Today there are also European Championships for Pony Riders, Juniors, and Young Riders; and an International Dressage Competition, first held in 1982, for which experienced European judges travel to Asia, South America, and Africa in order to evaluate and help emerging dressage nations there.

In top international competition, the single most important development in popularizing dressage as a sport was the introduction of a freestyle routine to music. It began in 1985, with the birth of the dressage World Cup series. Then in 1991 the first European Championship medals were awarded for Freestyle, alongside those for Grand Prix Special (a ride-off test for the top Grand Prix riders to decide the final result). In 1995, for the first time, the European Championship medals were decided on individual percentage points from the Grand Prix, Grand Prix Special, and Grand Prix Freestyle to Music. The following year this formula was used at the Olympic Games in Atlanta. The top 12 in the world performed. The stadium was sold out for the thrilling Freestyle finale.

The sport of dressage today

In competition, dressage riders perform a set series of movements or figures, each designed to demonstrate a certain level of skill. At the first level, the test consists of a simple pattern of large circles and turns in walk, trot, and canter. Depending on the national rules there may be as many as five levels – each with more complex movements – before the Prix St Georges, which is the first of the international tests. The highest level is the Grand Prix, ridden at international competitions and the Olympic Games.

Progression through the various levels tests the ability of horse and rider to carry out the movements with energy, obedience, confidence, harmony, and accuracy. The more

The passage, an elevated slow trot, is one of the movements performed in advanced dressage and requires years of training for horse and rider.

familiar the rider is with what is required for each test, the more able he or she will be to present the horse well. Riders have their own individual methods of memorizing tests, from walking through them on the ground to drawing diagrams on paper.

At every level, the competitor is evaluated on the performance of each set movement, which is marked out of 10, and on the judge's overall assessment of the horse's way of going, the quality of its paces, and the rider's position and effectiveness. These collective marks are also marked out of 10. The marks are added together, and then usually also expressed as a percentage. The winner is the combination of horse and rider with the highest score.

In a Freestyle to Music test, popular at all levels, the rider devises his or her own pattern or routine, incorporating all the required movements for that level. In Freestyle there are additional marks for artistic interpretation, which

PACES

WORKING PACES (trot and canter) fall between collected and medium and are asked for in the lower-level tests from horses not yet ready or trained for collection.

COLLECTED PACES (walk, trot, and canter) require a progressively higher level of lightness and engagement than the working paces. This is achieved as the horse becomes able to carry more weight on the hindquarters so the forehand or 'front end' lightens.

MEDIUM PACES (walk, trot, and canter) come between working and extended paces. While medium walk is only slightly more than the 'working' walk, in trot and canter medium requires significant lengthening, with plenty of energy and balance.

EXTENDED PACES (walk, trot, and canter) require the horse to cover as much ground as possible. Maximum extensions in trot and canter are advanced movements.

TRANSITIONS between the paces and within the paces, and their development from progressive to direct as the horse becomes more advanced, are a vital tool in both training and competitive riding.

makes it vital to choose music that best suits the horse's gaits and character.

The International Equestrian Federation (FEI) is the international governing body for the sport. At national level, each country must have a governing body affiliated to the FEI in order to hold international competitions and qualifiers for championships. The national governing body will administer and oversee the running of affiliated competitions, from preliminary level to Grand Prix. In addition, any club or organization is at liberty to run its own, unaffiliated competitions, and these provide a valuable training ground for novice horses and riders.

INTERNATIONAL CHAMPIONSHIPS At international championship level (European, Pan American, World, and Olympic), there are both individual and team competitions. A nation requires a minimum of three horses and riders to field a team. Each rider's performance is judged individually, and the top three scores for each nation are added together to give the team result.

WORLD CUP In the World Cup, the European qualifying rounds consist of an initial Grand Prix, from which the top 12 riders go forward to the Freestyle to Music. Each of the 12 receives qualifying points, depending on their final result, and those earning the highest number of points over the season win a place in the final.

Qualifying series are run slightly differently in continents other than Europe. North America, Australia, and latterly Asia and South America, with fewer competitors and greater

The rhythm and balance required to perform an even trot at full extension needs maximum concentration from both horse and rider.

distances to travel, hold their own league finals, with the winner qualifying for the World Cup final.

The arena

The test is always performed in an arena, increasingly these days on a prepared surface. For international competitions the arena must be 20 x 60m (about 66 x 197ft). Some national basic-level tests are performed on grass, in an arena of 20 x 40m (approximately 66 x 131ft). The arena

The spectacular arena at S'Hertogenbosch in the Netherlands is a popular venue and has played host to many international championships.

is traditionally marked out with white boards, with the starting and finishing points for movements indicated by letters of the alphabet.

The dressage horse

Clean, correct gaits are more important than extravagant movement when choosing a dressage horse. A regular four-beat walk with an ability to 'march' out, a rhythmic, balanced, elastic trot with some elevation, and a three-beat, uphill canter are ideal starting points. However, there are many successful horses with one weaker gait that has been improved by careful training.

Trainability, implying a willingness to learn, describes the ideal character of a dressage horse. In contrast to 20 years ago when the heavier, 'powerhouse' type of horse predominated, most top riders now favour a lighter, 'hot' horse, which may be difficult or naughty in the early days, but will develop the stamina, spirit, and presence of a winner. This transition from power to lightness and elegance can be attributed to the great combination of Nicole Uphoff and Rembrandt, who won dual gold medals for Germany at both the Seoul and Barcelona Olympics in 1988 and 1992.

Today's ideal dressage horse may therefore have a high percentage of Thoroughbred blood. The German and

The light elegance of Germany's Nicole Uphoff and Rembrandt, winners of four Olympic gold medals, changed the style of modern dressage.

Dutch Warmbloods, developed from the early working breeds, are favoured for dressage, having the desired movement, conformation, and trainability. Stallions are again becoming more popular because they tend to have an extra presence in the arena, as well as being more valuable for breeding once they have proved themselves in competition.

Key people

A winning performance in dressage demonstrates a unique partnership and harmony between horse and rider. Both, however, owe a huge debt to the skill, sensitivity, and patience of their trainer, and to the meticulous work of their groom. Running a dressage competition involves still another layer of experienced and dedicated officials and helpers.

THE RIDER A good dressage rider will have nurtured a trusting relationship with his or her horse by being sensitive to its temperament and ability. The

MOVEMENTS

LATERAL WORK The key lateral movements are shoulder-in, traverse, and half pass. In half pass, a major part of all advanced tests, the horse is bent slightly around the rider's inside leg and in the direction towards which it is moving. The horse's outside legs cross and pass in front of its inside legs.

PIROUETTES A half pirouette is where the horse's forehand moves around its hindquarters. At walk, half pirouettes are included in tests from 'medium' level upwards. At canter, half pirouettes are introduced at Prix St Georges. Full pirouettes are part of the Intermediare and Grand Prix tests.

PASSAGE A graceful, measured, highly collected and elevated 'trot' executed with great cadence.

PIAFFE A highly collected, elevated movement in which the horse appears to be 'trotting', with pronounced cadence, but remains almost in place.

Passage and *piaffe* are introduced at international level with the Intermediare II test. The most demanding *piaffe, passage,* and pirouettes, in conjunction with half passes, form the core of the Grand Prix Special and Freestyle tests, although the basic gaits trained to collection and extension are just as important in the judges' assessment.

horse will then be confident to give its best in the unfamiliar and often distracting atmosphere of the competition arena.

An expert dressage rider will direct the horse with almost invisible signals. A secure, poised, independent seat is a prerequisite for this, and riders must be prepared to work hard to attain it, by getting fit themselves as well as by having lessons on the lunge.

Dressage has much to do with presentation, so it helps if the rider has a degree of showmanship in the arena, along with the ability to concentrate on directing the horse to be both calm and expressive as well as accurate.

THE TRAINER Every success in international dressage is the combined product of horse, rider, and trainer. The rider can feel if the horse is moving well, but the trainer's 'eyes on the ground' are almost essential to achieving the standard required for top-level sport.

Training a dressage horse takes years of dedication and patience, and demands both sensitivity and discretion. Confidence building is an essential part of the process, and the trainer will always teach a horse a new movement it finds easy before one it finds more difficult. The trainer will also make sure the horse enjoys its work and is not pushed too hard when its muscles and mind are tired.

Trainers also ensure variety in the work of dressage horses. Interspersing training in the school with riding in the fields and even the occasional jump is more commonly part of the dressage horse's life than schoolwork day in, day out. Fitness is vital, too, especially at international championship level where the top horses have to give a demanding performance three days in succession. Competing on the international circuit involves a good deal of travel, and therefore some stress, so the trainer and rider must work together to ensure the horse is at peak fitness to do its best.

THE GROOM Dressage horses are invariably turned out beautifully. A gleaming, well-muscled horse is achieved not only through years of training but also through elbow grease and effort on behalf of the groom.

A proud neck is enhanced by a row of small, perfectly matched plaits that are often bound in white tape on a dark-coloured horse. Quarter marks brushed into the coat show off well-muscled hindquarters. The dressage horse is led out of the stables in immaculate saddle and bridle, wearing pristine white protective bandages that are *de rigueur* in the warm-up ring.

The groom is the stalwart charged with carrying down to the ring the last minute tidy up kit, and the rider's coat if it is a hot day; the one who holds the whip discarded just before the test, and who checks the progress of the previous competitor so the rider can time his or her warm-up to the second.

Afterwards, while the rider and trainer wait for the results of the class, the groom walks the horse in hand for a pick of grass after it has been washed off, to relax its mind and its muscles.

The groom, spending most time with the horse, is best placed to notice the first signs of stiffness or injury or if the animal is off its food. In unfamiliar stables the presence of the groom also offers the horse welcome reassurance.

THE JUDGE At international level, a panel of five judges scores each test. They judge independently from different parts of the arena, and the five scores are added together to give the total for each horse and rider. In international eventing tests, some national championships, and some smaller international dressage shows, there are only three judges; at the lower levels, one judge usually presides.

A good judge will have a thorough understanding of training, and many judges are (or have been) riders and/or trainers themselves (although active riders may not judge internationally). Different nations may have slightly different criteria for evaluating judges but, generally, the judge must attend instructional courses and usually sit an exam to be accepted on to a panel. He or she can then progress through the levels by attending seminars and 'sitting in' with more experienced judges before taking the qualifying exam necessary to officiate at a higher level. The highest level is that of Official International Judge. Only these judges are eligible to judge at championships and Olympic Games.

THE VET As with any athlete, peak physical condition is vital to a dressage horse's performance. Any athlete is also liable to stresses and strains. Muscles, joints, and tendons are the dressage horse's vulnerable areas. Injuries can be dealt with more easily if spotted early. A good relationship with a veterinary surgeon who has experience in dealing with competition horses and has a chance to get to know the individual animal is very important to horse, rider, and trainer.

The judges sit around the arena to watch the combinations performed from all angles. This judge and rider are halfway down the long side.

There are few movements more exciting to watch than the half pass, when the horse flows sideways across the arena in perfect balance.

RELATED TOPICS

Warmbloods	76
Westphalian	90
Lipizzaner	102
Eventing	156
A dressage lesson	174
Ceremonial and working horses	232

THE PHYSIOTHERAPIST Physiotherapy in the form of massage or any adaptation of the techniques used in humans, even simple stretching exercises, has become an integral part of many a dressage horse's way of life, whether to promote fitness and relaxation or to aid recovery from injury.

ALTERNATIVE PRACTITIONERS Acupuncture, chiropractic, and other alternative therapies under the direction of specialist equine practitioners are becoming more widely used in the treatment of injury. Homeopathy and herbal medicine may also have a valuable place in the care of the competition horse. They can provide both temporary pain relief and stimulate healing as an alternative to chemically based medicines during competition where drug controls are in force. Herbal remedies such as natural aids to relaxation can also help to produce the best in a dressage horse.

THE FARRIER Working much of the time on prepared surfaces, and less on rough ground or roads, the dressage horse will require a different type of shoe from the general-purpose horse or event horse. A lighter shoe, for example, can help a horse to show more expression in its paces. Foot balance and correctly fitting shoes are important for any horse, but especially when movement and straightness are the tools of the animal's trade.

TOP DRESSAGE NATIONS

Country	Main venue
Germany	Aachen, Wiesbaden
Netherlands	S'Hertogenbosch Rotterdam
Sweden	Falsterbo
USA	Florida
Denmark	Aarhus
Spain	Jerez
Britain	Hickstead
Switzerland	Geneva
France	Rennes
Finland	Helsinki

A dressage lesson

All succesful dressage combinations are trios of horse, rider, and trainer. Regular lessons are the rider's chance to gauge progress and obtain advice.

Before getting down to work, trainer and pupil will have a chat about how the horse has been going since the last lesson. The trainer needs to know what problems the rider may have been experiencing and hopefully what improvements have taken place. There may be a specific competition for which the rider is preparing. All this information helps the trainer assess what they should work on for this particular lesson.

Sometimes the trainer will sit on the horse for a while to make a correction, or to feel what the rider is experiencing. Carl Hester has been training dressage riders for many years – here he is training Jo and her horse, Hari.

▲ **1** Hari needs to be relaxed before work begins. Here, Jo begins by working Hari in a forward, swinging, working trot, encouraging him to stretch over his neck and back. She'll do this in the canter too, as the transitions between the paces get the horse listening to the rider.

▲ **2** Carl isn't happy. He would like to see Hari working in a rounder outline. In extended and medium paces, he should lengthen his frame but he is leaning on Jo's hands.

▼ **3** Carl gets them working on a circle around him so he can see what the problem is. Circlework helps establish suppleness, so Hari becomes softer in the contact.

▶ **4** In extended trot and canter sometimes the rider tends to lean back, pushing the horse with the seat, rather than keeping a soft, supple seat that allows the horse to use his back. Here Carl is aligning Jo's position in the saddle, reminding her to keep upright.

▼ **5** To help Jo and Hari practise the improved position, Carl gets Jo to make transitions within the trot and canter paces, known as 'on and back', through the half-halt. The half-halt is a signal used in preparation for a change in pace or direction, to balance the horse and keep him alert. Here, we can see Hari sit back and take more weight on his hindlegs.

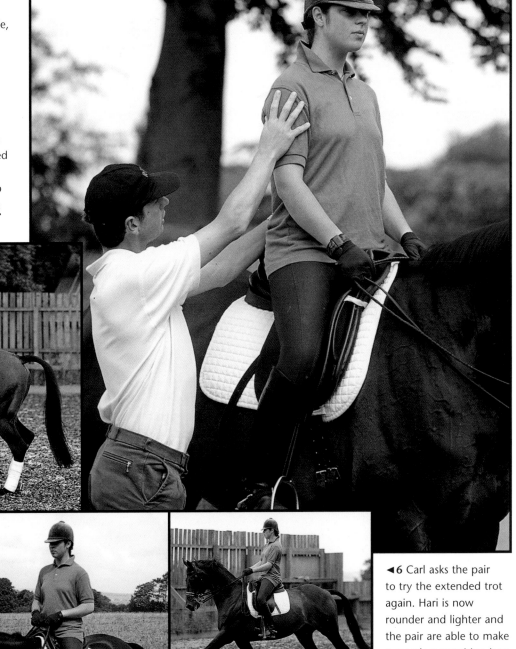

◀ **6** Carl asks the pair to try the extended trot again. Hari is now rounder and lighter and the pair are able to make a seamless transition into extended and back to collected trot. This would earn high marks in a test.

◀ **7** It is important that Hari is praised when he has done well. After achieving good progress in the lesson, Jo takes Hari for a relaxing walk around the fields. This gives his muscles the chance to relax and stretch. Also, ending a lesson with horse and rider in a good frame of mind means the next day's work will start positively.

175

SHOWJUMPING

The power, elegance, and sheer athletic ability of the horse are nowhere better demonstrated than when it is soaring over the challenging fences of the world's famous showjumping arenas.

From its relatively humble beginnings at local fairs in the 19th century, showjumping has become a highly organized sport that attracts the world's leading riders and huge audiences, both at home via television and at the showground.

Leaping contests

It is not known exactly when showjumping started but evidence suggests that 'leaping contests' were a feature of county fairs from the 1850s. Hamburg, Dublin, Paris, and New York all staged showjumping events from 1866. By 1900 Dublin's Ballsbridge arena had a spectacular course, which included banks, ditches, and water jumps. International showjumping was first staged indoors in 1902 at London's Olympia stadium, and at New York's Madison Square Garden in 1907.

Showjumping was first included in the Olympics in 1912, and for many years was dominated by military riders. After World War I the sport increased in popularity and at the 1936 Berlin Olympics 17 nations competed.

The developing sport

France, Germany, and Italy led the world of showjumping at this time. They had their own designers, creating such imaginative courses as those at Hamburg and Aachen (which is still one of the world's top showgrounds), the Borghese Gardens in Rome, and the indoor arena at the Grand Palais in Paris. The riders trained at excellent military equitation schools, and passed on their knowledge and expertise to younger generations.

It was not until after World War II that British showjumping reached the standard found in the rest of Europe. Although there were a few riders with military training, most had to rely on their natural ability and taught themselves as they went along. By the 1960s courses and fences began to improve, as designers developed ideas

inspired by visits to showjumping arenas in other countries, and the superb Hickstead course – one of the most popular in Britain today – was created in 1969.

With horse transport improving all the time, showjumpers could compete internationally much more frequently. Showjumping went from strength to strength not only in Europe but also in the Middle East, and North and South America, as well as South Africa, Australia, and New Zealand. The USA, in particular, began producing riders of international quality at this time, under the expert guidance of Hungarian trainer Bertalan de Némethy. Regional trials were held all over the country, and the most promising riders from these were brought together for training at a newly established equitation centre at Gladstone, New Jersey. This programme produced really successful horses and riders, many of them able to compete against the best in the world.

Today's riders spend the whole season travelling the world to international competitions, and it takes considerable organization to plan a programme that ensures the horses get the necessary experience at the top level to be able to hold their own among the world's best. The Whitaker brothers of Britain, Germany's Ludger Beerbaum, the young American Alison Firestone, and Jos Lansink from the Netherlands are just a few on the circuit. Perhaps the most brilliant showjumper today is the 1998 World Champion Rodrigo Pessoa from Brazil, who is an example, just as his father Nelson has been, to every rider in the business.

Showjumping today

International showjumping is dominated by two major annual competitions – the World Cup and the Samsung Nations Cup – and the two supreme challenges every four years of the Olympic Games

and the World Championships. For the North and South American countries there are Pan American Games every four years. In addition, every two years there are continental and regional championships. All international competitions are governed by the rules of the International Equestrian Federation (FEI).

WORLD CUP Introduced in 1979, the annual World Cup is run mostly indoors throughout the winter months. Riders are organized into different leagues, with the best from each league competing in the final held in April.

NATIONS CUP Nations Cup competitions for teams have been in existence almost since showjumping started, but the introduction of the Samsung Nations Cup in 1997 has done wonders for encouraging the spread of the sport all

Right: Francis Connors negotiates the famous Hickstead bank. This type of obstacle is generally found only in Derby courses.

Below: Michael Whitaker has been one of Britain's most consistent showjumping stars, along with his brother John.

Above: Many showjumpers wear girth attachments to prevent the horse striking itself with its front legs as it jumps a big fence.

Right: Open-fronted boots are a favourite with competitors. They are light, yet protect the horse's all-important tendons.

over the world. These are competitions in which four riders from each country jump two identical rounds. The scores of the top three riders in each round count. The winner is the nation with the least penalties over the two rounds.

WORLD CHAMPIONSHIPS AND OLYMPIC GAMES The aim of outdoor showjumping is to reach the World Championships and Olympic Games, which feature an individual and team competition. Both take place on a four-year cycle, two years apart. At the World Championships the top four competitors ride one another's horses, in a unique demonstration of their equestrian skills.

NATIONAL COMPETITIONS Nationally, each country organizes its own competition structure, holding classes at all levels to

bring horses and riders to the top of the sport. The rules are generally based on those of the FEI. National showjumping associations raise their own finance for the sport through membership and sponsorship.

Showjumping courses

At all levels of the sport, it is extremely important to have good showgrounds, with well-designed courses that encourage the riders to keep riding forwards. Most courses consist of 12 fences, which can be divided into uprights and spreads, specialized fences, and combinations.

Before the class, riders walk the course to work out how best to jump each fence. It also helps them to gauge the distances between jumps so they can adjust the horses' strides to suit.

UPRIGHTS These consist of a single vertical element with no spread (width) to it. They include such fences as gates, planks, single rails, and walls. The more solid and substantial these elements are, the easier they are for horse and rider to negotiate.

SPREAD FENCES These are fences with width as well as height. Spreads include oxers (parallels), which are either square or with ascending rails; triple bars, which get higher from front to back; fan fences, which are wide on one side and narrow on the other; and Liverpools, which are similar in profile to the fences at the Aintree racecourse, with a low rail at the front and a high rail at the back, and are always over water ditches.

COMBINATIONS These consist of two or three elements with varying numbers of strides (usually one or two) between them. They may consist of uprights or spreads or a combination of both. Two fences are described as a double, three as a treble. If a horse refuses to jump any one of the elements, the whole fence must be taken again. Closed combinations, where it is not possible to move outside the elements, are generally found in Derby courses.

The Six Bar competition, over six similar fences, demands that the horse is well balanced and athletic if it is to complete the line without faults.

178

WATER JUMPS These generally consist of a spread of approximately 3.6–4.9m (12–16ft) over water, with a small brush fence on the take-off side.

SPECIALIZED FENCES Generally found in Derby courses, specialized fences may include banks, ditches, steps, and a variety of other obstacles.

Competitions

There are a number of different kinds of competition and most international shows have classes for the top Grand Prix horses and for the speed horses. These shows are classified as *Concours de Saut d'Obstacles Internationale* (CSIs) or, if they have a Nations Cup (team class), *Concours de Saut d'Obstacles Internationale Officiel* (CSIOs). One CSIO is held in each country every year, except in the USA and Canada where two are held.

Showjumping classes

Showjumping classes fall into one of two basic categories, known as Table A and Table C; each of these has its own specific rules.

TABLE A Classes in this category are judged on the jumping faults or penalty points incurred, with four penalty points being given for each knockdown, and three for the first disobedience or refusal (see box on page 180). Winners of the first round then usually compete in timed jump-offs, consisting of further rounds over a shortened course, against the clock. The table A classes with jump-off are mostly for the better horses. Sometimes there is only one round judged on time.

TABLE C In this category, any jumping faults are converted into seconds. For every fence knocked down, seconds are added to a rider's time for completing the round, and the competitor with the lowest aggregate time is the winner.

There are numerous variations to the above depending on the type of class; these are stated in the show schedule and are always posted in the collecting ring for competitors to see before walking the course.

The main classes at international showjumping events are:

TOP SHOWJUMPING NATIONS	
Country	Main venue
Britain	Hickstead
Ireland	Millstreet, Ballsbridge (Dublin)
Canada	Spruce Meadows, Ontario
USA	New York, Washington, Southampton
Germany	Aachen, Hamburg, Wiesbaden
France	La Baule, Dinard, Paris
Netherlands	Rotterdam, Valkenswaard
Brazil	Saõ Paulo
Mexico	Monterrey
Spain	Madrid, Barcelona, Gijon
South Africa	Pretoria
Australia	Sydney

GRAND PRIX A Grand Prix can be run under a variety of rules over one or two preliminary rounds; the best qualify for a jump-off.

PUISSANCE This is a test of strength for the powerful, high-jumping horses and takes place over four to six fences, which are then reduced to two for the

final jump-off. Only single fences are used, and initially these may be up to 1.6m (5ft 3in) high; the height is increased with each successive round. Puissance records at major shows often exceed 2.2m (7ft 3in).

SIX BAR A class run over six similar fences, with two non-jumping strides between each one. The fences may be reduced to three after the second jump-off, and their height is increased with each successive round.

DERBY This competition requires an extremely fit horse, since it is run over a long course of approximately 1km (½ mile), which consists of fences that are as natural as possible. A Derby may be run under Table A, with or without a jump-off but against the clock, or under Table C.

Puissance classes are for the powerful, high-jumping horses. Those that can jump great heights, over 2m (6ft 6in), are exceptional.

In Europe, the two main Derbys are held at Hamburg, Germany, and Hickstead, England. Spruce Meadows in Canada has two Derbys each year. All these are held over one round with a jump-off. Monterrey, in Mexico, has a slightly easier course, which is run on time in the first round.

FAULT AND OUT Designed to test agility at speed, this competition is judged on both points and time.

There are also many speed competitions, judged under a variety of different rules. These include Accumulator, Hit and Hurry, Top Score, Take Your Own Line, and Knockout.

The showjumping horse

The showjumping horse must be tough, sound, and supple, and have an equable temperament to cope with the competitions, training, and travelling involved. Above all, the horse must be a brave and naturally athletic jumper.

SHOWJUMPING PENALTIES (TABLE A)	
Fault	**Penalties**
Knockdown	4 faults
Landing with one or more feet on the lath (edge), tape, or strip at a water jump, or in the water itself	4 faults
Fall at an obstacle anywhere on the course	Elimination*
First disobedience or refusal	3 faults
Second disobedience	6 faults
Third disobedience	Elimination
Jumping or attempting to jump an obstacle in the wrong order or in the wrong direction as indicated on the course plan, or omitting an obstacle included on the course plan	Elimination
A competitor or horse leaving the arena before completing his or her round or starting before the bell	Elimination

* except in Olympic Games, Championships, and Nations Cups

Training can improve its technique, but most top showjumpers show talent from the start.

Good jumpers are found among many breeds, but perhaps the German breeds have been most successful – the Hanoverians, Westphalians, and Holsteins, as well as the Warmbloods, which have been specifically bred for competition. Many Thoroughbreds have also reached the top, as have several Selle Français. Some excellent showjumpers have been influenced by pony blood, such as Connemara and Welsh Cob.

The showjumper needs good, strong limbs to cope with the stress of jumping; it must also be strong in the back, and have lots of scope (the ability to jump big fences). It must be agile and have quick reactions to enable it to respond immediately to the rider's demands, especially in jump-offs when speed plays an important part.

Key people

The success or failure of any showjumping competition depends to a large extent on the skill of the course designer. He or she must create an interesting and imaginative course that tests the ability of the competing horses and riders, and entertains the spectators. A paragon of efficiency is needed to co-ordinate arrangements for the event, and various officials to ensure it is conducted fairly and according to the rules. As in most other areas of the equestrian world, the sport is underpinned by the care and attention of the 'back-up crew' – vets, farriers, and the dedicated grooms.

THE RIDER To be successful, the showjumper must have a natural flair, with a great deal of patience, a will to win, and the skill to put the horse in the best possible position for any jump. Many at the top are sponsored, and must work hard to ensure they have a pool of good horses coming through.

In countries where there is a set style of riding, as in Germany, France, and the Netherlands, the leading showjumpers have up-and-coming riders who work on the young horses; both gain valuable experience under the watchful eye of the trainer.

THE TRAINER Although at the top level of the sport riders generally train their own horses, the less experienced often seek help from professionals who will work on improving the horse's basic schooling and jumping technique. Many hours will be spent developing the all-important canter, so that the horse can shorten and lengthen its stride on demand, to reach an appropriate take-off point for a particular fence. Jumping exercises with the use of poles on the ground and including variations in striding help the horse learn to balance itself in front of fences.

The trainer will also work closely with the rider to ensure he or she is in complete balance over the fence (the single most important aspect of jumping) and maintains a rhythm throughout the round.

COURSE DESIGNER A well-designed course is crucial to the success of every competition, at any level. By and large, the best results come from designers who have been competitors themselves. Factors the course designer must take into account range from the size of the

arena and (for an outdoor course) the position of the sun at various times of day, to the type of material and colours used for the fences. Careful consideration must be given to the height and spread of each jump, and the distances between them, in order to construct a course that challenges the riders without overfacing the horses.

The courses need to be readily adaptable for the various events taking place throughout the show, which may be held over a period of one or two days or, at championship level, may last for a week or more.

During the competition, the course designer must check that all jumps are reset correctly when necessary.

SHOW ORGANIZER The organizer must draw up a schedule and timetable for the whole event, and offer competitions suitable for the type of horses expected. At international events, both Grand Prix type horses and speed horses are likely to take part. A varied programme, consisting of fun competitions intermingled with the more serious jumping, is essential to maintain the interest of spectators.

The organizer is responsible for making all the arrangements for the show, inviting judges and officials, allocating duties, and planning the layout of the showground.

GROUND JURY The president of the jury must inspect every course with the course designer. The jury takes responsibility for the course and can ask for alterations to the height and spread of the obstacles, their spacing, or the course length. They must check the course plan and distances, oversee time-keeping, and ring the starting bell for each competitor. In fact, the ground jury is responsible for the running and scoring of the whole competition.

TECHNICAL DELEGATE This official has overall responsibility for major international competitions and works closely with the ground jury and the course designer in the arena and with the stewards on the showground.

SPONSORS For both individual riders and whole events or competitions, sponsors are increasingly important. They provide a great deal of the finance for showjumping today and, in return, deserve good media coverage and success from the riders. Appreciation from the commentators is essential, as is as much publicity as possible around arenas and on banners in the showground. Organizers must try to ensure a good and professional working relationship with the sponsors of an event, so that both parties gain as much from each other as possible.

The ground jury being escorted round the jumps by international course designer Pamela Carruthers at Britain's Hickstead arena.

RELATED TOPICS

Connemara	55
Thoroughbred	70
Warmbloods	76
Selle Français	82
Holstein	86
Eventing	156
The jump-off	182

The jump-off

To reach the jump-off is the crucial step to becoming a prize winner in a showjumping competition. Those that clear the first round of the overall competition are then required to take part in a jump-off. Sometimes this is against the clock, which makes for a most exciting finale.

The skill of a showjumper is particularly tested in the jump-off as not only must they jump clear over higher fences, the time they take is now absolutely crucial.

Jos Lansink is Holland's national champion and is a real professional in the ring. He treats each jump-off as if it is the most important round of his career, checking every detail in the ring to ensure he has the best chance of winning – as he did here at Hickstead's famous venue in England.

▲ 2 'I take a look at the overall course plan. It is vital to know exactly where the obstacles are at each jump-off. The coursebuilder decides what the first fence will be, so I pay particular attention when the jump-off doesn't start at obstacle one, where the start and finish lines are.'

▶ 3 'Before starting the warm up, I check that everything is okay. It is important to know whether the jumping arena is hard or soft, wet or dry. Then I decide which studs to put on my horse.'

▲ ▶ 1 'Before a class starts, riders, owners, and trainers are allowed to walk the course. This gives us time to work out the lines and distances of the course exactly. It is important that I, as a rider, think about my own horse: how good it is to ride, how much gallop it has, and how much experience. These are all important to consider when planning how best to tackle the particular course.'

◄ 4 'Every rider has a system for warming up their horse. The timing is also dependent on the weather conditions. If I have jumped my first round clear, I only jump a couple of fences before the jump-off, and stop as soon as my horse feels ready.'

► 5 'At a jump-off it is very important to ride the shortest way because the winner will be the rider with the least faults and quickest overall time.'

◄ 6 'I tackle the last fence and then must travel as quickly as possible to the finish line. Seconds are vital at this final stage as the competition is close.'

▼ 7 'This is what every horse and rider works so hard towards during the whole competition. Winning is a wonderful feeling; knowing that all the work I have put in has come together and paid off. Here, the competition sponsor, Douglas Bunn, is congratulating me on my win.'

RACING

The sport of racing is an exciting spectacle combining the speed, courage, and beauty of horses with the skill of their riders. The most popular form of the sport is flat racing, which started in England early in the 18th century and has since flourished in almost 50 countries. Steeplechasing – racing over a course of jumps – has a dedicated following, especially in Britain and New Zealand. The Thoroughbred is the racehorse for both flat racing and steeplechasing. Organized racing also thrives, but on a far smaller scale, for other breeds, such as the Arabian and the Quarter Horse.

The ultimate racehorse

Anyone who has ridden horses immediately recognizes the Thoroughbred as being different and special. Whether galloping on the flat or jumping fences, the combination of strength and speed creates for the rider a thrill that is difficult to surpass.

The breeding industry in England and Ireland, and subsequently in France, the USA, and Australasia, has had to respond to the extraordinary appeal racing has acquired. In recent years the popularity of racing as a spectator sport, and particularly as a medium for gambling, has encouraged countries such as Japan and Hong Kong to participate in a major way.

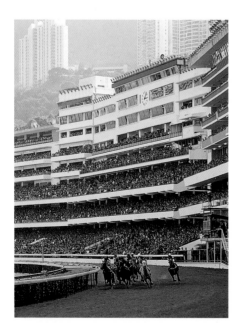

The growing interest in Thoroughbred racing in the Middle East, with the involvement of Dubai's ruling family, the Maktoums, as both owners and breeders, has given the sport a truly international flavour.

FLAT RACING

Horse racing dates back to ancient times, but its modern form evolved from the 'match' races of the 16th century, when one owner would match his horse against that of another. Gradually, races became more public events, as more and more runners entered the competitions. By the mid 17th century a wide variety of races had developed, with different conditions of entry to attract a range of different horses.

The breeders' determination to produce a better faster racehorse led to the creation of the Thoroughbred. Historically, the arrival in Britain at the end of the 17th century of three stallions noted for their outstanding speed and stamina – the Byerley Turk, the Darley Arabian, and the Godolphin Barb – marked the foundation of the breed, and all Thoroughbred horses are descended from these three animals.

The sport of kings

In England, races were held at Chester in the 16th century during Henry VIII's reign, and James I organized racing at Newmarket in the early 17th century; but it was Charles II who established racing as a national sport. King Charles actually rode in races himself and founded the Newmarket Town Plate in 1665, which is the oldest race still run in England today. Newmarket remains the headquarters of British racing, as well as being one of the country's main breeding centres.

The Jockey Club was formed in 1752, and for more than 200 years controlled

Left: The spectacular venue and huge crowds at Happy Valley in the centre of Hong Kong make this a unique racecourse.

Right: Jockeys demonstrate their determination to win as their horses thunder towards the finish at the USA's Gulfstream course.

all aspects of British racing. Sir James Weatherby published the first *Racing Calendar*, a record of racing, in 1773, and 20 years later compiled an Introduction to the General Stud Book, tracing the pedigree of every Thoroughbred and acknowledged as the official record of the breed in Britain. On behalf of the Jockey Club, the Weatherby family still publishes the calendar and stud book today. Since 1993, the sport in Britain has been run by the British Horseracing Board, leaving solely the rules and discipline to be administered by the Jockey Club.

RACING DEVELOPS IN THE USA Organized flat racing in the USA developed almost hand in hand with that in Britain. The first track there was opened in 1665 at Long Island by the governor of New York, who presented a silver cup to be run for twice a year. During the early part of the 18th century numerous Thoroughbreds were brought from England, but it was the importation of Diomed, the winner of the first English Derby held at Epsom in 1780, that gave

impetus to the breeding of racehorses in the USA.

In 1900 there were no fewer than 300 tracks in the USA and 43 in Canada, but anti-betting legislation forced many of these to close. Racing began to flourish again after the 1930s, and is now conducted in 43 different states at more than 80 different venues.

The bluegrass lands of Kentucky were long the main breeding grounds for American racehorses. Claiborne, Calumet, and Spendthrift are some of the great stud farms in the area today, and the sales pavilion at Keeneland, Lexington, has become famous for the auctions held there throughout the year. In recent decades Florida and California have also become major breeding and racing areas, and Saratoga's yearling sales attract buyers from all over the world.

ORIGINS OF FRENCH RACING Racing was officially established in France on 31 August 1805 when Napoleon issued a decree that racing would be held from the year 1807 in the country's seven

Starting stalls or gates ensure all horses have the opportunity of a clean break, especially important in sprint races if a good placing is to be achieved.

principal horse-breeding regions. A few English Thoroughbred stallions were imported between 1815 and 1830, and in 1833 the *Société d'Encouragement pour L'Amélioration des Races de Chevaux en France*, a national body governing the sport, was formed.

France's first racecourse opened at Chantilly in 1834 and, together with the Maisons-Laffitte course, opened in the 1840s, became the country's main training centre. Deauville was the next of the important French racecourses to evolve. It was created by the Duc de Morny, who commemorated there by the major race for two-year-olds over 1.2km (6 furlongs) – the Prix Morny. Deauville today remains a popular centre for French racing and for polo.

THE ITALIAN INFLUENCE Racing began in Italy in the first half of the 19th century, with tracks opening at Naples, Rome, Florence, Turin, and Milan.

Although Italy's bloodstock industry has always been tiny, the Italian Thoroughbred has had a worldwide influence out of all proportion to its numbers. One man was mainly responsible for this: Federico Tesio, who founded the Dormello stud on Lake Maggiore in 1898. Tesio bred Nearco, who many believe to be the breed's most influential stallion, and Ribot (foaled in 1952), who is considered by many to be the best racehorse of all time.

Flat racing today

In most countries, flat racing takes place on oval tracks, over distances varying from a minimum of 1km (5 furlongs) to a maximum of 4.4km (2¾ miles), such as the Queen Alexandra Stakes at Royal Ascot.

In Europe, the tracks are usually of grass, but in North America dirt tracks are commonly used, with smaller grass tracks inside them that have perhaps only a race or two a day.

There are usually six races at half-hour intervals on any one-day programme. Many courses hold two- or three-day meetings, but at Britain's Goodwood and Ascot a meeting may last five days, which naturally puts pressure on the turf. In the USA they will race every day for a month or more on some tracks – but the dirt surface can easily cope with this.

Types of race

Races generally fall into four different categories: maiden races, handicaps, group or pattern races, and claiming and selling races. These categories are found in both flat racing and steeplechasing.

MAIDEN RACES Only horses that have never won a race are eligible to enter maiden races.

HANDICAP RACES The weight that each horse has to carry is determined by the official handicapper, and has a range of 12.5kg (28lb) between best and worst (the better the horse, the greater the weight assigned). Handicaps are designed to give each horse entered in

Britain's Epsom Derby is one of the world's most important races. It is a testing course and needs a well-balanced and mature horse to win.

the race an equal chance of winning (in theory, all horses would cross the finishing line together).

GROUP OR PATTERN RACES Designed for the quality horses, these are races at level weights with allowances for age – the younger the horse, the less weight it has to carry – and sex – fillies get a 1.4–2.3kg (3–5lb) allowance. In some cases there are weight penalties for races previously won.

CLAIMING AND SELLING RACES For the moderate horses in training, there are in most countries 'claiming' and 'selling' races. In a claiming race, owners classify their horses by putting a price on them (the lower the price, the less weight the horse carries). An owner deliberately putting too low a price on his or her horse may win the race but risks losing the horse, since after the race it may be 'claimed' (bought) by another owner at the stated price. In a 'selling' race, the winning horse is auctioned afterwards, and in most cases any other runner may also be 'claimed' at a set price.

Famous races

One of the greatest racing feats, especially in Britain and the USA, is to win the Triple Crown, a series of three premier races ('classics') for three-year-olds. In England, the first race is the Newmarket 2000 Guineas, over 1.6km

(1 mile), usually run in early May. The Derby, the best-known race of the three, is run over 2.4km (1½ miles) at Epsom, about a month later. The final leg is the St Leger, run over 2.8km (1¾ miles) in September, at Doncaster.

The US Triple Crown consists of the Kentucky Derby, at Churchill Downs over 2km (1¼ miles) in early May and, two weeks later, the Preakness at Pimlico over 1.9km (1³⁄₁₆ miles). The third leg, the Belmont, over 2.4km (1½ miles), is run three weeks after that, at Belmont Park, Long Island.

The American Triple Crown has been won more frequently than its British

equivalent, and requires a fast, durable, and sound horse. In England, because of the very different distances and much longer time scale, a winner needs to be not only a fast horse, but a very versatile one. The only horse to have won the English Triple Crown since World War II is Nijinski, in 1970.

Highlights of the French racing year include the Prix du Jockey Club (the French equivalent of the English Derby), for three-year-olds, over 2.4km (1½ miles), which was established in 1836, and the Grand Prix de Paris, established in 1863. For a century or more, this was a 3km (1 mile 7 furlong) race for three-year-olds, but in recent years it has been reduced to 2km (1¼ miles). The Prix de l'Arc de Triomphe, an all-aged test over 2.4km (1½ miles) held at Longchamp on the first Sunday in October, is the most celebrated race of its kind in Europe.

The Gran Premio di Milano, inaugurated at San Siro, Milan, in 1921, and the Derby Italiano, first held at the Capanelle racecourse in Rome in 1884, are still Italy's two most prestigious races. Both races are run over 2.4km (1½ miles).

The Melbourne Cup run at Flemington, Melbourne is a handicap race over 3.2km (2 miles). It has for many years been the most important day in Australia's sporting calendar, attracting more than 80,000 people while the rest of the country listens on the radio or watches on television.

The sport's most valuable race is now the Dubai World Cup, held at Nad al Sheba. First run in 1996, it attracts the best of the world's three- and four-year-olds, who compete on a sand track over a distance of 2km (1¼ miles) for a prize of $5 million.

RACING RULES

There are thousands of racetracks and many racing associations around the world, but there is no one body that sets international racing rules. If a rider wishes to race in a different country, he or she has to adhere to the specific rules of that country. In the USA, rules on licensing, riding, and which horse drugs are acceptable differ from state to state.

The rules include medical, veterinary, and disciplinary procedures, as well as safety requirements on the racetrack. For steeplechasing there are also rules to cover types of fence and their dimensions.

Great horses and riders

The Italian-bred colt Ribot ruled the British racetrack in the 1950s, and the French horse Sea Bird II was believed to be the best for middle distance races in the 1960s. In the early 1970s Nijinsky, Mill Reef, and Brigadier Gerard were considered three of the greatest flat racehorses of all time. Dancing Brave, who won the 1986 Arc de Triomphe in electrifying fashion, was the best middle distance horse of the 1980s.

Man O' War, who was bred in 1917, is still considered the best of all American Thoroughbreds, and at stud he exerted a powerful influence on the breed. He was beaten only once in 21 races, and as a three-year-old broke seven American track records at all distances. Citation, Secretariat, Native Dancer, the gelding Kelso, Cigar, Skip Away, and Silver Charm are considered the most illustrious American flat racehorses of more recent times.

Jockeys Steve Donoghue and Gordon Richards dominated English flat racing in the first half of the 20th century and were succeeded by the extraordinarily talented Lestor Piggott, who was champion jockey 11 times and won the English Derby a record nine times, and almost every other big race all over the world. Piggott's main rivals for much of the 1970s and 1980s were the brilliant Australian jockey Scobie Breasley, and the Scotsman Willie Carson.

The two most notorious jockeys to ride in France since the last World War were Yves St. Martin, a champion jockey who won many times in the 1970s, and the American, Cash Asmussen, who first came to prominence in the 1980s. Other leading American riders today include Pat Day, Gary Stevens, Chris McCarron, and Jerry Bailey.

In the late 1990s the Italian Frankie Dettori and the French jockey Olivier Peslier won much acclaim and became the new international superstars, riding many winners in major races all over the world.

STEEPLECHASING

Steeplechasing is generally for older and bigger horses, and involves racing over jumps for distances generally from 3.2 to 6.4km (2–4 miles). Britain is said to be the home of the sport, where it is run by the National Hunt Committee of the Jockey Club. Steeplechasing is also very popular in France, Germany, and, in particular, New Zealand where they breed fine jumpers, many of which are then exported into Britain.

Steeplechase fences are typically made of birch and gorse and can be as tall as 1.4m (4ft 6in) high. Some

Britain's Princess Royal rode in a number of races during the 1980s, and won both on the flat and over fences.

involve hurdles – smaller obstacles, though these are not more than 1.1m (3ft 6in) high.

The sport takes its name from early races held between hunters riding across country, usually from one church steeple to another. The first recorded steeplechase took place in Ireland in 1752. In 1804 a three-horse 'chase was the first ridden in colours.

In England, Cheltenham and Aintree were two of the first racecourses to stage steeplechasing, in the 1830s, and they remain the two great National Hunt racecourses in the country. The English Grand National at Aintree, over 7.2km (4½ miles) and 30 big fences – up to 1.6m (5ft 3in) high with a 1.8m (6ft) spread – is the most demanding and exciting steeplechase in the world.

Steeplechasing in France started around the 1860s. The course at Auteuil – only a short distance from the centre of Paris – became the country's mecca of steeplechasing. The Grand Steeple, first run in 1874, over 6.4km (4 miles) is still the premier French race. The fences at Auteuil are much more varied than on an English course and *La Rivière* in front of the stands is an enormous and spectacular water jump.

The Velka Pardubicka, in the Czech Republic, is also run over a varied and formidable course, and is perhaps the most challenging race in mainland Europe today. In Germany steeplechasing usually takes place on the inside of the flat racecourses, and the jockeys often need compasses to help guide them around the twists, turns, and figures of eight.

POINT TO POINTING The amateur sport of point to point racing is immensely popular in Britain, and a great breeding ground for future steeplechasers and jockeys. Races are organized by the various hunts, and are held from January through May; in order to enter, horses must have been hunting a minimum of six times that season. Courses are usually 4.8–5.6km (3–3½ miles) long and consist of brush fences up to 1.4m (4ft 6in) high, some with ditches in front or behind.

TIMBER RACING In North America steeplechasing has never been as popular as in Britain, and there may be only a single 'chase on a card of six flat

races. Timber racing, however, which is more like English point to pointing and dominated by amateurs, has a devoted following. In these races, held over 3.2–6.4km (2–4 miles), the horses jump sturdy wooden rail fences usually about 1.2m (4ft) high. The most famous race is the Maryland Hunt Cup, run every year at the end of March over 6.4km (4 miles), with fences up to 1.5m (5ft) high. The equivalent race in England is the Marlborough Cup, which has been run since 1995.

Great steeplechasers

Of all the great steeplechasers, Arkle was, quite simply, the best, winning the Gold Cup at Cheltenham from 1964 to 1966. At Aintree, home of the British Grand National, Red Rum held sway in the 1970s; while in the late 1980s, the grey Desert Orchid became a favourite in the chasing world. The Fellow was the most notable French jumper during the 1990s.

HARNESS RACING

Trotting and pacing races in harness make up a distinctly different type of

Point to point racing began in the 17th century when riders raced from one church steeple to another, jumping whatever was in the way.

TOP RACING NATIONS		
Country	Number of major tracks	Recognized racing authority
Britain	59	The Jockey Club
USA	50	The Jockey Club, State Racing Commissions and Boards
France	23	France-Galop
Australia	20	Australian Jockey Club and State Turf Clubs
Germany	16	Direktorium fur Vollblutzucht und Rennen
Japan	10	Japan Racing Association
Italy	7	Jockey Club Italiano
Canada	4	Jockey Club of Canada
Denmark	3	Jockey Club of Denmark
Hong Kong	2	Royal Hong Kong Jockey Club

racing, in which the horses pull their drivers in small, lightweight, two-wheeled vehicles called sulkies.
The modern sport began in the form of impromptu road races in the eastern USA in the early 18th century. Today, it has a huge following throughout the USA and in parts of Europe, particularly France, as well as in New Zealand and Australia, commanding enormous prize money and drawing huge crowds of spectators.

It was at Long Island in 1826 that the first official American trotting race was held, and the sport spread through much of the country. In 1870 the first rules and regulations were drawn up by the forerunners of the United States Trotting Association, which today governs every aspect of the sport in the USA and much of Canada.

There are two Triple Crowns in American harness racing today, one for trotters and one for pacers (in trotting the diagonal pairs of legs move forwards together; in pacing, both legs on one side of the body move simultaneously). For pacers there is first the Cane Pace, then the Messenger Stakes, and the Little Brown Jug. Trotters compete for supremacy in the Hambletonian, the Yonkers Trot, and the Kentucky Futurity.

In Europe, trotting races were common from the early 19th century, but these were often under saddle (a practice that still exists today in France). The first French trotting race was known to have been held Cherbourg in 1836. Organized races also took place in Belgium, the Netherlands, Germany, Italy, Spain, Scandinavia, and some eastern European nations such as Hungary and Poland.

In 1879 French trotting races moved to Paris, to the flat track at Vincennes. In 1920 the international Prix d'Amerique was run at Vincennes, and is still classed as the European Trotter of the Year Championship.

Harness racing today

Today harness racing is run on oval tracks, usually over 1.6km (1 mile), although European races tend to be longer, varying from 2.4 to 3.2km (1½–2 miles) or even longer. Trotting races are slightly faster than pacing races, the latter mostly being held in

the USA, Australia, and New Zealand.
PACING HOBBLES It is a rule of the sport that the gait, whether trotting or pacing, remains true throughout the race, but this is not easy to re-establish if the rhythm is lost. Pacers wear straps called hobbles (or hopples) to link the front and back legs on the same side, making it easier to remain in rhythm, and so prevent the loss of stride (known as a 'break').

The harness racehorse

The outstanding harness racehorse is the American Standardbred, which was bred from Morgans, crossed with Thoroughbreds and European trotting horses. Standardbreds were widely exported and used to develop other trotting breeds. Most notable of these are the French Trotter, which dominates harness racing in Europe today, and the Russian Trotter, created by using Standardbred blood on the Orlov Trotter to give it extra speed.

Famous drivers

Billy Haughton, Del Miller, and Stanley Dancer were legendary names in American harness racing in the years following World War II. Their present-day counterparts include John Campbell, Luc Ouellette, and Walter Case, Jr. The latter headed the 1998 drivers' list by winning more than half of all his races to establish a new world record of 1079 wins. Equally dazzling was the 1998 record of the Leading Harness Horse and Leading Trotter of the Year, Moni Maker, who travelled

Harness racing is enormously popular, particularly in the USA and France, as well as Australia. There are races for trotters and pacers.

the world to win a dozen victories in 17 races, and earned almost $1,230,000 with Walter Hennessey at the reins.

KEY RACING PEOPLE

Producing a winning horse involves the hard work of a dedicated team – trainer, jockey, owner, breeder – and all play a vital part in the success of a racehorse's career.

THE TRAINER The trainer's role is the most crucial in the development of any racehorse. He or she is usually responsible for 'breaking in' the young horse, for its training right through its racing career, and for what happens to it once its racing days are over.

Each horse has to be treated as an individual and developed to achieve its maximum potential. The trainer must carefully choose the races the horse will enter, then concentrate on getting that horse to its peak for each one.

THE JOCKEY The stature of a flat race jockey is all important as the weight that horses carry varies from a minimum of 49kg (108lb) to a maximum of 64kg (140lb). All jockeys must initially go to a trainer to learn their craft and to work with the horses that, some day, they will ride. In most countries they have to take a concentrated course at a racing school before being granted a licence. The senior jockeys will ride in six races a day for six days a week and often travel abroad on a Sunday. Consequently they need to be extremely fit and dedicated. Some of the best jockeys will be retained by a particular owner or trainer, but the majority are freelance and through their agents seek rides whenever they can get them.

The racing life of the steeplechase jockey inevitably is quite short because they have so many falls. The flat jockey, however, whose own weight is constant, can often be effective into his or her forties and occasionally beyond.

THE OWNER Racing would not exist without owners who, in most cases, have to be wealthy people. They may breed the horse themselves, which in itself is costly, or must buy it at the sales. The owner selects a trainer not just to prepare the horse for a single race, but also to guide its career. In most cases owners receive very little credit for the success their horses achieve, but the enjoyment of winning makes up amply for the cost and the many disappointments along the way.

THE BREEDER Breeders determine the pedigree of racehorses and normally own their own stud farms where the broodmares reside. Each breeder chooses the stallion that will best suit that mare – depending also on the stallion fee they can afford. In most cases the mare will have her foal at the stallion's stud farm and be 'covered' soon afterwards. Eleven months later the foal arrives – and with it the great hopes and aspirations of the breeder.

THE DRIVER In harness racing the driver, trainer, and sometimes the owner, may be one person. Driving trotters and pacers require superb hands, keen judgement of pace and strategy, and a refined ability to get the most out of a horse without forcing it into a 'break'.

CLERK OF THE COURSE The organization of a day's racing lies in the hands of the clerk of the course. They decide, in advance, the value, distance, and type of each race (whether flat, hurdle, or steeplechase). They must be sure that the doctor, ambulances, vets, and farriers are all present before racing can actually start.

RELATED TOPICS

Thoroughbred	70
French Trotter	80
Quarter Horse	112
Standardbred	116
Orlov Trotter	125
Arabian	128
A day at the races	192

STEWARDS The stewards (amateur in Britain), helped by the secretaries appointed by each racecourse, control and administer the rules.

THE VET Apart from attending to injured or sick horses at a race meeting, the vet has the task of checking that no prohibited substances have been used. In every country nowadays horses will be dope tested at random. After the race, the vet takes a urine or blood sample and sends it off to the laboratory for testing. In addition, in all big races, the first three horses to finish will be dope tested.

Jockeys wear silks in the owners' colours. Goggles are an essential item to protect the face from mud and dirt kicked up by the horses.

BETTING All betting in racing countries operates through the totalizator, a computerized system which decides the odds of the horses by the amount of money that is placed on them. In Britain and Australia there are book makers who decide their own odds. Each individual bookie keeps the majority of his profits. The 'tote' is government-owned however a large part of its profits go back into the racing industry.

A day at the races

A day at America's Gulf Stream racecourse is filled with excitement, colour, and pageantry. It is a day that gives you the chance to see and cheer some of the most beautiful and well-conditioned animals in the world. Each one of them has been bred to compete, and they thrive on the competition of the race.

You can also put a wager on the horse and jockey of your choice and watch their progress from the comfortable viewing areas. In between races there are various dining areas to choose from.

There are normally eight to 10 races run each day, with about 30 minutes break between races. The most impressive parts of the day are each time the horses and jockeys charge down the home stretch toward that all important finish line, and you are swept up in the excitment of the moment.

▲ 3 The saddling paddock is where horses are saddled by their trainers prior to going out on the track to run their race. It is also where trainers give their jockeys their final instructions.

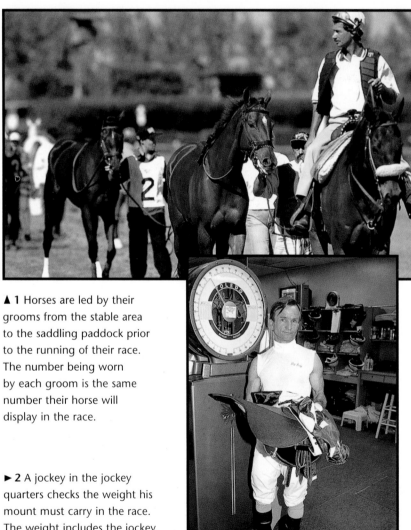

▲ 1 Horses are led by their grooms from the stable area to the saddling paddock prior to the running of their race. The number being worn by each groom is the same number their horse will display in the race.

► 2 A jockey in the jockey quarters checks the weight his mount must carry in the race. The weight includes the jockey, his boots, britches, and racing colours. It also includes his saddle and lead pad.

► **4** All the horses warm up on the track during the 10-minute post parade prior to the start of the race. It is during this parade that you can make your selection if you want to wager on the race.

▼ **5** At the betting windows spectators make wagers prior to the running of a race. The windows will be closed when the horses arrive at the starting line and will not reopen until the race result is made official.

▼ **6** The tension is high as a race begins. Horses start in post position order with number one starting on the inside next to the rail. Numbers on saddle cloths correspond to numbers on the starting gate.

▼ **7** A winning horse stands in the winners circle with the jockey, trainer, horse owner, and friends for the ceremonial picture following the victory. This ritual takes place after each race. Afterwards, the jockey will clean up and change into the colours to be worn in the next race.

DRIVING

Driving horses and ponies for sport first came to prominence with the chariot races of ancient Greece and Rome, and has continued in one form or another ever since. Horse driving trials, the modern form of competitive driving, arose in Europe in the early 20th century, and it remains a largely European sport. Coaching and pleasure driving have a strong following in Europe and the USA, and classes are held at agricultural and horse shows as well as at dedicated driving events.

Chariot racing

The ancient city states of Greece gave birth to the sport of competitive driving. Religious festivals and games nearly always included chariot racing, which took place before thousands of spectators in centres such as Delphi and Olympia.

The Romans copied the Greek example. Competitions were held all over the empire, but especially at the Circus Maximus in Rome, which measured a vast 600 x 200m (1970 x 660ft). Races were over seven laps of the track, always on the left rein.

The Greek and Roman horses were bred at stud farms in Greece, Italy, northern Africa, and Spain, and all were recorded in their own stud books.

They were broken to harness at three years old, and were ready for racing at five. Racing teams consisted of up to 10 horses driven abreast. They depended much on the strength of the outside horses (called funales), who were short coupled and full of quality.

Simple rawhide harness attached the horses to the chariot. A yoke across the withers was held in place by a neck strap and surcingle. The chariot was light and strong, with extremely wide axles to give stability when turning. The charioteer drove with the reins in two hands and stood well back in the chariot in a semi-crouched position. Four-horse chariot racing first took place at the Olympics in 680 BC; and many different driving races were run at ensuing Games.

THE SPORT OF COACHING

Chariot racing persisted into the Middle Ages but, with the eclipse of the Byzantine empire in the 15th century, it disappeared as a major spectator sport. Eventually, the 1870s saw gentlemen driving teams of four horses for pleasure, and these amateurs kindled new interest in the skill. They were inspired by the heroic deeds of the 'golden age' of coaching in the early part of the century.

The emerging sport gained enormous publicity in 1888 when, for a wager, the famous professional 'whip' James Selby drove the Old Times Coach from London to Brighton and back – some 190km (120 miles) – in the record time of seven hours 50 minutes. Soon driving clubs began to be formed around the world, notably in Paris, London, and New York, to cater to those wanting to drive teams, pairs, tandems, and single horses.

By the beginning of the 20th century, coaching was a well established sport. Amateur drivers wanted to keep alive the art of four-in-hand driving, which was dying out with the advent of motorized transport.

On 13 June 1907 the first coaching marathon took place at the Royal International Horse Show in London. Fourteen teams took part, starting at Hyde Park and following a 13km (8 mile) route.

In 1909, the first marathon for private and road coaches was held, also in England. Teams started from Hampton Court, some 13km (8 miles) from London, and drove to Olympia. The winner was a team of greys exhibited by the American Alfred Vanderbilt.

Coaching today

Since the 1950s, major agricultural shows have held classes for coaches.

Left: John Richards, President of the Coaching Club, wins the coaching championships at Royal Windsor Horse Show with this team.

Right: Thomas Eriksson, drives his team of Swedish Warmbloods through a water obstacle.

These are divided into sections for private, road, and regimental coaches, all judged on the turnout of horses and harness, and the overall appearance of the coachman, passengers, and grooms, as well as the horses' way of going. At some shows, the coaches take part in a marathon drive, usually 13–14km (8–9 miles) long. The judges assess the skill of the driver and the performance of the team, which is also judged at the halt.

PRIVATE COACHES Often called park drags, these are drawn by teams with great quality, action, and manners. The four horses must be perfectly matched, in terms of size and colour; excessive white markings are undesirable and thus avoided.

The coach is usually painted in discreet colours with a finer finish than a road coach. Often there is a crest or monogram painted on the door panels and the hind boot. The hind seat is big enough for two grooms in full livery. Park team harness is finely made, usually in brass and black leather.

When the coach is stationary, the head groom stands at the head of the horse next to the offside front wheel, with the second groom positioned in front of the leaders.

ROAD COACHES Heavier and more robust than a park drag, a road coach is painted in bright colours, with the names of the principal towns on the route it follows shown on the sides. The door panels are often painted with a device associated with the coach's name – such as a fox's mask for a coach called the Tally-Ho. This device is also carried through on the harness, which is heavier than that used on a park drag. The rear seat accommodates four people including the guard.

A road-coach team need not be perfectly matched: often, a grey or odd-coloured horse takes the offside lead.

REGIMENTAL COACHES A particularly British institution, regimental coaches are always park drags and are usually painted in regimental colours. The 5th Lancers was the first regiment to

An American Spring Perch Phaeton is used with a pair of Morgan Horses in a private driving class at Royal Windsor in 1992.

acquire a coach, in 1875, followed by the 6th Dragoon Guards in 1876. A beautifully appointed coach of the Household Cavalry competes in coaching marathons. Regimental coaches have no ceremonial duties, but appear regularly at many of the major British shows.

In Britain the Coaching Club issues guidance on the correct equipment to be used with park drags and road coaches, and provides a list of qualified coaching judges. Each show then organizes its own classes. Members of the Coaching Club have the privilege of being able to drive to the Royal Ascot race meeting and park their coaches in their own enclosure.

The Royal Windsor Horse Show is one of the acknowledged meccas of coaching. The first marathon there took place in 1947. Some of the most spectacular coaching classes are seen at the Royal Winter Fair held indoors at the Coliseum in Toronto. Here the arena is filled with magnificent entries from both Canada and the USA.

PLEASURE DRIVING

In former years, particularly in the 18th and 19th centuries, carriage driving was both a vital means of travel and a sport. After the motor car became the most popular means of transport, enthusiasts kept the art of driving alive. Thanks to them and their descendants, many traditional vehicles have been restored and preserved, and there has been a rebirth of carriage making.

Pleasure driving classes vary from nation to nation, but all offer drivers the opportunity to demonstrate their abilities at the reins, their turnouts, and the qualities of their horses or ponies.

The international scene

In Britain, the British Driving Society (BDS) is the major organization dedicated to driving, with some 300 shows affiliated to it each year. Classes are categorized for particular breeds and vehicles and include singles, pairs, and tandems. There are also classes for trade vehicles and costers, and a thriving section for disabled drivers. The BDS Annual Show held at Smiths Lawn, Windsor, has four rings and is one of the largest and most prestigious driving shows in the world.

The American Driving Society (ADS) has drawn up rules for show classes, and the American Horse Shows Association also has a driving committee. Many shows are run independently. The five-day Pittsford Carriage Association's Walnut Hill Show is the largest and most successful of its kind in the USA. Its wide range of classes include some run under ADS rules for turnout, working, and reinsmanship, together with novelty classes. The Devon Horse Show in Pennsylvania, held in the last week in May, is equally famed. In Canada, the Central Ontario Pleasure Driving Club holds an annual driving show similar to the Walnut Hill event.

There is considerable interest in pleasure driving in the southern hemisphere, especially in Australia,

where the Australian Driving Society, founded in 1970, has helped to promote a number of other affiliated clubs and associations. There is a long tradition of pleasure driving in New Zealand, where a variety of two- and four-wheel vehicles is used. The New Zealand Driving Society is well established, with a growing membership.

Pleasure driving classes are now run at many of the major shows in South Africa. Among the most popular vehicles used is the Cape cart, a two-wheeled vehicle drawn by a pair of horses, instead of the usual one. The cart was specifically designed for farmers to enable them to drive safely across rough and difficult country.

SCURRY DRIVING

Scurry driving is an exciting sport that is derived from American barrel racing, but is particularly popular in Britain, and also thrives in other European countries such as Germany and the Netherlands. Pairs of driving ponies race at speed through a course of cones, and the pair with the fastest overall time wins. The competitions are easy to stage and often dramatic to watch, and are held at both local and national shows.

The ponies must be at least four-year-olds, and compete in two groups –

TOP DRIVING NATIONS	
Country	Main venue
Germany	Aachen
Britain	Windsor
Hungary	Tapioszentmarton
Netherlands	Breda
Switzerland	St Gallen
Poland	Poznan
USA	Gladstone, New Jersey
Sweden	Asbo

those of 122cm (12 hands) and under, and those over 122cm (12 hands) but not exceeding 148cm (14.2 hands).

The carriage must have four wheels and be equipped with a working brake. Wire-spoked wheels and pneumatic tyres are not allowed. The track width must be at least 130cm (4ft 3in). The distance between the cones must be 40cm (28in) wider than the width of the carriage. The course usually consists of 12 to 14 'gates' or obstacles.

One groom must sit behind the driver at all times during the competition. The groom may help to balance the carriage, by leaning out, but it is against the rules for him or her to give directions to the driver or assist in moving the vehicle in any way.

All the speed, drama, and skill of scurry driving is clearly shown as this competitor successfully negotiates a set of cones with her pair of ponies.

DRIVING TRIALS

Horse driving trials developed in Germany in the 1930s. The Aachen and Hamburg shows were the first to hold international driving classes, with four-in-hand dressage and cross-country competitions. At that time, the teams came mostly from Germany, Hungary, and Switzerland.

When the Duke of Edinburgh was elected President of the International Equestrian Federation (FEI) in 1964, he suggested the FEI might produce rules for the burgeoning international driving competitions. In 1969, the FEI published the first set of international rules. Two years later the Royal Windsor Horse Show staged an international competition for four in hands, and the first European Championship was held in Budapest, Hungary; the first World Championship was held in 1972.

The sport has continued to grow in popularity ever since. There have been many amendments to the rules, and striking changes in the style and construction of carriages and harness to withstand the strains and rigours of the competition.

The modern competition

The modern driving trials competition is based on the ridden sport of eventing. It is held over three or four days, and divided into three sections: presentation and dressage; the marathon; and cone driving.

PRESENTATION AND DRESSAGE This stage takes place in an arena, which measures 100 x 40m (328 x 131ft). At major international events, presentation is judged at a standstill, and the proper fit of harness as well as the maintenance of national traditions are carefully considered. The coachman, horses, harness, grooms, and carriage must be turned out to the highest standards.

Dressage involves a set series of movements designed to test the horse's obedience, paces, and suppleness – and the driver's ability to handle the reins. Among other things, the judges look for freedom of movement, regularity of paces, impulsion, and the correct positioning of the horses. Horses or ponies driven in multiple turnouts are judged collectively, the judges looking for harmony within the turnout. The drivers are also marked on their ability to produce a fluent, accurate, and obedient performance. Reins, voice, and whip are the only permitted aids.

MARATHON Designed to test the fitness and stamina of the horses, the marathon is run over a maximum of 22km (13½ miles), on roads and tracks and across country, and is usually divided into five sections.

The first four sections are time trials, which have to be driven at a set pace. Penalties are incurred for being too fast or too slow. There are two compulsory halts, with veterinary checks to monitor fitness. Horses not considered fit to continue are retired.

The final section of the marathon includes a maximum of eight obstacles. These are designed to test the ability and obedience of the turnout to negotiate narrow gates and tight turns at speed. Competitors may view the obstacles before the start of the marathon, to plan the fastest route through the gates.

Cone driving is equivalent to the showjumping phase in eventing. Horses and carriages are always turned out to a very high standard.

CONE DRIVING This is the final phase of the driving trial and, like the dressage test, it takes place in the arena. It is designed to test the fitness, obedience, and suppleness of the horses after the rigours of the marathon. After walking the course, competitors drive a set route through narrowly spaced pairs of cones. A ball is placed on top of each cone; penalties are given if it is dislodged, or if the time allowed is exceeded. This makes for an exciting finale to the event, as competitors compete in reverse order of placing.

RULES

International horse driving trials are run under FEI rules, but for domestic competitions most countries have their own rules, which may vary slightly. The regulations cover the format of the competition and specific matters such as the type, weight, and width of carriages, and the number of people to be carried.

THE MARATHON COURSE

This is a typical marathon course for driving trials, divided into five sections, and showing the distance and times for each section for both horses and ponies.

	Max distance (Horses/Ponies)	Pace	Max speed (Horses/Ponies)
A	7km (4½ miles)/ 6km (4 miles)	Free	15kmph (10mph)/ 14kmph (9mph)
B	1km (½ mile) —	Walk	7kmph (4½mph)/ 6kmph (4mph)
C	4km (2½ miles) —	Trot	19kmph (12mph)/ 17kmph (11mph)
D	1km (½ mile)/ 1km (½ mile)	Walk	7kmph (4½mph)/ 6kmph (4mph)
E	9km (5½ miles) —	Free	14kmph (9mph)/ 13kmph (8mph)

SCORING Penalty points may be incurred during each of the three phases of the event, and are cumulative. The overall winner is the competitor with the fewest penalties.

In the dressage test marks are awarded for each movement, and these are then subtracted from the optimum score, to give the total number of penalties for the section. Presentation is scored in a similar manner.

In the marathon phase, penalties are incurred for being under or over the time allowed for each section, and for breaks of pace. Each obstacle is timed individually, and penalties are given for every second spent within the obstacle. Extra penalties can be incurred for infringing the rules, such as turning over the vehicle, knocking down a collapsible element, or a groom dismounting. Competitors may be eliminated for failing to correct an error of course, failing to pass through one of the gates, exceeding the time limit of five minutes at any one obstacle, or failing to pass between the entry/exit flags.

Britain's George Bowman with his famous team of Cumberland Cobs negotiating an obstacle during the marathon phase.

In the cone-driving phase, penalty points are given for displacing a ball, a disobedience such as refusing to pass through a pair of cones, a groom dismounting, and exceeding the time limit. Competitors may be eliminated for such errors as taking the wrong route, or the groom indicating the course to the driver.

A variety of classes

Classes are run nationally for the following turnouts: horse teams; pony teams; horse pairs; pony pairs; horse tandems; pony tandems; single horse; single pony; and at most events novice single horse and novice single pony.

There are now international championships for horse teams, pony teams, and horse pairs. In 1998 the first World Championship for single horses took place at Ebbs in Austria, and was won by Arja Mikkonen of Finland.

Carriage development

In the very early days of the sport, competitors drove traditional vehicles. Often this meant that original carriages, of considerable age, were being used. However, these soon proved unsuitable for the punishment of competitive driving, and new

methods of carriage construction were developed. It quickly became apparent, too, that competitors should use vehicles of a standard width and weight for their class.

The carriages used for the marathon are usually different from those used for the presentation, dressage, and cone-driving phases of the event. For the latter phases, the same vehicle must be used, and the axle (the rear axle if a four-wheel vehicle) must not exceed a set maximum width. Usually the vehicle is of traditional style, although most are of modern construction.

For the marathon a much more robust type of carriage is essential. Rules govern the weight and minimum width of the carriage. As the sport has evolved, so has the art of building marathon vehicles. Features that are fitted as standard today, such as disc brakes and delayed steering, were unheard of 30 years ago.

Types of harness

Most driving competitors use two sets of harness. For presentation and dressage in a major competition, the correct harness is black leather and brass or white metal, with a neck collar. The marathon harness is much more

robust and is generally used with a breast collar. Modern materials such as nylon webbing make it strong and easy to maintain. Stainless steel quick-release fittings are widely used and are most helpful in the case of an emergency. There are quite a few distinctive national styles of harness, and examples of these are exhibited by the old established studs of Hungary, Poland, and Slovakia. Irrespective of the style of harness, the judge will be looking to see if it fits correctly and that it is clean and well maintained.

Driving successes

The nations that have the longest traditions in driving are Germany, Britain, Hungary, the Netherlands, Switzerland, Poland, and the USA. Since the late 1980s European driving has produced many great horse-team World Champions. Notable among these have been Tjeerd Velstra and Ijsbrand Chardon from the Netherlands, Felix Brasseur from Belgium, Laszlo Juhasz from Hungary, Michael Freund from Germany, and Thomas Eriksson from Sweden as well as one of the most consistent international drivers, George Bowman of Britain, who has had unparalleled success since the 1970s. Other distinguished champions include Imri Aboni, Georgy Bardos, and Sandor Fulop of Hungary, Jan Eric Pahlsson of Sweden, and Auguste Dubay and Verner Ulrich of Switzerland. The horse pairs have also produced fine World Champions, such as Zoltan Lazar from Hungary and George Moser of Austria.

In the recently introduced international pony team class, Georgina Frith of Britain won the European Championships in 1995 and 1997 with her exceptional team of Welsh Ponies.

Emil Bernhard Jung had great influence competing with his Holstein team in the USA. He started an exceptionally strong team driving tradition, built on by Dierdre Pirie, Bill Long, Tucker Johnson, James Fairclough, and others.

The driving trials horse

Many breeds have outstanding records in horse driving trials. In Germany, Holsteins, Hanoverians, and Oldenburgs have been used most successfully, while Dutch and Swedish Warmbloods, Gelderlanders, and Friesian and Hungarian half-breds have also established formidable reputations in the sport.

The Russian Orlov Trotters have great speed and stamina. The Lipizzaner, the Kladruber, and the Polish Wielkopolski, which is closely related to the Trakehner, have featured prominently. Former World Champion team driver Felix Brasseur of Belgium drives a team of Lusitanos, which are

trials; pure- and part-bred Welsh Ponies have proved very successful. Hackney ponies have also demonstrated that they are more than capable of competing at the highest levels and are not just adornments for the show ring.

Key people

Driving is a team sport, even when it involves a single horse and driver. Horses, grooms, and drivers all work together to create a successful performance, and the event itself would be nothing without judges, technical experts, and even people with the wisdom to settle occasional disputes.

DRIVERS The successful driver (also called a 'whip') is intuitive, with quick reactions, and has good hands ensuring a sensitive contact with the horse's mouth. He or she must be calm and level headed, and have a burning desire to succeed. Only the driver is allowed to hold the reins and carry the whip, and should sit in a strong and upright position on the box seat.

GROOMS The number of grooms varies according to the turnout, but they should always be neatly and appropriately dressed. During the dressage and cone-driving phases of the event, the grooms must remain silent at all times and offer no assistance whatsoever to the driver. In the marathon, one of the grooms navigates and keeps time, and helps to balance the vehicle through the obstacles and on difficult terrain.

JUDGES AND OFFICIALS Driving trials rely on an army of unpaid helpers. International judges are appointed by the FEI, while each country has its own official panel of judges for national events. Judges must be totally conversant with the test they are assessing, and written observations should be helpful and concise. They must recognize lame horses that need to be withdrawn from the event and understand the rules, especially when judging the cone-driving competition, which frequently calls for quick decisions. It is important, too, that the ground referees and time-keepers are fully proficient in their duties.

The technical delegate's job is to approve the construction and layout of the dressage arenas, and the marathon and cone-driving courses. He or she is responsible for ensuring that the technical side of the event runs according to the rule book.

Should a dispute arise, a competitor may take a grievance to the appeal jury. The competitor may be asked to lodge a sum of money with the jury, which will be lost if the appeal is unsuccessful.

Above: Georgina Frith of Britain drives her team of home-bred Section B Welsh Ponies through a water hazard at Windsor.

Right: The groom uses her weight to balance the carriage during the tight turns of this obstacle for Lady Russell and her pair of Connemara Ponies.

also known for their tremendous strength and athleticism.

The future of the Cleveland Bay, one of the oldest established breeds of English horse, was secured by the British Royal Mews' breeding programme. Cleveland Bays were for many years driven by the Duke of Edinburgh. Welsh Cobs have also been driven successfully, and the renowned British driver George Bowman has driven a mixed team of Hackney horses and others, which he has given the generic name Cumberland Cobs.

In Britain, 16 breeds of light horses and ponies have taken part in driving

RELATED TOPICS

Welsh Pony and Cob	58
Cleveland Bay	74
Warmbloods	76
Lipizzaner	100
Orlov Trotter	125
Ceremonial and working horses	232

WESTERN RIDING

Western riding has appeal to many different nations, but it is distinctly American. For many, it is a traditional style of riding that provides a link back to the pioneering days of the Old West. For others, it is a high-energy sport pitting rider and horse against cow and clock. But regardless of whether riding just for pleasure or competitively, Western riding has its own roots, its own rules, and its own unique attitude.

Classical beginnings

Although the Western style of riding evolved with the American cowboy, it had more classical beginnings. During the 1600s, when the Spanish began to explore the New World, they took with them not only their fine Barb and Iberian horses, but also their classical riding methods, which were those used by the military. Over the years, the Spanish developed a saddle and way

of riding that gave them security and comfort during the long hours spent exploring on horseback. This early version of the Western saddle had a high cantle and pommel and long stirrups, similar to Australian stock saddles of today.

Western riding has its origins with the Spanish explorers, and this influence can still be seen in today's Mexican rodeos.

The Spaniards did not settle only in North America. They also spread through Central and South America. Soon the people of Mexico began adopting a similar style of horsemanship, and Mexican *vaqueros* became skilled in the ways of cattle roping and herding. American colonists who headed west in the 1800s, usually with draught horses pulling their covered wagons and Quarter Horses working under saddle, took up the new form of riding. They adapted the Spanish saddle to make it more workmanlike, adding a horn at the front from which to dally a rope that could be used in holding cattle.

Because of the nature of their work, whether hunting, ranching, or farming the new land, settlers had to spend long periods on horseback, and they had to be secure during the sudden sprints made by the cow horse – and so evolved the style known today as Western riding. The rider sits deeply in the saddle, with a tall posture and a long leg. The legs do not have significant contact with the horse's sides, but instead the horse responds to the barest of cues from the rider's heel. Rowelled spurs help to cue the horse without having to kick. Split reins (two reins unattached) are held together in one hand over the saddle horn, and the horse is guided through light rein pressure on the neck, called neckreining. Traditionally, the cowboy rode with one hand, usually the left, and neckreined the horse while holding the rope in his right.

Cowboy entertainment

Rodeos developed as a way for the cowboy to let off steam. Initially nothing more than an informal get together to test the mettle of a group of ranch hands, rodeos became more formalized over the years. Travelling Wild West shows, featuring such colourful characters as William F Cody ('Buffalo Bill'), were popular in the late 19th century, and teams went from town to town performing trick roping, trick riding, and shooting. From these events grew regular horse show competitions and rodeos.

Pleasure riding also took a turn from the many different forms of riding found in the rest of the country. The English saddle remained a staple of the

Above: Western-style shows are often competitive, and riders make a large investment in silver-laden tack and trendy show apparel.

Right: The Western saddle features a high cantle, a deep seat, a pommel with a horn, and wide leather fenders to which the stirrups are attached.

eastern states, while the flat 'Lane Fox' saddle used for saddleseat riding was typically found in the south. Western riding, however, became synonymous

with trail riding, and today it is difficult to go on an American trail ride in anything but a Western saddle.

Western shows and competitions today

Today's competitions strive to keep the frontier tradition alive. There are several different events in which a Western rider can take part, all of which exemplify the well-trained horse and the skill of the rider or handler. There are many classes, both halter (or in hand) and ridden.

HALTER CLASSES The purpose of showing a horse in hand is to present the animal's classic stock-horse conformation to the judge. The judge observes how impeccably the horse is groomed and presented, how well it

'sets up' (that is, adopts the showing stance of standing square with a level topline), how easily and willingly it responds to the handler's subtle cues on the lead rope, and how much its conformation and/or colour matches the standard for the breed.

SHOWMANSHIP This is another halter class, but this time it is the handler who is judged on how well he or she can manoeuvre and cue the horse to follow a particular in-hand pattern or routine. All competitors enter the arena at the same time and each one performs the pattern designated for that show, then returns to the line-up. The handler cues the horse invisibly, and must 'set it up' without touching it. The only communication used is subtle body language and a few instructions via the lead rope.

WESTERN PLEASURE This is a ridden class, in which the horse is judged on its way of going. The original aim for the class was to select a horse that would be a pleasure to ride on the trail. The horse is judged at the walk, jog, and lope (canter), and each of these is performed in a slow, easy, relaxed frame, with the horse exhibiting a level topline, and pushing with the hind legs well

Western saddles differ in many ways from other types, including the method of cinching – or girthing – them up.

The sport of reining, known for its spectacular sliding stops, is performed with very subtle cues from the rider.

underneath the body. This is one of the most competitive classes, and a world-class pleasure horse is generally born to the event, not made.

HORSEMANSHIP Also known as an equitation class, in which the rider is judged more than the horse. Each rider performs a pattern that demonstrates control and riding skill at the walk, jog, and lope, and during turns on the haunches, lead (or leg) changes, and reinbacks. Good scores from the judge depend on smooth transitions between each of the gaits and excellent use of the reins. After the individual displays, the whole class may be asked to ride around the arena.

TRAIL CLASS The trail class poses a unique set of challenges to the horse and rider, presenting them with obstacles that might be met on a regular trail ride.

A trail horse must be confident and trusting of its rider, and must be seasoned to approach any object that the course designer presents. The horse must not only deal successfully with every obstacle within the designated time, but must also approach them in the correct order and at the right gait. The horse may be expected to sidepass over poles laid parallel on the ground , back up through an 'L' pattern, go over an artificial bridge, manoeuvre through a gate opened and closed by the rider from the saddle, go up to a mail box, tackle a water obstacle, and jump a small cross-rail. The horse may also need to be used to 'ground tying' – when the rider simply drops the reins to the ground and the horse obediently stays put.

WESTERN RIDING Similar to the horsemanship class, the Western riding class also has the horse and rider performing a pattern, but this one involves the horse changing leads via a series of serpentines through cones. The horse is judged on the smoothness of its lead changes, its transitions from one gait to another, and its obedience.

A cutting horse in action in the arena. A good cutting horse will automatically use tactics to prevent a cow returning to its herd.

The horse moves out a little more freely than a Western pleasure horse and performs smooth flying lead changes.

Working horses

There are other events for performance or working horses – animals that reflect their ranching heritage, and move in a much freer, less collected manner than show horses.

REINING Horse and rider perform an athletic, rhythmic pattern including circles at the lope and gallop, multiple 360° spins at breakneck speed, flying lead changes, and rollbacks (180° pivots on the hocks). The most spectacular movement is the sliding stop, where the horse gallops and then shifts all its weight to its haunches, appearing as though it is sitting down and sliding to a halt, while the front legs keep moving to make the stop as long as possible. The movement is accentuated by the back shoes, called sliding plates, which allow the horse to exaggerate its stop.

To succeed in a reining contest, the horse must be extremely obedient and responsive, moving off with the subtlest of cues.

CUTTING A fast-growing sport that shows the skill and talent of a true cow horse. The rider has two and a half minutes in which to separate a cow from the rest of the herd and keep it in the middle of the arena. (The cattle in these events are usually yearling heifers or steers; adult cattle are rarely used.) The rider usually selects the particular cow to be worked, then the horse takes over completely, cutting out the designated cow and manoeuvering so as to prevent it returning to the herd.

Good cutting horses are amazing to watch, with fluid, cat-like action in their wiry bodies. They have been known to flatten their ears, bare their teeth, and snap at cows to intimidate them, and some have actually dropped to their knees in front of the cow to get at eye level and mirror its next move.

WORKING COW HORSE There are many phases to this event, which is designed to demonstrate the horse's willingness, responsiveness, and athleticism, as well as its herding ability. The horse performs a reining pattern first, then the horse and rider must work a cow in a variety of ways.

The Western horse

The Quarter Horse and the Appaloosa, as well as the Paint Horse and the Palomino, are popular for Western riding, and most shows are put on by their breed associations. These breeds have both the conformation and the attitude for the events.

A good Western horse is typically on the small side, standing about 157cm (15.2 hands) high, and is muscular and somewhat stocky. The horse generally has an unflappable nature, and if startled merely holds its ground. Its gaits are slower than those of hot-blooded horses (the Thoroughbreds and Arabians), and are easy to sit on. Western horses are responsive to light leg and rein aids, being 'broke to the bridle', carrying their heads low and in an unwavering fashion. Western horses tend to be very tolerant by nature, and all are willing workers.

Each of the specialized events requires a different type of horse, to meet the challenges of the sport. The reining horse is close coupled, with a relatively short, muscular neck, and flexible joints for speed and agility. The cutting horse is small, wiry, and muscular, but not stocky. It must be

able to move at a moment's notice, and out-think the cow. The Western pleasure horse is slender yet muscular, with a thin neck and small head, and a naturally level topline. The halter horse has ample muscling and a stocky build, with a 'bulldog' jowly face, short neck, straight legs, and unblemished coat. A horse that competes in the working cow horse event has a more all-round build, exemplifying the versatility needed for the sport.

Key people

As with any horse show, the competitors and the judges are the focus of a Western riding event, but the day depends on the efforts of a number of diligent workers.

SHOW RIDER Everything worn by the show rider is neat and fitted, to accentuate the silhouette in the saddle. Although fashions change, there is one enduring rule: nothing the rider wears should detract from the performance. The show rider's outfit consists of jeans and shirt (women can also wear a vest or waistcoat or fitted jacket), leather or artificial suede chaps, and a beaver felt hat (or a woven straw hat in summer). Men wear Western scarves tied at the

Right: Most Western performance events have their roots in real-life ranching and demand true co-operation between horse and rider.

Below: The Palomino is one of the most popular coat patterns in Western riding, and is to be seen both on working ranches and in the show arena.

throat, while women can choose from a range of different neckwear. Boots are not the pointed-toe cowboy boots that are most associated with Western wear, but fringed, lace-up 'ropers' styled like a paddock boot.

THE JUDGE He or she must observe the whole class and individual contestants and, using the rules set by the show's governing organization, select the competitor who most closely meets the ideal for that event.

RELATED TOPICS

Appaloosa	104
Quarter Horse	112
Palomino	134
Rodeo	208
A day at the rodeo	210
Showing	246

THE STEWARDS It is the steward's job to make sure that the horses are wearing the appropriate tack for the class, and to check that they are not being prepared with anything that is against the rules (for example, improper training equipment, or the wrong bit). The steward also ensures that obstacles such as cones for riding horsemanship patterns are set up correctly.

TRAIL COURSE DESIGNER Following the rules laid down by the show's governing organization, the trail course designer sets up a sequence of obstacles such as bridges, mail boxes, water crossings, and jumps – all designed to test the horses' obedience and training.

RING CREW Help set up the trail courses or prepare the arena for each event.

GATE PERSONNEL Ensure that each contestant entering the arena is in the right class.

RANCH VACATIONS

Staying as a guest at a working ranch offers the opportunity to experience the full variety of Western riding. Besides taking part in the day-to-day life of the ranch, guests may get involved in driving cattle, have lessons in various activities such as cutting, reining, or roping, and join organized trail rides through often spectacular countryside. The majority of horses used are Quarter Horses. Most ranches have animals of varying ability, so that even the most inexperienced rider can feel comfortable in the saddle.

RODEO

An offshoot of Western riding, rodeo is derived from traditional ranching skills. The tasks that were performed in order to break saddle horses, as well as rope, brand, and herd cattle have developed into a phenomenal international entertainment. There are rodeos all over the world, but none attracts support and funding as the American rodeos do. The Professional Rodeo Cowboys of America (PRCA) sanctions hundreds of events annually, and these are qualifiers that lead up to the December finals in Las Vegas, Nevada.

The most coveted title in professional rodeo is the PRCA World Champion All-Around Cowboy. He or she who earns the most prize money in a year while competing in at least two events, earning a minimum of $2000 in each, wins the crown. The Texan Ty Murray won the 1998 title (his ninth time), with earnings of $264,673 for that year.

The rodeo today

There are two types of contest in rodeo today: roughstock riding and timed events. Those in which horses play a major part include:

SADDLE BRONC RIDING This event has its origins in the Old West, where ranch hands would often compete among themselves to see who could display the best style while riding wild horses.

The ride begins in the chute (a small, tall-sided holding pen) with the rider's feet over the horse's shoulder to give it the advantage. When the chute gate is opened, the horse comes out bucking, an action enhanced by a strap buckled tightly around its flanks. The rider holds on with one hand to a rope rein attached to the horse's halter; he or she is judged on the degree of control throughout the ride, the length of the spurring stroke, and how hard the horse bucks. The rider must stay on for eight seconds, and will be disqualified for touching the horse, themselves, or the tack with their free hand, or for losing a stirrup, dropping the rein, or failing to have their feet in the correct position when coming out of the chute.

The late Casey Tibbs of South Dakota is perhaps the best-known saddle bronc rider. Between 1949 and 1959, he won six saddle bronc riding titles, as well as two all-around titles and a bareback riding championship.

BAREBACK RIDING The cowboy has only a surcingle-like strap, called 'rigging', to hold on to during the ride. As with the saddle bronc riding, the horse wears a flank strap, and comes out of the chute bucking, and the cowboy must stay on for eight seconds. Scoring is based on the horse's bucking performance, and the rider's spurring technique and control. Contestants are disqualified if their free hand touches their body, their equipment, or their horse.

In 1995, Marvin Garrett won $156,733 while qualifying for the year-end finals, and has won the title of World Champion Bareback Rider four times.

STEER ROPING This event also has its origins on the American ranch, where it was used to get cattle off their feet for branding or veterinary attention.

In the saddle bronc riding event, the horse comes out of the chute bucking, and the cowboy is judged on degree of control throughout the ride.

The steer must be roped around its horns, which are wrapped for protection, then the cowboy rides to the left, pulling the animal to the ground. The horse keeps the rope taut, while the rider dismounts and runs to tie three of the steer's legs. The steer must remain tied for six seconds after the tie is complete.

TEAM ROPING Rodeo's only true team event, involving two horses and riders. The 'header' races into the arena on horseback, chases a running steer and ropes it around the horns (which are wrapped for protection) or neck, or around the head and one horn. Then the header must turn the steer to the left, giving the second contestant, the 'heeler', a chance to rope its hind feet. The run is completed when the steer is secured and pulled off his feet. One of rodeo's fastest events, this is usually accomplished in five seconds or less.

BARREL RACING Although many barrel racing events are also held at gymkhanas, the most prestigious take place at sanctioned rodeos. Most barrel racers are women, and it is a sport that requires skill and guts.

The rider enters the arena at full gallop, triggering an electronic timer. He or she must then ride a cloverleaf pattern around three barrels, then sprint back out of the arena, tripping the timer and stopping the clock.

There is no penalty for touching or moving a barrel, but knocking one over incurs a five-second penalty. Times are compared in hundredths of seconds, so overturning a barrel usually means the rider is out of the competition.

One of the most famous barrel racing horses is Scamper, a bay Quarter Horse owned and ridden by Charmayne James. Together they won 10 consecutive World Championships between 1984 and 1993.

The rodeo horse

Quarter Horses are the most popular breed for rodeo, although saddle broncs and bareback broncs are generally of any breed that has a good buck in it – some saddle broncs are even Thoroughbreds. Contrary to what many people believe, these bucking horses are not wild Mustangs.

Ethical treatment of animals

With its abundant use of livestock in various manners, rodeo is not without its critics, who allege that animals are mistreated in any number of ways, from the equipment used on them to their living conditions, as well as in what happens to them when they are no longer useful as 'roughstock'.

There are small, unsanctioned rodeos run without any regulations. However, the PRCA has drawn up more than 60 rules designed to protect the animals at its events and ensure that they are treated humanely. These govern all aspects of animal welfare, including their care and treatment, conditions of travel, and how they are used in competitions. Vets are required to be present at all PRCA events.

Some of the contentious issues relating to animal welfare in the rodeo world include:

THE FLANK STRAP This is a fleece-lined strip of leather, with a quick-release buckle, tightened behind the horse's ribcage in the flank area to enhance bucking action. The rules specify that no sharp or cutting object may be placed under the strap.

Those in favour of this equipment argue that, because the horses used in rodeos are not wild animals, they may not instinctively buck unless they have the tight strap in place.

Opponents of the flank strap say that it is often tightened around the horse's genitals, and has been known to be pulled so tight that it damages the skin. They also argue that the horse stops bucking once the strap is released, which must mean it causes the animal intense irritation.

SPURS Dull spurs are used in three riding events and, according to guidelines issued by the PRCA, must have blunt rowels about 3mm (⅛in) thick, so that they cannot cut the animals. A rider who uses any other type of spur is disqualified.

Those who support the use of spurs in rodeo claim that the hide of a horse is much thicker than human skin, and so resists cutting or bruising, and that

RELATED TOPICS
Quarter Horse   112
Western riding   202
A day at the rodeo   210

On the final whistle, the pick-up men must move in immediately, riding alongside the roughstock to help the rider get to safety.

the spurs used at PRCA rodeos usually only ruffle the animal's hair.

Opponents of excessive spurring note that while horses do have thicker skin than humans, they also have different nerve endings within it, and are sensitive enough that they can feel the weight of a fly on their sides.

ELECTRIC PRODS Also called 'hot shots', these deliver a small electric shock, but cannot burn the animal. They are generally used to herd animals into holding pens and not actually used while the livestock is in the chute, but allegations exist of their misuse at unsanctioned events. However, the PRCA is taking steps to monitor their use in all their sanctioned rodeos.

Key people

Local, unsanctioned rodeos can be run with a body of volunteers and a handful of staff, but for major PRCA rodeos, hundreds of people work behind the scenes to put together an event.

RODEO COMMISSIONER Keeps track of the budget and, with the larger rodeos, uses a board of directors to help supervise the staff running the event.

RODEO ANNOUNCER He or she announces the classes, the competitors, and their scores; they must have a good voice

and keep up the energy of the event. Announcers usually do their homework well, so as to provide the most up to date information on the competitors.

OFFICIALS When a ruling is to be made, the judges' word is final. They ensure that each event's rules are enforced (for instance, that a bareback rider is disqualified for touching the horse with their free hand, that a steer stays roped for the official six seconds).

STOCK CONTRACTOR A vital component of any rodeo, the stock contractor provides the cattle, and the bareback and saddle broncs for the event.

LIVESTOCK SUPERINTENDENTS AND CHUTE BOSS Their task is to oversee the rodeo stock, caring for the animals and making sure that they are ready to compete at the appropriate time.

PICK-UP MEN These cowboys work in the arena in events such as bareback or saddle bronc riding. After the whistle is blown to signify the end of the ride, two pick-up men ride alongside the roughstock to help the cowboy to get safely away from the bucking horse.

A day at the rodeo

Cattle bray in the stock pens as the brass band strikes up 'The Star Spangled Banner'. It's Sunday, the final performance of the Pikes Peak Rodeo in Colorado Springs, Colorado, USA. Months of preparation go into this five-day event, which attracts the top competitors from throughout the 10,000-member Professional Rodeo Cowboys Association, which sanctions more than 700 annual rodeo competitions. As more than 6000 spectators look on, hundreds of mounted cowboys and barrel racers parade through the arena in the grand entry. When the pageantry ends, a bareback bronc rider tries to settle the nervous bronc below him. Ready, he nods his head, the gate swings open, and the horse breaks from the chutes. A cheer erupts from the grandstands when the cowboy completes an eight-second ride. The rodeo has begun.

▲ 2 Rain or shine, the rodeo always goes on. A barrel racer and her magnificent Quarter Horse take a deep turn around the first of three barrels, hoping to squeeze out a fast time in this sprint race against the clock. Electronic timing devices are necessary in this event as it is often decided by hundredths of a second.

▼ 3 Next comes team roping. Two horses and riders endeavour to snare a steer using ropes. First, the 'header' catches the horns, then turns off to allow his teammate, the 'heeler', to swoop in and catch the steer's hind legs. Failure to rope both hind legs results in a penalty of five seconds. Time stops when both ropers turn and face one another, with the captured steer stretched between them.

▲ 1 A calf roper, loop at the ready, gives chase. A quick toss of the loop, and the calf roper will slide to the ground, sprinting down the taut rope stretched from saddle to calf. In a blur, he will lift the calf, drop it to its side, and truss three legs, then throw his arms in the air to stop the official's watch. A winning run takes less than nine seconds.

▼ 4 This is bronc riding. This bareback rider demonstrates excellent form, with his hand securely grasping the suitcase handle of the rawhide bareback rigging. Laid back, a bareback rider must have great strength, balance, and excellent timing to weather eight seconds on a bucking horse. In saddle bronc riding, the rider is aided by a modified western saddle and a thick braided rein.

► 5 Specialty act Jerry Diaz, a Mexican-American Charro raised in San Antonio, Texas, and his Quarter Horse Grano de Oro perform at the Pikes Peak. Fancy roping and horsemanship are the hallmarks of the charro. Most rodeos hire contract acts to entertain the audiences during intermissions. A top performer like Diaz is as much a part of the rodeo as the contestants themselves.

◄6 Three-time world champion bull rider Richard 'Tuff' Hedeman signs autographs after capturing a win in his event. Typically, a championship contender like Hedeman will compete at 100 rodeos a year; all but a handful of rodeo contestants specialize in a single event. Each pays his or her own expenses and entry fees, and is paid only the prize money if they win. Hedeman is one of about 20 cowboys to surpass $1 million dollars in career earnings.

ENDURANCE

In the long collaboration between horse and human, there has developed a partnership of mutual support and understanding. The horse has lent strength, speed, and stamina, while the human has brought the power to reason and the ability to provide for the horse's physical needs. In these essential aspects of the horse/human alliance lie the seeds of modern endurance riding.

Many hundreds of rides take place each year, through some of the world's most demanding countryside. Each one is a breathtaking challenge – overcome by a unique partnership.

Military origins

Modern endurance riding developed from horse trials conducted by European and American cavalry units, designed to find the best horses to carry weight at speed over long distances. The science of equine exercise physiology had yet to be invented, and the trials sometimes

had tragic results. However, in the 1920s the Arab Horse Society in Britain demonstrated the superiority of the breed for producing cavalry horses. Each horse carried 83kg (183lb) and covered nearly 500km (300 miles) in five days. In 1936 in the USA the Vermont 160km (100 mile) ride was inaugurated. It was ridden to a standard speed and also developed from the search for cavalry mounts.

Silver buckles

It was in 1955 in the USA that modern endurance riding took root with the first Tevis Cup. This gruelling test through the Sierra Nevadas of northern California was named after Lloyd Tevis, a former president of Wells Fargo, the express company founded to serve the American West in the 1850s. Today, anyone completing the ride receives a silver buckle depicting a horse and rider of the Pony Express, the famous mail delivery service of the time.

The ride was the brainchild of Wendell T Robie who, with a group of friends, wanted to prove that modern horses were as tough as those of the pioneer days. They rode the old emigrant and mining trails from Squaw Valley to Auburn, 160km (100 miles) of high, forested, sometimes snow-capped mountains and deep, blisteringly hot canyons. Overall, the trail gains more than 5000m (17,000ft) in altitude and descends over 6600m (22,000ft).

Today, to a select band of riders, the Tevis forms part of the 'four buckle challenge', where the aim is to complete the world's three major 160km (100 mile) rides, the Tevis in the USA, the Tom Quilty Gold Cup in Australia, and the Florac ride in France, a world championship event. No one has yet achieved this.

The Quilty began in 1966, originally in the Blue Mountains of New South Wales, but it now moves from state to state each year. The first ride was won by an Arabian stallion, Shalawi, ridden bareback by Gabriel Stecher.

The endurance rider has the opportunity to travel through stunning countryside, such as that found on the Florac ride in southern France.

Florac, in the Lozère region of southern France, is the toughest of several challenging French rides. To date, France has proved the most successful nation in terms of international medals won in the sport, followed by the USA and Britain.

The Summer Solstice is the oldest established British 160km (100 mile) ride. Run by the Endurance Horse and Pony Society, it changes its location roughly every three years.

Coming right up to date, in a new and exciting move, the countries of the Arabian Gulf have developed an interest in the sport: 1997 saw the first endurance World Cup successfully run in Qatar, and in 1998 the World Championships took place in the United Arab Emirates (UAE).

Endurance riding today

Officially, an endurance ride is a competition to test the speed and stamina of the horse and the horsemanship of the rider. At a more fundamental level it is the partnership of horse and rider, over natural, often wild, terrain and against all that the elements can throw, with the aim of finishing with a sound horse in good condition. Achieving all this at winning speed is the ultimate added factor.

International endurance riding is governed by the International Equestrian Federation (FEI), working through national federations to apply a consistent standard to major competitions. In 1998, the sport was upgraded and given its own standing committee, alongside the other major equestrian disciplines. Official international championships have been run since 1984. The Endurance and Long Distance Riding International Conference (ELDRIC) is an independent body that, in tandem with the FEI, provides an international forum for debate on the sport. This unique organization includes countries such as Brazil, San Marino, and Slovakia, as well as major European nations. It runs its own international trophy competitions, under FEI rules, co-operates with the FEI endurance committee, and provides a useful link between the FEI, individual riders, and endurance riding organizations. In the USA the American Endurance Rides Conference has its own rules and ride sanctioning system and is now working with the FEI.

A young and developing sport is bound to experience growing pains. In many countries this has resulted in more than one organization trying to promote their own version. Britain, for example, has the internationally recognized British Endurance Riding Association, but rides are also run by the Endurance Horse and Pony Society and the Scottish Endurance Riding Club. Fortunately, co-operation among these bodies is increasing, and there is now little divergence of rules.

Types of ride

Rides fall into two basic categories. Lower distance rides, including qualifiers and competitive trail rides of between 30 and 80km (20–50 miles), often with fixed upper and lower speed limits, are primarily designed to introduce novice horses and riders to the sport. In some countries placings are given for these types of ride, based on a combination of speed and the horse's recovery rate, which is judged

All kinds of terrain may be encountered in the course of an endurance ride: at the waterfront the sand will be at its most firm and consistent.

at the veterinary inspections during and after the ride. In other countries, no placings are given, but awards are made to horses that achieve the required standard.

Endurance rides of 80km (50 miles) and over, up to the classic championship distance of 160km (100 miles) in one day, represent the senior level of the sport and are judged on a combination of first past the winning post and the veterinary inspection. Any horse that fails veterinary judging is automatically eliminated from the competition, even after the finish.

An anomaly that seems peculiar to Britain is the longer distance, set speed ride, of which the Golden Horseshoe, held on Exmoor, is a typical example. Riders receive gold, silver, or bronze

Tough hill work can be very tiring, so many riders dismount and walk alongside their horses to give them a break.

awards for completing the 160km (100 miles) over two days at a designated speed and to a veterinary standard, but there are no placings, so there is no actual winner.

Until recently, in keeping with the spirit of a truly amateur sport, prize money has been prohibited, especially in Britain and the USA. However, it is increasingly found in major European events and will inevitably be a feature of future international competition, especially in view of the injection of funding as a result of the growing interest of the Arab countries.

This new development is bringing fresh life to the sport in various ways. Major world events, attracting more public interest and media coverage than ever before, have boosted hopes that eventually endurance may become an Olympic sport. Of more immediate effect, breeders are turning their attention to producing horses

specifically for endurance, rather than relying on rejects from showing and racing, and the advent of specialized training yards is clearly on the horizon. In the past, endurance has been very much a sport for the individual, one-horse owner/rider.

Despite these advances, the overriding principle of the sport remains that the welfare of the horse is paramount. Endurance is the only equestrian sport where the horse's health, condition, and fitness are judged throughout the competition and as an integral part of it. The stringent requirements of the veterinary inspections ensure that, despite the tough demands on both horse and rider at the top level, endurance is an extremely safe sport for the horse.

The endurance horse
Endurance is strongly associated with the Arabian horse and the breed does have excellent natural qualities of resilience, stamina, weight-carrying ability, and courage. However, other breeds have also been successful. For example Nelson II, who won the 1997 European Championships for France and, after being sold to the UAE, the 1998 World Championships dress rehearsal ride, was originally acquired from a trekking stable and his breeding is unknown.

The ideal horse for endurance is 152–63cm (15–16 hands), with good, athletic conformation, and lean, rather than chunky, muscles, which dissipate heat more easily. Excellent feet and an enthusiastic, outgoing temperament, coupled with the ability to 'switch off' when not working, are essential.

Key people
As an amateur sport, endurance until recently involved only the horse, rider, and a back-up crew of family or friends

RULES

An endurance ride is a competition of 80km (50 miles) or more, to be completed within a specified maximum time. The winner is the first horse that passes the finishing post provided that it also passes the veterinary inspections as 'fit to continue'.

Lower distance and set speed competitions have a variety of rules depending on the country in which they are run and the organizing society.

RELATED TOPICS
Thoroughbred	70
Arabian	128
Eventing	156
A vet check at an endurance ride	216

VETERINARY STANDARDS

Veterinary inspections take place before the start of the ride, at set points during it, and within 30 minutes of the horse passing the finishing post.

Any horse exhibiting lameness will be eliminated from the competition. Elimination also results if the horse has injuries likely to be made worse by continued participation; and if the horse's heart rate fails to recover to an acceptable level fixed for the ride, which is usually 64 beats per minute maximum.

on the participants' side. With the growing interest of Middle Eastern countries, the sport is beginning to see professional trainers and riders, with employed grooms acting as crew.

On the organizational side, a ground jury or team of stewards to implement the rules is required, depending on the level of ride, together with numerous helpers such as time-keepers, vetgate managers, and checkpoint stewards. Of primary importance are the veterinary judges and, in major events, the vets themselves.

THE RIDER Endurance riders have always believed that to be successful you must train your own horse, developing a partnership along the way. On the toughest rides, such as the Tevis Cup, where access for crews is limited, horse and rider are alone together on the trail for many miles at a time. The horse must be trained to maximum fitness if it is to cope with the task without injury or strain.

The rider must depend on excellent horsemanship, both in equitation and in the care of the horse along the route, to have any hope of success. Riders must know when they should slow down and when it is safe to increase their speed. They must ride efficiently, causing the least disturbance to their horse and allowing it to conserve energy as much as possible. They must be aware when the horse is tiring or overheating and needs water or even a rest and some food, when to give electrolytes, and whether the horse is moving on freely or developing some problem of action. The rider must be equipped to cope in all these situations.

When the horse is fit and strong, the rider must know how to ride the race to win and use tactics to outperform the opposition.

THE TRAINER The professional who is responsible for training riders as well as horses is a new and developing phenomenon. The aim of training is the same for both the professional and the traditional owner/rider – to produce the horse at the peak of readiness for a major competition. Bringing an endurance horse to 160km (100 mile) level takes at least three years of steady, progressive work to build up the animal's strength and durability, as well as its mental capacity to cope with the rigours of the sport. In addition to fitness training, schooling for suppleness, balance, and muscular strength is necessary, as is varied work to prevent boredom.

THE CREW The principal task of the crew – variously termed pit-crew, back-up, strapper, or *suiveur* (follower) in different countries – is to prepare the horse for the veterinary inspections. This involves cooling the horse down, checking for injuries, making sure its shoes are in good order, monitoring its heart rate, and generally ensuring that it is presented in good condition. Once

A dedicated back-up team is an essential part of the competition. Their day is long and strenuous as they follow their charges throughout the ride.

the horse passes the inspection, the crew takes care of it during the 'hold' or rest period, and prepares it for the next stage of the ride.

The crew's secondary task is to water the horse at meeting points during the ride, and to keep track of the progress of both the rider and the opposition. Being part of a back-up crew is a busy, strenuous, but fascinating task.

THE VETERINARY JUDGE The judgement of vets is integral to the sport. The ultimate welfare of the horse rests on their expertise and, fortunately, through many years of experience and research, the controls used at vet checks now ensure that very few horses suffer any serious problems in what can be a high risk sport. At inspections throughout the ride, set criteria are used to decide if a horse should be eliminated or passed 'fit to continue'. An overall clinical inspection confirms the decision.

A vet check at an endurance ride

The welfare of the horse is an integral part of an endurance ride and veterinary checks before, during, and after a competition ensure that horses are under constant supervision. They will be taken out of the race if they seem to be at risk of exhaustion or are suffering from an injury. The veterinary surgeons act as judges and there is no appeal against their decision.

The vetgate is laid out with a preparation area, followed by numbered vet stations and trotting lanes, and then an exit through to the hold area, where horses rest before continuing onto the next stage of the ride.

The vet check can be a nail-biting time for the competitor, while they wait to see if their horse can continue onto the next stage. In major rides, minutes gained or lost in the vet check can mean the difference between winning and losing the race.

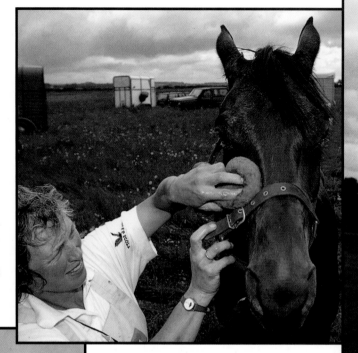

▲ **1** The clock keeps running while a rider and crew prepares their horse for the vet check, so cooling their horse down quickly is important.

◄ **2** The vet takes the horse's pulse first, to check if it has recovered adequately from its exertion.

▼ **4** The vet takes a fold of the horse's skin between his finger and thumb. Once he releases his hold, the time until the skin returns to normal is counted. A count of more than three seconds indicates that the horse is becoming dehydrated.

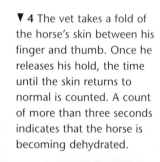

▲ **3** The horse is then trotted away to at least 30m (100ft) and back to check there are no signs of lameness. One minute from the start of the trot, the pulse is again taken. If the horse's pulse is still elevated it indicates that the horse is tiring.

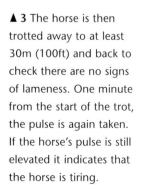

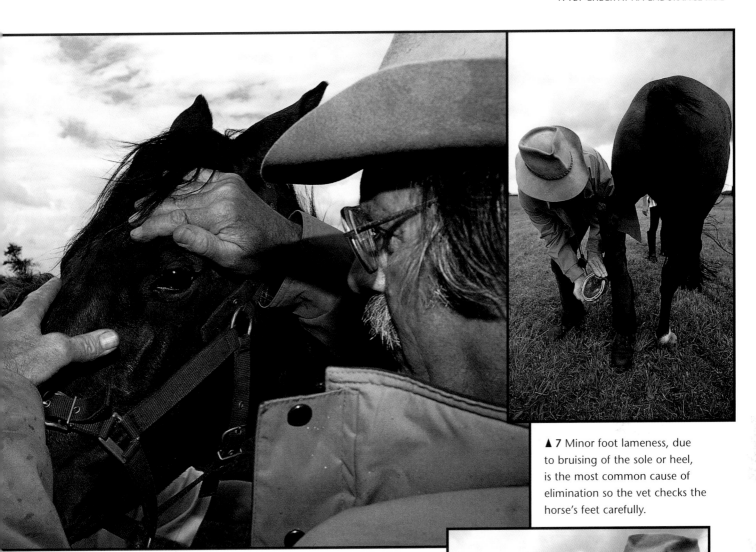

▲ **7** Minor foot lameness, due to bruising of the sole or heel, is the most common cause of elimination so the vet checks the horse's feet carefully.

▲ **5** Eyes also show signs of dehydration so the vet checks that the mucous membranes are not getting red and congested.

▼ **6** If the vet notices that the horse's lips or gums have been bruised by the bit he can eliminate the horse from the ride.

▲ **8** Hours of wearing the saddle make the horse's back a particularly vulnerable area, so it has to be checked for sores, galls, or pain on touch.

◄ **9** At the end of the check the horse is given a chance to relax and eat and drink before the next stage of the ride.

VAULTING

Vaulting – gymnastics on a cantering horse – was originally devised to improve the skills of cavalry riders and has gradually developed to be an international sport in its own right. Today it is a spectacular amalgamation of equine strength, balance, and endurance, as well as of gymnastic performance and artistic choreography.

Ancient beginnings

The art of vaulting can be traced back to the early attempts at taming the horse. Drawings from the Bronze Age found in southern Scandinavia illustrate such movements, as do ancient wall paintings in Africa and Greece. Over 2000 years ago the Greek historian Xenophon described vaulting in his *Art of Horsemanship*, and competitions were included in the big festivals held in and around the Parthenon in Athens in the 5th century.

The current method of vaulting – with the horse cantering in a circle on a lunge rein – can be traced back to the Romans, although other kinds of exercises on moving horses were practised in eastern Europe and Asia. In western Europe, vaulting was used for training cavalry officers from the 16th century onwards. In the 18th century many riding masters in Europe found themselves out of work and turned to trick riding as a means of earning money, using horses galloping in a straight line. This form of vaulting can still be seen in France, eastern Europe, and the USA.

Today's vaulting exercises are directly derived from the skills required of the cavalry in battle, when agility on a moving horse was of paramount importance. The sport was represented by soldiers at the Olympic Games between 1896 and 1920 under the title of 'Artistic Riding'. When the horse lost its importance for the military, interest in vaulting also waned; for a long time it was practised mainly as a pastime for children, by trick riders in American rodeos, and by circus gymnasts.

Vaulting today

The modern discipline of vaulting is enjoyed in at least 30 countries, mainly by teenagers, both competitively and recreationally. The sport offers fun and fitness, while promoting the best qualities in young people, working in a group with the horse at its centre. Most countries hold regional and national competitions, with rules based on German ones laid down in 1958.

Keen vaulters aspire to international level, with rules introduced by the International Equestrian Federation (FEI) in 1983. European and World Championships take place in alternate years. Vaulting is included in the World Equestrian Games, held every four years, and was a demonstration sport at the Los Angeles Olympics in 1984.

Today international vaulting includes three disciplines: team classes with teams of eight vaulters (of both sexes) plus one reserve member; individual classes (both male and female); and *pas de deux* (mixed pairs). Team vaulters must be 18 years and under, but there is no age limit for individuals.

Each class has two sections, consisting of compulsory exercises and a freestyle programme. Both are performed on a cantering horse on the lunge, moving counter-clockwise in a circle of at least 15m (50ft) diameter.

The 'barrel' or 'wooden' horse, often constructed from empty oil drums, is used for training, to help vaulters perfect their technique.

FREESTYLE PROGRAMME. Vaulters perform an artistic routine to music; this must last one minute for individuals; two minutes for the *pas de deux*; and five minutes for teams.

At international level there are two rounds of competition, held on consecutive days. Each of five judges awards marks that take into account the technical skills of the vaulters and the harmony between vaulters and horse. The degree of difficulty, the composition, and the performance of the freestyle exercises may earn extra marks. The horse is judged on the quality of the canter, the cadence, submission, and balance when working on a consistent circle.

The vaulting horse

The horse is the most important member of the team and it must provide a calm and stable base for every performance. The team vaulting

TOP VAULTING NATIONS	
Country	**Main venue**
Germany	Aachen/Rhede
Switzerland	Berne
USA	Saratoga
Sweden	Malmo
Austria	Ebreichsdorf
France	Saumur
Slovakia	Sala/Nitra

COMPULSORY EXERCISES Individual vaulters perform eight compulsory exercises: Mount, followed by Basic Seat, Flare, Mill, Ground Jump, Scissors, Stand, and Flank. For teams, the sequence is split into two, each part starting with Mount followed by a set of three exercises (the Ground Jump is omitted). A team must complete all exercises within eight minutes, but there is no time limit for individuals.

RULES

Countries participating in competitive vaulting all use rules based on the those laid down by the FEI, although these may be modified, especially in the novice grades, to suit local circumstances. The rules govern such matters as contestants' eligibility for entry, time limits, scoring, and procedures following falls. Many novice competitions include work on both left and right rein, and some countries include work in walk and trot as well as canter. France also has rules for vaulting *en ligne*.

horse has to be an exceptional animal, since at any one time it must carry up to three vaulters, who may be balanced high above the horse's centre of gravity. The horse must, therefore, have incredible strength, good balance, and fitness to remain in a steady canter for eight minutes in the compulsory section followed by five minutes in the freestyle section.

Many types and breeds of horse are used. They have to be seven-years-old (for competition) and have received a basic training to 'medium' (bronze) level dressage. They are usually about 163–73cm (16–17 hands), and all must possess a marvellous temperament.

Key people

Vaulting requires a team for competition, consisting of the trainer, the lunger, and the athletes themselves.

THE VAULTERS The athletes may be of various shapes and sizes, to suit the different kinds of exercise. They must all be thoroughly dependable, since every member of the team has to be able to rely completely on the others.

THE LUNGER The person on the end of the lunge rein is a crucial member of the team. He or she trains and controls the horse, and their relationship is the foundation of every performance.

THE TRAINER He or she co-ordinates the team and works closely with the lunger. In some cases one person may take on both roles, but often it is more efficient to share the tasks. Then the trainer can watch from outside the circle and enlist the help of physiotherapists and gymnasts where necessary. The trainer also supervises work on the barrel horse, correcting technique and developing the choreography.

THE JUDGES There are at least three but more usually five judges at an international championship, positioned at different points around the arena to ensure each performance is viewed from all angles. They have often been international vaulters or coaches themselves, and undergo similar training to dressage judges.

The German vaulting team performs at the World Equestrian Games held in 1998.

RELATED TOPICS	
Norwegian Fjord	62
Pony Club	226
Ceremonial and working horses	232

POLO

Imagine two Thoroughbreds thundering towards each other at a combined speed of 95–130kmph (60–80mph), and passing with only inches to spare. This happens time and time again in polo – which is one of the fastest games ever invented, and probably the most thrilling.

Polo consists of two teams, each of four mounted players, who attempt on a field not more than 275m x 183m (300 x 200yd) to strike a ball through the opponents' goal. Every match is divided into between four and eight periods known as 'chukkas' or 'chukkers', each of which is between seven and seven and a half minutes long. Whichever team ends with most goals on the scoreboard is the winner.

Eastern origins

Polo is an ancient sport that originated over 2000 years ago in Persia. Matches were often played as entertainment for the king, and the cavalry were ordered to play as a means of improving their horsemanship and fighting qualities.

From Persia, polo spread across to China, Tibet, and eventually to India.

The player in blue, though hard ridden by his opposite number in white, executes a near-side backhander – the most difficult shot in polo.

British army officers were introduced to the game while serving on India's north-west frontier, and they brought it back with them to England, where the first match took place in 1869. The Hurlingham Polo Association, founded in 1873, drew up rules for the game, and before long it was being played throughout Europe, the Americas, and in Australasia. However, it was probably in India that the game was played most. Here, the wealth of the maharajahs, the lightning-fast grounds, and the ready availability of British and Indian cavalry officers and their horses, all added lustre to the sport.

World War II brought polo to a halt throughout Europe for seven years, but gradually the game has been restored to its former eminence. In North and South America it continued to thrive, dominated by Argentina, which since 1936 has consistently triumphed in the Cup of the Americas at the expense of the USA; the USA in turn has successfully resisted the challenge of Mexico in the General Manuel Avila Camacho Cup, first played for in 1941.

The game today

Polo today is played on every continent and in more than 60 different countries. This figure is still on the increase. In

The player taps round in a clockwise semi-circle. The pony is balanced and watchful, and clearly enjoying the game.

each country players are handicapped according to ability in line with international standards, each being awarded a rating between zero (in some countries minus two) and an optimum of ten; the four individual ratings are added together to give a handicap rating for the team. In most matches the side with the lower handicap receives a starting advantage in goals of the difference in handicap. Tournaments are arranged to accommodate teams of similar handicaps: in Britain, for instance, 'low goal' tournaments are for teams totalling between 4 and 8 goals; 'intermediate' between 9 and 12, 'medium' 12–15, and 'high' 17–22.

The best polo in the world is played in Argentina, where the national finals can be contested by two teams each containing four 10-goal players. The Argentinean team would almost certainly defeat the best side that the rest of the world could put together. In order to widen the base of international competition, the International Polo Federation (FIP) was founded in 1983, on Argentina's initiative. Countries

RULES

In every country the rules of the game were originally based on those of England's Hurlingham Polo Association. Although some variations have inevitably crept in, great efforts are currently being made to standardize them once again throughout the world.

The main consideration is for the safety of players and ponies. 'Riding off' is permitted, that is, bumping an opponent's pony at angles of up to about 40°, but always with the strict proviso that the player who is riding most closely to the line of the ball has the right of way. Another player crossing the line, in such a way that may cause a collision, is committing a foul.

Penalties consist mainly of free hits from a selection of spots on the field, so that the severity of the penalty relates directly to the seriousness of the foul committed. In the event of players arguing with or abusing the umpire, the severity of the penalty can be increased.

Ends are changed only when a goal is scored, not at the start of each chukka.

Ponies await their turn to play on the frozen lake at St Moritz. Special shoeing ensures that there are very few falls.

TOP POLO NATIONS	
Country	Number of clubs
Argentina	151
USA	130
Australia*	47
Britain*	40
Brazil	39
South Africa*	34
New Zealand*	23
Pakistan*	13
Zimbabwe*	12
Mexico	11
Nigeria*	10
India	9
Malaysia*	6
France*	5
Germany*	5
Spain	5
Chile	4
Kenya*	4
Brunei*	1
Dubai*	1
Philippines*	1
* Playing under HPA Rules	

belonging to the FIP can compete in a World Polo Championship at a 10–14 goal level every three or four years. Initially teams have to qualify by winning within their own zone – Europe, Asia, North America, South America, Africa/Australasia – before proceeding to the finals the following year; here they meet the other zonal winners, plus teams from the host nation, and the winners of the previous tournament. Except in Europe, where teams can transport their own horses relatively easily, the host nation has to supply every side with a pool of 30 ponies. All matches are played on handicap over six chukkas.

The FIP has also produced a set of rules under which all international matches are now played, and a committee with representatives from Argentina, Britain, and the USA is currently examining these rules and their own with a view to bringing about global consistency.

EQUIPMENT The polo ball is made of willow, bamboo, or plastic, and must not exceed 9cm (3½in) in diameter or 125g (4⅜oz) in weight. Sticks (or mallets) have bamboo or composite fibreglass and carbon shafts and hardwood heads. Helmets with chin straps are compulsory for players,

and knee guards and face guards are commonly worn.

The ponies' legs must be protected with boots or bandages. To prevent slipping, a single 1.3cm (½in) stud or calkin is normally placed on the outer edge of each hind shoe. The gag snaffle is the most popular bit, and a standing martingale is almost invariably used.

Alternative polo

Arena polo is an alternative form of the sport. It is played in an enclosed space such as a riding school or an outdoor manège, about 90 x 37m (100 x 40yd). There are three players per side, a soft ball is used, and the game has its own rules and handicap system. It is popular with spectators because they are, of course, much closer to the action than in the original game.

Another winter variation of polo is played on the frozen, snow-covered lake at St Moritz in Switzerland. As with arena polo, each team has three members, and the game is played with a soft ball. The ponies need special shoeing to meet the conditions.

Polo ponies

In the original rules, there was a height limit for polo ponies of 142cm (14 hands). This was increased to 147cm (14.2 hands) in 1902, but subsequently abolished altogether. Since then the ideal height has proved to be 152–7cm (15–15.2 hands): a pony this size is small enough to be 'handy' (able to stop, turn, and accelerate quickly), but big enough to move at top speed as well as being able to carry weight.

Traditionally polo ponies have come from native stock: the Australian Waler in New South Wales, for example, and the Criollo in Argentina. The latter, refined by crossing with Thoroughbreds, have now been bred specifically for polo in ever increasing numbers for over a century, and consequently provide the bulk of polo ponies throughout the world. However, as the game has become faster and faster, the very best pony nowadays is the pure Thoroughbred, irrespective of where it comes from.

Curiously the vast majority of playing ponies are mares. For some reason they seem to take more readily to the game than geldings, perhaps because

they are neater in size and action, or perhaps because their temperament is better suited to the sport.

Ponies are always changed after each chukka but, especially in low-goal polo, they may come back to play a second chukka later in the game.

Key people

Skilful players are the essential elements of a polo game, supported increasingly these days by team patrons or sponsors, and overseen by eagle-eyed umpires and referees. In the pony lines are the grooms, many of whom have amazing knowledge about the sport and the ponies, and the vitally important vets and farriers.

THE PLAYERS The four players on each team are assigned positions designated by numbers. One and two are the forwards, three the pivot man, and four the back. Each player attempts to 'cover' his or her opposite number

(number one covering the opposing number four, and number two the opposing number three). For reasons of safety, left-handed players are not permitted. Female players, however, are, and their numbers are very much on the up and up.

MATCH OFFICIALS Two mounted umpires supervise the game from the field. In the stands is a 'third man' or referee whom the umpires can consult if they cannot agree. In addition there is a judge behind each goal, a time-keeper, and a scoreboard attendant.

SPONSORS Most teams nowadays have either commercial sponsorship or an individual patron, who may or may not play, but is responsible for financing the players and the ponies.

A good pony knows exactly where it is going, and takes the player to the ball on an even, level stride. The umpire watches closely.

RELATED TOPICS

Thoroughbred	70
Criollo	120
A day in the life of a polo pony	224
Pony Club	226

A day in the life of a polo pony

A polo pony is in a unique position within equestrian sports because it is required to assist its rider in a game. A well-trained polo pony will have a responsive mouth, a low action, and, most importantly, the athleticism required to stop and spin around then to accelerate at great speed. Polo ponies get to know and enjoy the game and can often be seen watching the play attentively waiting for their chukka. The most distinguishable feature of a polo pony is surely its benign temperament. It is handled constantly and is always part of a team – it is exercised with other polo ponies, travels with them, and comes in close contact with them during the game.

The speed and agility required of a polo pony during a game demand that the pony is extremely fit and performing at its best at all times. A player will rely on his or her pony – it is said that the pony is 75 per cent of the game. The players therefore ensure that they have competent grooms who each take care of six or seven ponies. During the polo season, depending on the level of player and tournament, an average pony will play approximately three games of polo per week. Prior to the season, the ponies will be brought in and exercised daily for six weeks.

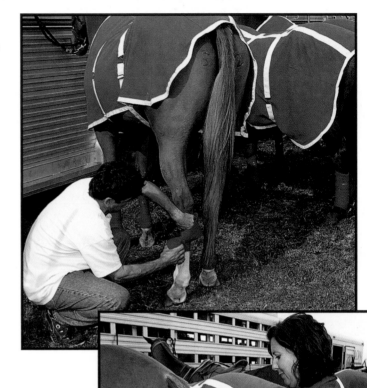

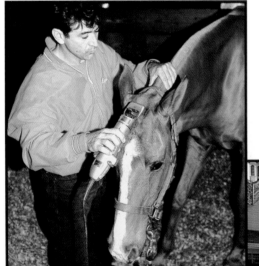

▼ **2.00pm** Once the groom has prepared and checked all the tack required for the game and it has been loaded onto the truck, the pony is then also led onto the truck for the journey.

▲ **10.30am** An average polo day starts with the grooms arriving at 6.30am. The rugs are taken off each pony and they are led out of the stables and given a brush before each is taken out for 40 mintues of exercise. After feeding and mucking out, the morning is spent preparing the ponies. Each mane has to be clipped to prevent a mallet or the reins becoming entangled in the hair during a game.

▲ **2.30pm** On arrival, the pony is tied up either to the truck or to the designated polo pony lines. It is given a brush and the groom puts rear studs into the shoes to prevent slipping during the game. All four legs are bandaged in the team colours. Tendon boots and over-reach boots are put on the front legs and the tail is plaited. Next comes the tack: a team saddle cloth, saddle, breast plate and surcingle, bridle, martingale, a caversom and drop nose band, and gag and draw reins.

◄ **3.30pm** The pony is warmed up for a minute with a canter on both legs, the girth is tightened, and everything checked by the groom. While the ponies are standing waiting for the chukka bell they watch the game with ears pricked forwards in anticipation. Polo ponies have to be very fit and agile, although each chukka is only 7½ minutes long.

▼ **3.35pm** The player will have given orders to the groom earlier in the day as to which pony he would like to ride in each chukka. In between chukkas the player will come off the field, dismount, and remount a fresh pony (or in some cases hop from one pony to the next).

▲ **3.40pm** The chukka begins. During the chukka the pony will go from a walk to a flat gallop within seconds. The player will also ask the pony to 'ride off': it will need to ride another pony off the 'line' so that its player then has the right to strike the ball. When the chukka bell rings the pony's work is over and it will be stripped down and given a wash.

► **6.00pm** On returning back to the yard the pony will be checked for any possible injury and any swelling will be attended to and bandaged. The grooms check the pony's water, give it some hay, put one or two rugs on it depending on the climate, and leave the pony to rest for the night.

PONY CLUB

The Pony Club is the largest international association of riders in the world. It is here that children learn the basics of horse care, receive instruction on riding and how to take part in the numerous equestrian disciplines, and meet hundreds of other young people with similar interests. The Pony Club began in Britain in the late 1920s, and today is represented in 15 countries, with worldwide membership exceeding 100,000.

Beginnings of the Pony Club

In 1928, the Institute of the Horse, Britain's governing equestrian body, started a training scheme to encourage riding. It was intended primarily for adults, but also included events for children in the form of paperchases and gymkhanas, generally called mounted games. The first recorded Pony Club gymkhana was organized that year by the Oxted (Surrey) Branch.

In 1929 the Institute of the Horse inaugurated a junior branch, which it called the Pony Club, 'for the purpose of interesting young people in riding and sport and at the same time offering the opportunity of light instruction in this direction'. Under this scheme the country was divided into districts corresponding with the different hunts, each under the control of a district commissioner. Most branches were named after the local hunt or a local feature or town. Several American branches became affiliated in the 1930s.

Today there are 364 Pony Club branches in Britain and 2195 in the rest of the world, in countries ranging from the USA to Botswana. The US Pony Club was founded in 1954 as a separate organization, and today numbers over 600 clubs with more than 12,000 members. The Euro Pony Club runs along similar lines in Europe, but it, too, is a separate organization.

The Pony Club today

The Pony Club is open to boys and girls up to 21 years of age. Ordinary members are those who are under 18 at the beginning of the current year and associate members are 18–21 years. There is no minimum age. Members pay a small annual fee to their local branch, which constitutes membership of the club as a whole.

In Britain branches of the Pony Club are administered by a volunteer district commissioner and a local committee. The country is divided into 19 areas, each of which is under the control of an area representative chosen by the district commissioner. All area representatives are members of the Pony Club Council.

The Pony Club can rightly claim to have been extremely influential in the early training of many of the world's top riders.

The Council of the Pony Club (again all volunteers) manages the local branches through the headquarters, which employs a chief executive, development officer, general manager, and a small secretarial staff.

In other countries, the organization has a similar structure, adapted to suit local needs.

Pony Club activities

The Pony Club organizes a myriad activities for its members, variously designed to improve riding skills, teach practical pony management, or introduce children to the world of competitive equestrian sports.

AFFILIATED NATIONS		
Country	Number of branches	Approx. membership
Antigua	1	14
Australia	950	70,000
Botswana	1	50
Britain	364	40,000
Canada	195	3760
Cyprus	4	75
Dubai	1	50
Germany	7	212
Hong Kong	1	301
Ireland	60	4280
Kenya	5	157
Malta	1	19
New Zealand	305	10,450
South Africa	40	1007
USA	615	12,000
Zimbabwe	9	463

PONY CLUB AIMS

The objectives that were laid down at the foundation of the Pony Club in 1929 remain much the same today:

To encourage young people to ride and to learn to enjoy all kinds of sport connected with horses and riding.

To provide instruction in riding and horsemastership and to instil in members the proper care of their animals.

To promote the highest ideals of sportsmanship, citizenship, and loyalty, thereby cultivating strength of character and self discipline.

WORKING RALLIES These are the main activity of the Pony Club, and the backbone of the organization. Working rallies are held as frequently as possible throughout the year, and every member is required to attend those organized by their branch. At a rally, participants can expect some instruction in equitation, and various aspects of horse care, tack cleaning, stable management, and first aid, as well as to take part in mounted games and sports.

A group of riders take their mounts for a welcome drink after a hard day's training during Pony Club camp.

PONY CLUB CAMP For most branches, the highlight of the year is the Pony Club camp, which is generally held in the summer, during school holidays. Camps usually last from three days up to a week; some are residential, at others the riders attend daily. Instruction takes place throughout the day in all the various disciplines of dressage, showjumping, and cross-country riding, as well as polo, tetrathlon practice (which involves riding, swimming, running, and pistol shooting), and, in some cases, vaulting. Lectures and demonstrations are usually given, and visits to interesting

equestrian establishments are sometimes made. For all who attend, there is a great deal of fun, as well as sound instruction, with many new friendships being made.

COMPETITIONS Team competitions are organized, the main disciplines being eventing or horse trials, showjumping, and dressage. In addition tetrathlon, mounted games, polo, and polo cross competitions are held.

There are area qualifying competitions in each main discipline, culminating in a national championship. The accent is on

development of team spirit. There are very few international riders who have not started their competitive lives in the Pony Club.

TRAINING AND EFFICIENCY CERTIFICATES
The third main feature of the Pony Club is the Training and Efficiency Certificate. The Pony Club tests start at 'D' level for the very young and go up to the well-respected 'A' test, attainable only by those with a great deal of knowledge and skill.

The 'D' test includes having to tack up a pony and lead it, as well as tackling simple mounted exercises in the different paces. Care of the pony and stable management form a vital part of the tests, and greater riding skills on the flat and over fences are required at each of the higher levels. Those passing their 'A' test are considered quite capable of coping alone with horses and having sufficient knowledge to know when to call the vet, farrier, or feed merchant, as well as being competent riders in all disciplines. Many regard the 'A' test as one of the best all-round proficiency certificates for riders.

The popularity of the Pony Club is evident as several riders perform their tests at the British Championships at Weston Park.

The Pony Club also publishes its own training manuals and *The Manual of Horsemastership* is widely recognized as one of the best textbooks available on all aspects of horse care, management, and riding.

The Pony Club ponies

The ponies come in just about every breed, colour, and type, but all have one thing in common: an amazing patience and willingness to perform well for their young riders. These amicable animals need to be tough enough to stand up to a heavy programme of activities, especially during school holidays; they must also be very versatile, and able to take part in a huge variety of sports. Although some older children ride horses, many remain on ponies and these compete against the larger animals with ease, their agility and speed often making up for their lack of height.

Key people

The Pony Club relies on the goodwill of tens of thousands of volunteers who give freely of their time and expertise, in order to nurture youthful enthusiasm for equestrian sports.

Above: All the determination needed to succeed is shown by this young jockey as she and her willing pony fly round the cross-country course.

Right: An energetic trainer helps his young charge gain confidence over a jump. The earlier a rider can start, the easier it is to succeed.

THE DISTRICT COMMISSIONER He or she organizes all the activities and draws up the annual programme of events. The district commissioner has to be sane, fair, sensible, and extremely patient to cope not only with the children but also with their often difficult parents, some of whom have an overweening ambition to see their young offspring shine above the others.

THE TRAINERS These are dedicated, often voluntary helpers who teach at camp or various rallies in the course of the year. They are responsible for the content of the lessons, which may be mounted or consist of lectures, visits to equestrian events, or an equestrian quiz or video show. Expertise varies, as the trainers themselves range from Olympic stars to newly qualified or trainee instructors.

THE PARENTS Few Pony Club activities could take place without the sheer dedication of the parents, who spend untold hours ferrying ponies and children to and from the numerous events throughout the year. They also help in setting up all the different activities, with catering, or with any other task that comes their way.

RELATED TOPICS

A day at the Pony Club
camp 68
Eventing 156
Dressage 168
Showjumping 176
Polo 220

MOUNTED GAMES

Over the years Pony Club gymkhana or mounted games have provided enormous fun for countless children, as well as helping to improve their riding. Balance and co-ordination, the all-important partnership between pony and rider, and the art of sportsmanship are all learned at an early age – helping to justify the Pony Club's claim to be the breeding ground for top international riders in all spheres of equestrian competition.

Origin of the games

Games on horseback have been played for several thousand years, either as a form of recreation or as part of military training, but it is only relatively recently that organized competitions for children have come into being.

The suggestion to hold organized games for children and their ponies was first made by HRH Prince Philip, the Duke of Edinburgh, to Colonel Sir Mike Ansell, then director of Britain's indoor Horse of the Year Show, with the idea that they emulate in some way the popular competitions traditionally held by the cavalry.

After approaches to the Pony Club, a committee was formed under the chairmanship of Lt Colonel Charles Adderley with a view to devising games that would both test the skills of young riders and give them a lot of fun. Prince Philip knew that a competition of this sort would be a huge attraction at the Horse of the Year Show and

Handing over a baton or similar object encourages good hand and eye co-ordination. These two young riders are doing well.

Being able to vault on and off the pony is one of the essential skills for any young rider wishing to compete in gymkhana or mounted games.

agreed to give a Perpetual Challenge Cup to the winners. The first competition took place in 1957, and ever since has been known as the Prince Philip Cup.

In the mid 1970s the idea of mounted games for children was enthusiastically adopted by the Netherlands and France, after teams from the British Pony Club gave demonstrations at shows in Amsterdam and Paris. In 1976 teams from the USA and Canada travelled to Britain for a highly successful international competition; and in 1985 the USA's National Horse Show included mounted games run on similar lines to those in Britain.

Mounted games today

In Britain there are 19 area games every year, followed by five zone finals and a runners-up competition, before the winners of these six events compete at the Horse of the Year Show. The competitions in most other Pony Club nations follow a similar format.

The upper age limit for competitors has always been 15 but, over the years, it was realized that the much younger children were finding it difficult to compete against the older riders. A junior competition, with its own finals, was introduced with an upper age limit of 12 years, allowing these riders to compete on equal terms.

There are well over 100 different games, competed for individually or in

pairs or teams (usually consisting of three to five members). Some of the most popular are:

FLAG RACE The teams work in relays, racing to transfer a number of flags in buckets from one end of the arena to the other.

FLOWER POT RACE This is another team game, in which each rider in turn races up to a line of upturned flower pots, dismounts, and, while leading the pony, runs along the tops of the pots. He or she then vaults back onto the pony, dashes back to the rest of the team, and passes the baton on to the next rider.

BENDING RACE A universal favourite, this involves zigzagging through a line of poles at breathtaking speed.

OBJECTIVES

Britain's Prince Philip Cup provides the Pony Club with a competition requiring courage, determination, and all-round riding ability on the part of the rider, and careful, systematic training of the pony.

Like the similar contests staged by other nations, its objective is to encourage a higher standard of riding throughout the Pony Club and to stimulate a greater interest in riding as a sport and as a recreation.

SWORD LANCERS A game for pairs or teams in which riders use a wooden sword to hook rings from poles, passing the sword from one to another until all the rings have been collected.

The skills

In the course of training for the mounted games, riders develop great balance and control of their pony as well as considerable hand and eye co-ordination (which is particularly well demonstrated by handing over batons to fellow team members when riding at speed). The pony also benefits greatly from this training and learns to change leg in the bending races, turn closely around an obstacle, or pause momentarily as the rider collects or puts down an item of equipment.

Mounted games will help even the youngest riders, and they will soon learn the ultimate skill of vaulting onto a moving pony. This is spectacular when done at great speed and builds huge confidence. They will also learn how to fall off safely – a technique sure to be needed even by the best of riders.

The gymkhana pony

The ideal gymkhana pony responds immediately to its rider's commands. Usually fast, wiry, and intelligent, they need only a few training sessions to learn what is required for the different games. They must be well behaved and remain calm in the excited atmosphere of the competition.

Many ponies get recycled within the various Pony Clubs as children grow out of them. The 'professional' mounted games pony is highly sought after by those who take the games seriously.

Key people

All the usual Pony Club helpers are involved in the mounted games. They help to prepare both children and ponies, taking them through the qualifying stages of the competition.

THE COMPETITORS The children who take part in the mounted games must have a natural balance and affinity with their ponies. Always keen to succeed, they are generally bold, confident, and quick thinking, and not afraid of speed.

THE OFFICIALS In most cases, the parents take on the duties of competition officials; they lay out the equipment needed for each game, and help to ensure fair play.

Some of the bigger Pony Clubs have professional trainers, responsible for arranging the practice sessions that enable the teams to compete in finals or league games.

Precision, speed, and the ability to keep the pony moving in a straight line are all vital ingredients when riding in this most competitive sport.

RELATED TOPICS
A day at the Pony Club camp   68
Pony Club   226

CEREMONIAL AND WORKING HORSES

Even today, in many parts of the world, horses are crucial to the indigenous way of life. In Mongolia for instance the herdsmen use ponies to patrol their land and control their herds (they also milk the mares). In developing countries where agriculture is still small scale, people depend entirely on native horses, for working the land and gathering the crops and as a means of transport. Horses still work too in the midst of developed societies: for example, the draught horses used by breweries, cow ponies ridden by the gauchos of Argentina, or the police horses that remain a feature of daily life in so many countries.

Ceremonial horses do their work as part of a deliberate spectacle, which may be Trooping the Colour, demonstrating the highest form of a national system of equitation, or providing entertainment at the circus.

CEREMONIAL HORSES

While horses were once fundamental to military life, mechanization made them virtually redundant. However, they are still an important part of military ceremonies, whether accompanying and conveying royalty and heads of state on formal occasions, or providing a guard of honour for a state funeral.

CEREMONIAL DUTIES Each unit or regiment has specific duties and uses particular horses for the task. In Britain, for example, the King's Troop, Royal Horse Artillery, uses relatively small, light horses, often Irish-bred, to pull its guns. The gun carriages are generally drawn by three pairs of postillion-ridden horses, which are usually bay; for state funerals, when a gun carriage is adapted to carry the casket, black horses are used. The King's Troop performs ceremonial duties such as firing royal salutes on special occasions, as well as giving demonstrations of a spectacular galloping musical 'drive'.

The Household Cavalry (which consists of the Life Guards, and the Blues and Royals) accompanies royal processions and mounts guard at the army headquarters in London's

BECOMING A CEREMONIAL HORSE

Potential ceremonial horses undergo a very thorough basic training, then, when they are three years old, they will be assessed by a panel of experts. Temperament is a primary concern – there is nothing worse than a horse that 'blows up' on parade. Size is important too, and not just for a visual effect. Royal carriage horses usually stand at least 163cm (16 hands) high, since they must be big enough to help pull a heavy carriage as well as bearing the weight of a rider (the postillion).

Those selected will be 'broken in' for riding and, if appropriate, driving. This phase takes about a year, during which time the young horses will be very gradually introduced to 'nuisances' likely to be encountered in the course of their public life, such as crowds, flags, bands, bangs, swords, and traffic. When confident enough alone, they will begin working in company. Those that pass their tests go to the stables of their designated units to start ceremonial life.

If a horse accepts ceremonial life in the first year, it may graduate to a more difficult role (attending noisier, more important events) in the second and third years. At this stage, its training should be complete.

Whitehall. They always use black horses, which are of hunter type, again bred mainly in Ireland.

The Household Cavalry drum horses, however, are piebald or skewbald, and are possibly the most spectacular of all the ceremonial horses used today. They are descended from the great Shire

horses, crossed with big Dutch coloured horses and gypsy ponies. Standing more than 183cm (18 hands) high, they have to carry not only their rider, but also the silver kettle drums, each weighing over 45kg (100lb).

They are controlled by special reins attached to the rider's stirrups, which leaves his hands free to play the drums. When standing still, the horses do so with their legs outstretched to ease the weight on their backs.

The mounted branch of London's Metropolitan Police has the honour of providing horses for VIPs at the Trooping the Colour ceremony, held to celebrate the Queen's official birthday; they also lead the processions for the state opening of Parliament and for visiting heads of state.

ROYAL STABLES Perhaps one of the most interesting stable grounds in the world is the British Royal Mews at Buckingham Palace. Here are stabled some 40 horses including the famous Windsor Greys, which are used only for drawing the carriage of the Queen or Queen Elizabeth the Queen Mother; the other horses are bays, used for conveying ambassadors and other foreign dignitaries by coach on their presentation to the Queen.

Denmark and Sweden still maintain royal stables but, next to Britain, the Netherlands has the largest working royal mews in Europe. Situated at The Hague, it has a complement of 30 horses, which are mainly Dutch Warmbloods and Gelderlanders, with some Friesian horses. There are a number of very ornate carriages, the most famous of which is the Golden Coach used by the monarch to open Parliament each year.

Some North African countries, such as Morocco, have royal or presidential mounted guards using Arabian and Barb horses. The Gulf States maintain royal and presidential mounted police forces, some using Arabian horses, some imported animals.

Left: Britain's Royal Horse Artillery escorts the coffin of Diana, Princess of Wales, in one of the most poignant ceremonial events in recent times.

Right: The splendid Household Cavalry Drum Horse parades at the Royal Windsor horse show. The reins are attached to the rider's stirrups.

THE MOUNTIES More formally known as the Royal Canadian Mounted Police, the Mounties were founded in 1873, primarily to bring law and order to the vast regions of Canada. Nowadays, the horses have largely been replaced by motor vehicles. However, there is still a mounted unit, based in Ontario, which provides ceremonial escorts and takes part in parades and celebrations, both in Canada and in other countries.

The Mounties' musical ride is renowned worldwide. Performed by some 32 horses, it is ridden at the canter and lasts for over 20 minutes, with a variety of wheels and turns all carried out very precisely. The Mounties breed their own horses at their stud and training centre at Pakenham, Ontario. All black, and 163–73cm (16–17 hands) tall, they are of mainly Thoroughbred and, more recently, Hanoverian blood. Over the years the stud has established a good-looking, tough type of horse capable of working for many hours at a time.

CAISSON PLATOON Members of the Caisson Platoon of the 3rd US Infantry maintain a mounted honour guard at Arlington National Cemetery, Washington, DC. Some of the dead from every war in which the USA has taken part are buried here, as are many of the country's military leaders, and former presidents such as Franklin Roosevelt, Dwight D Eisenhower, and John F Kennedy.

A team of six horses, only three of which have riders, pulls the flag-draped casket on a caisson or gun carriage. In a full-honour funeral, a riderless, caparisoned horse is led behind the caisson, wearing a saddle with a pair of boots reversed in the stirrups.

The horses used by the Caisson Platoon are not of any particular breed, but are matched for size and colour (which may be black or white). All must have quiet temperaments to do the job required. They are stabled at the entrance to Arlington Park.

Display horses and riders

In many countries, ceremonial horses serve another function: to promote a particular system of equitation or a certain breed of horse, and to help riders attain the highest standards with which to represent their country in equestrian competitions such as the Olympic Games.

THE CADRE NOIR The French national riding troupe known as the Cadre Noir was founded in 1828, although the black uniform from which the troupe takes its name, and which is still in use

Right: The spectacular finale to the displays given by the Cadre Noir, the élite French riding troupe, has enthralled audiences at home and abroad.

Below: Canada's famous mounted police, nicknamed the Mounties, perform their musical ride in countries all over the world.

today, was not introduced until later. Integrated with the National School of Equitation, just outside Saumur, in 1972, the Cadre Noir has about 50 horses, and the élite team of riders is normally limited to 22.

The equitation practised by the Cadre Noir is based on that taught by François Robichon de la Guérinière, riding master to King Louis XV and author of the enormously influential

book on equitation *Ecole de Cavalerie* published in 1731. The Cadre Noir mainly uses three breeds of horse: the Thoroughbred, the Anglo-Arabian, and the Selle Français. In addition, Lusitano horses are kept to demonstrate the baroque riding style of the 16th and 17th centuries.

The lighter types of horse (the Thoroughbreds and Anglo-Arabians) excel in the movements of Grand Prix dressage, as ridden at the Olympic Games. Such displays may be performed individually, or as *pas de deux* (pairs), *de trois* (trios), or *du quantité* (larger groups), and may be either in hand or ridden. Then there is a grand reprise, in which 10 horses and riders are led by the troupe commandant into the arena and out again, performing a slow, elevated walk known as the *pas de manège*.

The heavier Selle Français horses are used to display the 'airs above the ground', the movements formerly used in close-combat fighting on the battlefield to dislodge the enemy. In the *courbette*, the horse stands up on its hind legs; in the *croupade* it stands on its front legs and kicks out with its hind legs; in the *capriole* the horse jumps in the air and kicks out with both front and hind legs.

THE SPANISH RIDING SCHOOL OF VIENNA

This world-famous school was founded in the 16th century, to perpetuate the art of classical riding. The splendid white stallions used there were descended from Spanish stock, brought to a stud at Lipizza (now Lipica, in Slovenia) by Archduke Charles II. In 1735 Emperor Charles VI opened a new indoor riding hall at the Hofburg Palace in Vienna, which is where the school is still based today.

The white Lipizzaners are small, powerful, and athletic, and lend themselves especially well to the intricacies of advanced dressage. The methods used at Vienna, like those of the Cadre Noir, are based on the teachings of the 18th century French royal riding master François Robichon de la Guérinière.

Standards at the school today are as strict as they always were. The young stallions receive a basic training then, as they grow stronger, are schooled in the collected work. At this stage, each stallion will be assessed to determine whether it has the ability to perform the most difficult movements, the 'airs above the ground'. It is the belief of the school that the complete balance necessary to perform each one of these 'airs' can be achieved only through consistent training. The riders are given as thorough a schooling as the horses. Young riders are put onto trained horses without stirrups or reins, and they work under the close supervision of an instructor until they have achieved the balance, suppleness, and independence of seat that enable them to become one with their horse.

Spanish Riding School horses demonstrate 'airs above the ground' in breathtaking style, and have given such performances for well over 400 years.

Performances at the Spanish School today include individual and *pas de deux* displays, as well as more elaborate routines. The Grand Quadrille consists of 16 horses in formation working through walk, trot, and canter, including flying changes, *piaffe*, and *passage*.

All the riders wear the traditional 18th-century uniform of dark brown frock coats and tricorn hats; the horses have red and gold saddle cloths.

THE DOMECQ SCHOOL The Spanish Royal School of Equestrian Art is a much younger institution than its French or Austrian equivalent. In 1973, the Domecq family (renowned as much for their expertise in the bullring as for their sherry) founded their own riding school to preserve both the art of classical riding and the Andalusian horse. In conjunction with the government, the family undertook the building of a magnificent indoor arena at Jerez de la Frontera, with seating for over 1400 people and stabling for 60 horses. Opened in 1982, it soon became the Royal School.

Here, young riders and young horses are taught all the movements of classical equitation, including the 'airs above the ground' and the Spanish walk. Spectacular equestrian displays are given regularly at the school, as well as at royal functions and at such ceremonies as the opening of the Ryder Cup golf tournament at Sotogrande, Cadiz, in 1997.

THE CELLE STUD One of the great German state studs, Celle is famous for its display unit, which is used to show off the Hanoverian horses that are bred there. One of the special features of the display involves riders long-reining one horse while riding another. Each autumn, young stallions are put through their paces to demonstrate their conformation, movement, and trainability, in order that they can be assessed for breeding purposes.

THE REJOINDERS In Portugal, where bullfighting is regarded as an art (and the bull is not killed in the ring), the *rejoindors* (mounted bullfighters) give spectacular ridden displays before the fights begin. The horses they use are Lusitanos, which are supremely brave and athletic, with a remarkably calm nature. These proud horses are never allowed to be touched by the bull. The penalty to the rider is very severe if a horse is injured.

PARADE HORSES Parades provide a wonderful opportunity to show off the speciality of a particular breed. This may be a distinctive colouring, such as the golden coat of the Palomino horse with its flaxen mane and tail, or it may be an unusual gait, such as that of the Tennessee Walking Horse or the Missouri Fox Trotter. In Colombia and Peru, the Paso horses are the dominant parade horses. They are amblers or pacers, with a fairly high-stepping gait. Riders wear special cloaks and hats when showing them off at displays.

The Charro riders of Mexico, wearing sombreros and elaborately decorated costumes, parade on horses bedecked with silver-embossed saddles and bridles. The reins are held in the left hand but, although the bits used look severe, they are hardly touched as the horses wear a rawhide noseband known as a *bosal*. Equally, the long spurs are there for show, the rowels revolving and making a noise.

The Charro riders evolved from the native Indians who played games on horseback with cattle. The Charros still hold competitions for calf roping and calf tailing, and are accompanied by the Mariachi trumpet bands that are peculiar to Mexico.

Circus horses

Horses have always been fundamental to circus entertainment, tracing right back to the chariot races held by the Romans at the Circus Maximus. In more modern times, the spectacular displays given by performing horses, with and without riders, are the centrepiece of most big circuses.

A number of circus families are still operating today. In Britain the Chipperfields, the Smarts, the Roberts, and the Gandeys still tour, but very often abroad. The Swiss National Circus is run by the Knie family, probably the foremost trainers of circus horses in Europe, employing the likes of Georg Wahl, late of the Spanish Riding School, to help train their horses. Circus Gruss in France and Circus Knone in Germany are other well-known circuses. In Russia there is the Russian State Circus, and Hungary produces the Cisio bareback riders.

The horses used in circuses fall into three categories: Haute Ecole, Liberty, and Rosinback. Pure white, pure black, and golden are favourite colours. The riders match their costumes to the colour of their horses and to the theme of the performance.

HAUTE ECOLE These perform an advanced form of dressage, a sequence of highly collected movements carried out with barely perceptible cues from the rider. Haute Ecole horses are very often Andalusians, Lusitanos, or Friesians because of their spectacular appearance, particular ability, and exceptional temperament, which is unusually calm and tractable.

In a typical routine, the horse and rider enter the ring at the gallop, halt for a dramatic salute to the crowd, then move away at trot with small circles and lateral work on both reins; once in the centre of the ring, the horse bows, then moves off into canter, with pirouettes and flying changes. Next come the polka and the Spanish walk, followed by *piaffe, passage,* and a spectacular finale.

LIBERTY HORSES The Liberty horses, which are mostly Arabians, perform without a rider. They wear colourful harnesses, usually with loose side reins, and follow the instructions of their handler, who uses only a whip (or guider) to direct them to stop, turn, or go backwards.

A troupe of Liberty horses usually consists of six to eight animals, sometimes more. At the end of a routine, one of the horses may put on a special display such as walking on its

Circus horses carry out a variety of routines in small circular arenas, sometimes with riders performing amazing balancing acts.

Horses have found a new role in the entertainment business, appearing in films ranging from Westerns to period dramas.

hind legs round the ring. Liberty horse acts are still a feature of such American circuses as Barnum and Bailey.

ROSINBACKS The Rosinbacks are used for voltige, when the rider performs an acrobatic routine on the horse's hindquarters, which are usually dusted with resin for better grip. These horses are often Bretons or other European heavy breeds, which are squarely built and not too tall, and maintain a good rhythm at canter. Several performers may mount the horse at the same time.

WORKING HORSES

Since the advent of the tractor and other motor vehicles, many working horses have disappeared, and those that remain are being preserved by breed societies. However, in parts of the Western world horses are still worked in the traditional way.

In the USA, the Amish religious community relies solely on the horse. Originally from northern Germany, the Amish have a modest way of life. They use only horse-drawn transport for both people and goods, and till and gather their crops with teams of six or eight horses and some mules.

In Britain, some breweries use Shires to pull their drays, mostly to keep the breed going and to promote their beers. Clydesdales still work to some extent pulling out trees felled in the Scottish forests and in Ulster. The Suffolk Punch is used in small numbers

for ploughing and general farm work in eastern England. In Scotland, the Highland Pony still carries deer and other game after a day's stalking.

Work horses are used considerably in Normandy, northern France. Most are of the Boulonnais type, a strong, muscular horse that is also popular for farm work in Belgium. In Germany a number of different breeds can still be found working in agriculture, for tilling the land and bringing in crops such as potatoes and carrots, as well as drawing floats for the famous beer festivals. In the Netherlands, Friesians and Gelderlanders are perhaps the most popular work horses.

In Hungary the Cisko horses and the Shagyas are still used to round up cattle. In Romania and Bulgaria some Lipizzaner blood is used to produce horses for work on the land, and in Switzerland and Austria the tough Haflinger ponies are used in the Tyrol mountains for agricultural purposes. The great horses of Kladruby in the Czech Republic are still popular with farmers as well as driving enthusiasts.

COW PONIES Spain's Doma Vaquera horses, used to work cattle on the farms, are true working horses, of stocky appearance and with a short tail. The rider holds the reins in his left

hand, and carries a very long pole in his right hand to control the cattle. In competitions, the horses perform walk, canter, gallop, reinback, and sliding halt, as well as full passes and pirouettes – all movements used in their work with cattle.

The American cowboys' style of riding evolved from Doma Vaquera techniques, which spread throughout the Americas with Spanish explorers. Although often kept for competition these days, American cow ponies are still used on some ranches, such as in California, Wyoming, and Texas, to control cattle over vast areas of land.

In various parts of Australia, too, cattle stations depend on working horses. Each station breeds and trains its own horses for use on the farm. Usually a Thoroughbred stallion is turned out with a herd of station-bred mares. Nowadays some of the offspring are sold and they have proved exceptional eventers.

The Argentinean gaucho rides a pony that is part Thoroughbred, part Criollo. The Criollo is descended from Spanish stock, and is noted for its hardiness. These ponies, usually standing about 152cm (15 hands) high, are used to work cattle and to capture wild horses, by galloping alongside a particular animal while the gaucho lassoes it. Polo ponies are often of this breeding.

TELEVISION AND FILMS Most recently, the horse has found a new metier in films and in television commercials. Perhaps best known is the hitch of Clydesdales used to advertise Budweiser beer in North America. Hollywood has its own stables of stunt horses, and its own store of chuck wagons and the like. These are run by expert horsemen and can be seen in films from westerns to dramas such as 'Gone with The Wind'. In Britain, Pinewood Studios near London has its own horses, mostly Spanish, for film work; the Norwich Union insurance company's horse-drawn carriages are often seen in films and on television, and circuses use their horses for similar work. Little Hollywood near Marbella in Spain also has access to horses for use in films.

A fine Percheron carries out its traditional work at Bloss National Stud in France. In some parts of the world the working horse is still widely used.

RELATED TOPICS

Lipizzaner	100
A day in the life of a draught horse	152
Dressage	168
A day in the life of a police horse	242

A day in the life of a police horse

The use of horses in police work is worldwide and not just confined to Europe, where virtually every country has its own Mounted Police Unit. In Great Britain 15 police forces currently retain an active mounted branch, of which the largest is the Metropolitan Police in London.

The average Metropolitan Police horse commences its service at four or five years of age, and will have a working life expectancy of about 16 to 18 years. Initial training lasts for six months, at the end of which the horse will be able to: go across country in parks, common land, and open spaces; go quietly through the heaviest of traffic; stand rock steady during the pomp and circumstance of a State occasion; and remain completely responsive to its rider in the emotionally charged furore of a political demonstration.

Whatever the surroundings, the function of a mounted police officer is identical to any other police officer. It is, however, during large public gatherings and situations involving large scale public disorder that the police horse becomes an invaluable partner to its officer, justifying the reason for which it was trained.

▶ **11.10am** Escorting troops to and from barracks through heavy London traffic causes the least possible inconvenience to other road users. The high profile of the mounted police officer provides a clear and helpful focus to drivers, while the gentle but persuasive demeanour of the horses keeps pedestrians on the footway.

▲ **10.00am** Long before the London rush hour reaches its peak, the horses at Great Scotland Yard Stables are fed, groomed, and saddled up. They leave for their duties immaculately turned out.

◀ **11.30am** During the height of the summer season, an estimated 5000 tourists regularly turn up to watch the Changing of the Guard at Buckingham Palace. Working in dense crowds, orderly or otherwise, calls for a high degree of training for both horse and rider in order to ensure the safety of members of the public, whose regard for their own personal well being is often overshadowed by their enthusiasm for a better view – or often obtaining that extra photo opportunity.

▶ **12.00pm** A horse is prepared for duty at a football match. Horses have been acknowledged as the most effective means of controlling large, and sometimes violent, crowds at scenes of potential disorder. Such has been the level of violence towards horses and riders in recent years that is has been necessary to fit extra protective equipment to the horses: perspex blinkers to protect the eyes, nose guards, knee pads, leg protectors, and fireproof quarter sheets to protect the loins.

◀ **1.00pm** A group of horses travel to the match. The riders can also wear protective gear: reinforced helmets with visors and neck guards, elbow and forearm protectors, reinforced gloves, and leg protectors worn over boots to shield against slashes when attacked with sharp instruments.

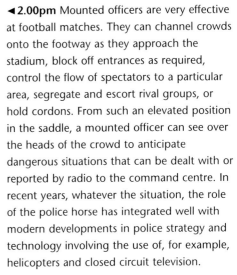

◀ **2.00pm** Mounted officers are very effective at football matches. They can channel crowds onto the footway as they approach the stadium, block off entrances as required, control the flow of spectators to a particular area, segregate and escort rival groups, or hold cordons. From such an elevated position in the saddle, a mounted officer can see over the heads of the crowd to anticipate dangerous situations that can be dealt with or reported by radio to the command centre. In recent years, whatever the situation, the role of the police horse has integrated well with modern developments in police strategy and technology involving the use of, for example, helicopters and closed circuit television.

SHOWING

Showing has become one of the most colourful and varied of activities in the horse world, with thousands of competitive classes held each year at shows and agricultural fairs across the globe. The animals, which may be ridden or shown in hand, range from tiny ponies with their diminutive riders on the leading rein to magnificent draught horses in full harness, and gaited American breeds with spectacular movement. All are there with one aim in mind: to demonstrate that they are the perfect example of their breed or type, or the best for a particular purpose.

Skilful and meticulous presentation is the essential ingredient in producing horses and ponies for the show ring. Here every aspect of the animals' conformation, type, movement, behaviour, and style may be under scrutiny. The judge will be trying to determine which is the supreme example of what the class demands before awarding the coveted first prize.

Origins of showing

In times past, people throughout the world sold horses and ponies – whether for riding, driving, or farm work – at country fairs, race meetings, and markets, and buyers sought the opinion of experts before agreeing to a deal. In the 18th and 19th centuries, agricultural shows held classes for farm animals, including horses, and from the 1850s 'horse leaping' contests became one of the big attractions. By the early 20th century dedicated horse shows were beginning to appear.

Since the 1920s, shows have gradually become more organized, and now cater for virtually every height, type, and breed of pony or horse, with classes to suit all age groups, both human and equine. Most breed societies hold their own national shows for both in-hand and ridden exhibits. Horse shows are designed not only for the exhibitors themselves, but also to provide entertainment for the general public, with demonstrations by equestrian military or police units, enthusiastic performances by Pony or Riding Club teams, or hugely popular

displays of dressage or Western riding, to name just a few. The wide variety of trade stands that accompany the larger shows are also a big attraction.

Showing today

Most shows are one day affairs, but in Britain and the USA in particular, many take place over several days to accommodate the huge number of classes involved. In the USA, the American Horse Shows Association (AHSA) is the sport's governing body. AHSA rules govern all the major shows, and the AHSA is responsible for registrations, records, and judges' certification. American shows may feature classes for everything from ridden hunters and in-hand Arabians to equitation and showmanship.

In Britain and Ireland shows are often affiliated with societies for specific breeds, and provide needed information to entrants and public alike. As a rule, only society members and registered animals can compete in affiliated shows. This situation also sometimes prevails in the USA.

Other European countries, including those in Scandinavia, and Australia and South Africa run similar shows, each catering to local interests and many having showjumping classes and special displays for entertainment. Some are more formal than others, but all have one common theme – a passion for horses and all things connected with them.

PROFESSIONAL SHOWMEN Some riders and handlers are more experienced than others, and may prepare and show animals professionally. There are, however, certain classes that debar professionals from taking part, leaving the competition open only to amateurs.

The classes

Showing classes generally require the animals to parade in front of the judges

A beautifully presented mare and foal celebrate their success in front of the camera at Britain's Three Counties show.

and show their paces. Depending on the class, animals may perform individual shows or tests, and in some cases the judge will ride the horses or ponies to assess their way of going and their manners.

In classes divided into sections for different heights (such as for Riding Ponies) or weights (as for hunters), the winners of each section may come forward to a championship to determine the overall winner. Certain classes serve as regional qualifiers, with a final held at a prestigious show such as the Horse of the Year Show at Wembley in Britain.

IN-HAND CLASSES The in-hand show horse must be perfectly trained if it is to be shown to best advantage in front of the judge. Many in-hand classes are for youngsters, and early handling and training is essential to ensure they behave impeccably, despite the distraction of being among numerous other horses or ponies. In certain classes, especially those for Hackneys and some of the American breeds, the animals must be shown in a particular stance, and this should always be thoroughly rehearsed before the event. The handler must be appropriately dressed for the class and wear suitable shoes to present the horse in the required manner.

Exhibits are presented in neat show bridle and bit suitable for the class in question; they must be in the peak of

Plaiting a tail takes practice to perfect but in some classes is considered essential to the correct presentation of the horse.

health, with a gleaming coat and oiled, well-manicured feet. The mane and tail may be braided or plaited according to the rules for the class. With young animals, who may be immature, certain tricks of the trade will prove useful, helping to accentuate good points and disguise weaker ones by clever plaiting and general presentation. For example, using a broad noseband will help to shorten a long head, and placing plaits high on a weak neck can help it look more muscular.

RIDDEN CLASSES Whatever the class, and there are literally hundreds of different types, the ridden show horse must be beautifully schooled to perform the tasks required, whether jumping, displaying a particular gait, or simply standing still. Correct conformation, good movement, and manners are vital. Months of patient training are essential to ensure the animal performs confidently, happily, and correctly on the day.

In a large class, with many competitors parading round the ring together, it can be difficult to stand out from the crowd, and it is the exhibitors who present themselves in a positive, confident manner, one that suggests 'I am the best', who catch the judge's eye.

Key people

The success of every show depends on its exhibitors. Their role is to prepare

RELATED TOPICS
Showjumping 176
Western riding 202
Ceremonial and working horses 232

Riders await the final verdict of the judge in this show class in the USA. In some cases the winners will go on to a championship.

and present their exhibits to the best of their ability, and to accept the judge's decision with good grace. The show officials – the organizer, judges, and stewards – each play a part in ensuring the event is an enjoyable occasion for all concerned.

THE ORGANIZER For any horse show, the organizer has to be level headed and extremely efficient to ensure the whole event runs smoothly. The many tasks that must be tackled – or delegated to others – include finding judges, stewards, and sponsors, and providing prizes, catering, public address system, security, parking, and entertainment.

THE JUDGE The task of a judge is never easy, since generally he or she will be able to please only one person in a class – the winner. The judge must be not only knowledgeable and experienced, but also fair and consistent, and must stick to the rules and requirements for the class.

STEWARDS Every judge relies on a good steward, who ensures the exhibitors follow the format for the class, takes notes for the judge if necessary, and records the numbers and placings for the show.

HUNTING

People have hunted for food, and to defend themselves and their livestock against predators, for thousands of years. The thrill of the chase is part of any kind of hunt, and riding a horse hard across country in pursuit of the quarry adds elements of challenge and danger. Although hunting is no longer a necessity, it continues as a leisure activity in several countries, especially Britain, Ireland, France, North America, Australia, and New Zealand.

How hunting developed

Bears, lynx, wolves, and wild cattle have all been hunted on horseback, but today the major quarries are the fox, deer, and boar.

Fox hunting originated in England, at least as early as the 15th century. Then the landed gentry most often hunted deer; but many deer parks and deer were destroyed in the Civil War, and fox hunting became more and more popular. British colonists took the sport to North America, and the first American hunt to be run along modern lines was held in north Virginia in 1747.

In England, during the 18th and early 19th centuries, millions of acres of open farmland were enclosed by hedges and fences to improve agricultural efficiency. To ride across this altered countryside called for faster, more athletic horses. By the 1840s the conventions of fox hunting were well established, and they have changed little in essentials since.

Hunting today

Today in Britain and Ireland there are well over 200 packs of foxhounds, and North America has nearly the same number. In the USA, both the red and grey fox are hunted and, in many of the 36 states with recognized packs, hounds may encounter coyotes, hybrid coy-dogs, and the occasional bobcat.

Hunting rules are laid down by the Masters of Foxhounds Association (MFHA), which controls the sport internationally. These cover the general conduct of hunting, and the stipulation of a closed season that ensures that crops are protected from damage, and that fox cubs have time to mature.

Hunting takes place generally during the autumn and winter months. The hunt 'meets' at a specific spot and then moves off to 'draw' (flush a fox out of) a particular wood or field. Only the 'huntsman', his or her assistants (the 'whippers-in'), and the hounds are involved with the actual hunting. The mounted followers (the 'field') allow the hounds to work unhindered, following only when the fox has left cover.

Then, in an often exhilarating chase, they ride at speed over hedges, ditches, or other obstacles. Some hunts install special small fences, particularly in areas with many wire fences. In Australia and New Zealand, horses are taught to take wire in their stride.

A bold horse and a secure rider are necessary when crossing the country at speed over a variety of terrain.

POINT TO POINTING An amateur form of National Hunt steeplechasing, point to pointing is a popular country pursuit peculiar to Britain and Ireland. The races are organized by the various hunts in order to raise funds, either for themselves or for charity (the entry fees and the gate providing the money).

Horses qualify for entry in a point to point race by attending at least six days' hunting in a season, and they must have their entry cards signed by the hunt secretary. The races are regulated by the hunt and include members' and adjacent hunt's races as well as open races and those restricted to ladies. They are usually run under similar rules to those of the Jockey Club for steeplechasing.

The hunter

The hunter needs to be robust enough to carry its rider for up to six to eight hours in the field. It requires stamina, speed, and intelligence to cope with the demands of crossing often difficult country and to keep up with the hunted quarry. Temperament is paramount, since the horse must remain calm during the many breaks that take place while the hounds find the scent.

Although it may come in any shape and size, and be of any breed, the traditional hunter is a Thoroughbred, or a Thoroughbred crossed with an Irish Draught, one of the native breeds, or a Warmblood. In fast country, hunters with more Thoroughbred blood are best; over very hilly ground, where agility rather than speed is more important, the cob and smaller pony breeds are generally most popular.

The hounds

Most foxhounds are pedigree animals, bred for their skill in coping with different kinds of quarry and terrain. They must have good noses to follow the scent, and be tough, agile, and quick. They should also have good voices when they 'give tongue', and be able to accept discipline. A pack usually consists of between 15 and 20 'couples' of bitches or dog hounds.

Key people

A good day's hunting depends largely on the expertise of the small team of hunt officials, and the enthusiasm of the riders who follow the hounds.

THE MASTER OR JOINT MASTERS The master is in charge of the hunt. He or she may also act as huntsman, but increasingly this role is taken by a professional. The master arranges with local landowners when and where meets will be held, and is responsible for ensuring that the hunt follows MFHA rules and code of practice.

The master may also have a hunt secretary, who is responsible for administration and finances.

THE HUNTSMAN This is the person who manages the hounds, controlling them in the field by a series of calls on the hunting horn. The huntsman also oversees the hounds' day-to-day management and care.

THE WHIPPERS-IN These are the huntsman's assistants, usually riding on the flanks of the pack. They help to control the hounds during a hunt, making sure they carry out the huntsman's orders.

THE FIELD The riders who accompany the huntsmen are generally paying members of a particular hunt club or hunt. Their subscriptions pay for the upkeep of the hounds and the salaries or fees of the hunt's professionals. Some hunts are still private, such as the Duke of Beaufort's in Britain, or

A pack of foxhounds waits obediently at a meet before moving off under the direction of the huntsman. The field will follow at a distance.

Mr Stewart's Cheshire Foxhounds in the USA and in these cases the hounds are owned by a particular individual, and riders join the hunt only by invitation.

THE FIELD MASTER The field follows the hounds at a safe distance under the control of the field master, who has expert knowledge of the locality. He or she must know which land the field may or may not ride across, and selects the best and safest route.

HUNT FOLLOWERS The hunt followers often outnumber the field and are supporters who go out on foot, by car or bicycle to follow the day's events.

DRAG HUNTING

Drag hunting is a non-competitive cross-country sport involving plenty of galloping and jumping, which takes place through the autumn and early spring. Hounds are generally trained to follow an artificial trail, laid by dragging a cloth soaked in a substance such as aniseed. Sometimes Bloodhounds are used, and they follow human scent. Up to six trails are laid over suitable farmland incorporating a variety of fences. The field follows the trail behind the master.

RIDING HOLIDAYS

Throughout the world, riding holidays of every description are now emerging. Some have a historical flavour, following pioneering routes or touring battle grounds; some take the form of a riding safari, or offer a taste of the American West, staying on a working ranch; others consist of steady trekking over miles of spectacular country impossible to see from a vehicle.

Riding holidays are ideal for families and for those seeking a more active vacation. The exercise taken during the day provides healthy relaxation, and the companionship between horse and rider is both therapeutic and enjoyable.

Riding for leisure

Horses have been used for sport almost since they were first domesticated, with chariot racing, hunting, and mounted games for the cavalry dating back thousands of years. However, only in the 20th century has riding become popular as a leisure activity, with the opening of many new riding clubs and stables giving far greater numbers of people access to the horse.

The tourist industry has recently begun to promote riding as the ideal way of getting back to nature and seeing the countryside close at hand, a rare privilege nowadays with so much land having restricted access.

Types of holiday

Riding holidays vary considerably. Some involve several hours of riding each day, staying at different

destinations along a set route. In others, much of the riding takes place at a riding school or on a ranch, with perhaps daily rides out into the surrounding countryside; those who have never ridden can usually receive instruction on the basic techniques.

Those who want a short break can go on a riding weekend, which is very popular. For the more committed, training holidays provide lessons in most aspects of equestrianism, from polo to showjumping and dressage, side-saddle to cross-country riding. They may vary in length from two days to a week or more, with tuition being given for between one and four hours a day. In many cases visits to local attractions and other sports facilities may be laid on as well.

Riding standards and safety

Most tour operators offer a range of holidays to suit riders of different abilities and experience. Often, there may be the facilities for riders to take their own horses. If not, it is essential that the organizers know the capability of prospective riders so that they can

Staying on a ranch provides an unusual and exciting holiday, giving visitors the chance to experience first hand the day-to-day working life.

provide suitable horses; they may also be able to advise first-time riders on the most appropriate holiday for them. Whatever the rider's level of expertise, it is important to bear in mind that the horse, however experienced it is, can be frightened by sudden noises or strange objects and may on occasions be unpredictable and unco-operative.

CLOTHING For comfort and safety it is essential to wear sensible clothes. A safety hat with chin strap, and low-heeled shoes are the basics for most situations. (For Western riding, standard Western wear is more appropriate.) Hats are usually provided, but ideally riders take their own. Tough, comfortable jeans, or better still riding jeans or jodhpurs, will help to prevent chafing or soreness. Tights or thin longjohns worn underneath these are the key to preventing discomfort. Thin gloves will help to prevent blisters on soft hands.

TACK INSPECTION Before riding, always check the tack is clean, well oiled, and flexible, and that the stitching is intact.

Riding holidays around the world

Horse holidays can be taken virtually anywhere nowadays: the choice of destination is endless. In Europe most holidays provide rides through areas of outstanding natural beauty. A trek through the Black Mountains of Wales, a five-day course of polo instruction in the English countryside, a tour of the Highlands in Scotland, and quiet hacks, cross-country gallops, or trail rides over the Wicklow Mountains in Ireland are just a few possibilities.

Riding in the Caucasus Mountains in Russia. There are few better ways of exploring the countryside than on the back of a horse.

Italy, Hungary, and France offer numerous beautiful scenic rides, often in conjunction with other sightseeing trips. In Spain, mounted on splendid Andalusian or Lusitano horses, riders may visit the famous horse fairs or enjoy exhilarating gallops along the coast. In Iceland, they may experience the unique *tolt* pace of the native horses. Finland has stunning winter riding breaks, which include sleigh rides in the snow. Winter riding is also available in Switzerland, where all manner of equestrian sports take place, from polo to skiing behind a horse.

The USA has an amazing choice of riding vacations such as staying on a working ranch or riding through the 'big sky country' in Montana with its breathtaking scenery, wildlife, and wonderful carpets of wild flowers.

Wyoming, South Dakota, and Texas all offer myriad riding holidays, ranch breaks, and treks through their famously dramatic landscape. Similar holidays may be found in Argentina, Cuba, and Chile, each one unique to the country and the local culture.

The valleys and mountains of the Himalayas and the vast Mongolian steppes feature equally dramatic scenery. On these holidays riders live with the horses and see a world that has changed little for centuries. Some safaris in Africa offer an unforgettable combination of riding and game or bird watching. In New Zealand and Australia, riders can follow very old pioneering trails, camping along the route or, for those who enjoy a greater degree of comfort, staying each night in a farmstead.

RELATED TOPICS	
Showjumping	176
Western riding	202
Polo	220

CONTRIBUTOR BIOGRAPHIES

Lord Patrick Beresford started playing polo as a young cavalry officer in 1954. He has since played in over 30 different countries around the world. In 1992 he formed the British Polo Pony Welfare Committee. Since 1997 Patrick has acted as Steward of the Hurlingham Polo Association.

Ian Balding became the master of Park House Stables in 1964 and inherited such influential owners as Paul Mellon and Her Majesty the Queen.

Ian was one of the first trainers to realize the huge benefits to be gained by campaigning abroad and in the intervening years has topped the overseas' trainers' table on three separate occasions and the English table once. Ian is responsible for the winners of over 1400 races, including 160 Group and Stakes events throughout Europe.

The horses he has handled have been among Group 1 winners and have included Mrs Penny, Glint of Gold, Gold and Ivory, Diamond Shoal, Forest Flower, Dashing Blade, Silver Fling, Silly Season, Selkirk, Lochsong and Tagula as well as the European Champion and Derby winner, Mill Reef, one of the finest horses to have raced on this side of the Atlantic.

Austin Brown was born in Tryon, North Carolina February 5, 1927. He grew up riding and fox hunting with his father who had his own pack of hounds. He became a licensed Amateur Steeplechase Rider at age 16 and in 1951 was the American Champion Amateur Steeplechase Jockey. He rode the winner of the famous Iroquois Steeplechase three times. He was also a successful Steeplechase Trainer and later became a Racing Official.

For 12 years Austin was Vice-President and General Manager of Delaware Park, a thoroughbred race track in Wilmington, Delaware. He and his wife Sally now live in Camden, South Carolina where he is Chairman of the Carolina Cup Racing Association, which conducts the Carolina Cup and Colonial Cup Steeplechase Meetings, and operates the Sprindale Training Center.

Pamela Carruthers has designed and built courses at Hickstead, England and in the US, Canada, Australia, New Zealand, South Africa, Iran, Middle East, Germany and Mexico. She was designated a 'sports ambassador of the USA' by president Nixon in 1974.

She was elected to the Showjumping Committee of the FEI and was the first woman to officiate at the Olympic Games as TD at Seoul in 1988. She was awarded the BEF Medal of Honour and inducted into the US Showjumping Hall of Fame in 1996 (the first non-American to receive such an honour).

Dennis Colton left the British Army in 1946, joined the Mounted Police Force in 1948 and retired 25 years later as Chief Inspector in charge of training at the Mounted Police Training Establishment at Imber Court.

When Dennis retired he was invited by BHS to work as Approvals Officer inspecting and reporting on riding establishments that applied for approval to their list.

For 35 years he was showing steward at the RIHS and HOYS and regular steward and judge at Riding Club and Pony Club Championships.

Gavin Ehringer is rodeo columnist for Western Horseman and has covered the sport for a decade. He writes an annual report for the *Encyclopedia Britannica's Book of the Year* and is co-author of the book *Rodeo in America: Wranglers, Roughstock and Paydirt* and has written numerous articles on rodeo, Western equitation and performance riding as well as skiing.

Kevin Flynn is the head coachman of the Youngs Brewery in Wandsworth, South London where he is responsible for the training and welfare of the horses and the daily deliveries in the area. He arranges numerous displays and demonstrations.

Bernadette Faurie, an international equestrain journalist and commentator, is a chief correspondent for *Horse International* and in 1996 was voted 'Journalist of the Year' by the International Dressage Trainers Club. She edits a transnational crime and security journal, has written *The Horse-Riding Handbook* and co-written, with Carl Hester, *Down to Earth Dressage*.

Moira C Harris is Editor of *Horse Illustrated*, the leading all-breed, multi-discipline magazine in the United States and *Horse USA*, an annual publication dedicated to selecting, purchasing and caring for horses. She has many years of riding experience, first as a western rider and later as a hunter and jumper. Now she concentrates exclusively on dressage and competes at the lower levels with her thoroughbred London Exchange. She currently lives in Southern California.

Carl Hester won the National Young Rider Dressage Championship in 1985, has amassed sixteen further national titles including three Grand Prix Championships, and has represented Great Britain on World, European and Olympic teams. A leading trainer, Carl is Dressage Trainer to the New Zealand Event team and has co-authored the book *Down to Earth Dressage* with Bernadette Faurie.

Andrew Hoy won Burghley CCI at his first attempt and was Australian national champion in 1991, individually taking fifth place and then team gold at the Barcelona Olympics in 1992. In 1996 he won Llumhlen CCI and team gold at the Atlanta Olympics. He was winner at Bramham CCI in 1997 and took third place at the British Open Championships in 1998. Andrew teaches regularly throughout the world and returns to Australia when his commitments allow.

Jane Kidd was twice a member of Gold Medal Showjumping teams at Junior European Championships and a member of senior teams. She has competed internationally in dressage up to Grand Prix levels and is an International Dressage Judge, a member of the British Dressage Board and Chairman of the International Dressage Teams Committee.

She is the editor of the *Official British Dressage* magazine. She also acts as a contributing writer to numerous equestrian magazines.

Chrissy Kieley was brought up in Kenya and married in 1989 after working with the Windsor Park Team for Geoffrey Kent.

She spends April to July in England, August to September in Soto Grande in Spain and October to July in Australia where she and her husband jointly train polo ponies – mostly thoroughbreds off the track on their polo farm. They also run holidays for those wanting to improve their polo skills and conduct correspondence courses for schools.

Tadzik Kopanski is Polish by birth and has lived most of his life in Britain. He was in the Kings Troop Royal Horse Artillery, and retired as Lieutenant Colonel. He was the Chef d'equipe for the British even team in 1978 and 1979, when the team won the European Gold medal and all three individual medals.

He has run a major riding establishment in Somerset with his wife and daughter, both successful Horse Trials riders themselves.

Jos Lansink has been Dutch showjumping champion eight times between 1991–8 and has ridden in three Olympic Games. He has twice won the Bronze medal at the European Championships and has also won the Volvo World Cup in 1997. Jos is a regular member of the Dutch team.

Jenny Leggate has been actively involved in most of the equestrian disciplines, with her main interest being eventing. She has competed and trained horses to international level and has trained the vaulting horse for the British Team since the 1990 World Equestrian Games. Jenny enjoys training students and is involved with the RDA both here and abroad.

Jennie Loriston-Clarke, one of Britain's leading dressage riders and trainers, was the first British rider to win a dressage medal, the bronze, at the World Championships in 1978 on Dutch Courage. She has represented Britain in four Olympics.

Jennie has enjoyed an outstanding career with horses, having bred and trained everything from show ponies, hacks, hunters, competition horses, and her own Olympic dressage stars, and is renowned for her long reining and side saddle displays.

Jennie is a Fellow of the British Horse Society, holds the National Pony Society Diploma, and is an examiner for both. She judges show horses and is a List 1 dressage judge. She was awarded an MBE for her services to British Equestrianism in 1978.

Susan McBane has been described by the Equestrian Book Society as 'one of Britain's most highly represented equestrian authors'. She lectures to equestrian groups around the country and has written, edited or contributed to over 30 books on horse care and management and related subjects. She has also written countless articles for most of Britain's leading horse magazines as well as overseas publications the last 30 years.

In 1978 she co-founded the Equine Behaviour Study Circle (now the Equine Behaviour Forum) with the late Dr Moyra Williams, and still edits its quarterly journal, *Equine Behaviour*.

In 1980 she founded *Equi* magazine and was its editor until it ceased publication in 1985. In 1995 she became founder editor of *EQ* magazine, and is now its Technical Editor.

Bettina Overesch, the current European Champion for Germany, is based in England. She has represented Germany internationally for several years, was seventh in the World Equestrian Games in 1994, ninth in the Olympic Games in 1996, and second in the 1997 Open European Championships – all with Watermill Stream. In 1998 she won the two star Bonn-Rodderberg CCI in Germany and was a team member at the World Equestrian Games at Pratoni.

Marcy Pavord is a freelance equestrian writer and contributor to *Horse & Hound* and *Horse & Rider*. She has authored *Endurance: Start to Finish* (J A Allen) and *Long Distance Riding* (Crowood Press) among others. She is an FEI international candidate judge for endurance riding and a member of British Endurance Riding Association Training Committee. She now breeds and trains endurance horses on a Welsh hill farm and competes in endurance up to international level.

John Richards is the president of the Coaching Club and the Chairman of the Carriage Foundation, founder and president of the Celebration of the Horse, California and Chairman of the British Driving Society 1975–83. He is a founding committee member of the Combined Driving Group of the British Horse Society and represented Great Britain at four World Driving championships and one European Driving Championship. He was editor, publisher and managing director of *Horse and Driving* magazine 1975–85.

Sylvia Stanier was taught to ride by Sam Marsh. She worked in Ireland from 1950 to 1975 for the Hume Dudgeon's and was Chief Instructoress 1968–75, schooling horses for six successive Olympic Games. Her Best Show wins are Dublin, Champion Light Weight 1965, Champion Side Saddle 1965 and she did an outstanding long reining display at Wembley HOYS in 1966. She was stand-in at the Trooping the Colour for HM the Queen 1968–86 and rode circus High School 1978–97. She wrote *The Art of Lungeing* and *The Art of Long Reigning*.

Amanda Sutton is owner of Harestock Stud Physiotherapy Centre in Winchester, England and Senior Physiotherapist in a two women practice and co-ordinator of an animal physio training programme. She lectures in animal physiotherapy and is an author on the subject. She was the Official Physiotherapist to the British Three Day Event team in 1994–7 and is the Official Physiotherapist to Burghley, Blenheim, and Windsor Horse Trials.

SPECIAL CONTRIBUTORS
Nadine Ronan is a student at West Kington stud and competition yard at Church Farm in Wiltshire, England. She has recently competed in her first three day event.

Louisa Brassey has been active in her local pony club for over five years and hopes to make the team for dressage, showjumping, or eventing. She is a very successful show rider and has had many wins with her ponies.

Tony Pavord is an official FEI vet for endurance and has been the British team vet for Intermediate International teams for several years. He vetted at international events worldwide and was responsible for the emergence of endurance in the Emirates. He has officiated at many world and European endurance events.

Acknowledgements

Jane Holderness–Roddam would like to thank all the expert contributors for their valuable time, patience and expertise, Tessa Clarke and Sandra McCallum for their secretarial assistance, Claire Musters and Kenny Grant at Mitchell Beazley for their help in compiling the book and Lesley Riley for her outstanding editing.

Mitchell Beazley would like to thank Lesley Riley for her tireless editorial work, and Hilary Bird and Michelle Pickering for indexing and proofreading respectively.

INDEX

A

Adderley, Lt Colonel Charles, 230
Akhal-Teke, 20, 12 2–3
alternative medicine, 173
American Driving Society (ADS), 197
American Horse Shows Association
  (AHSA), 246
American Saddlebred, 114–15
Amish, 240
Andalusian, 94–5, 240
Anglo-Arabian, 237
animal welfare, 164, 209
Ansell, Colonel Sir Mike, 230
Appaloosa, 104–5, 206
Arab Horse Society, 212
Arabian, 20, 128–30
  circus horses, 240
  endurance riding, 214
  racing, 184
Ardennes, 146–7
arena polo, 222
Argentina, 220, 241
Asmussen, Cash, 188
asses, 19
Australia, 188, 241
Australian Driving Society, 197
Australian Stock Horse, 126–7
Australian Warmblood, 78–80

B

Bailey, Jerry, 188
Barb, 132–3
bareback riding, rodeos, 208
barrel racing, rodeos, 208, 210
Bashkir, 23
Basuto Pony, 64
Bausil, Captain Paul, 156
Beerbaum, Ludger, 176
behaviour, 30-5
Belgian Warmblood, 78
body language, 33–4, 37
'bonding', training, 37, 40
bookies, 191
Boulonnais, 240
Bowman, George, 200, 201
box walking, 35
Brabant, 144–5
Brasseur, Felix, 200–1
Brassey, Louisa, 68–9
breaking in, 36–7, 44–5
Breasley, Scobie, 188
breeders, racing, 191
breeding, 8–11
Breton, 240
Britain: ceremonial horses, 234–5
  endurance riding, 212, 213, 214
  hunting, 248
  mounted games, 230
  police horses, 235, 242–3
  Pony Club, 226
  racing, 184–6, 187
  shows, 246
  steeplechasing, 189

  working horses, 240, 241
British Driving Society (BDS), 197
British Warmblood, 78
bronc riding, 208, 211
brushes, grooming, 27
Byerley Turk, 72, 184

C

Cadre Noir, 236–7
Caisson Platoon, 236
Campbell, John, 190
camps, Pony Club, 68–9, 227–8
Canada, Mounties, 236
Canadian Horse, 102–3
Caprilli, Federico, 156
Carson, Willie, 188
Case, Walter Jr, 190
cavalry, 8, 10, 156, 212, 218, 220, 230
Celle stud, 239
ceremonial horses, 234–40
chariots, 8, 194
Charles II, King of England, 184
Charro riders, 239
circus horses, 239–40
Cisko, 240
Cleveland Bay, 74–5, 201
clipping, 23
clothing, riding holidays, 250
Clydesdale, 138–9, 240
coaching, 194–7
Coaching Club, 196
coat, 21–3
  clipping, 23
  grooming, 27
'cock horse', 194
Cody, William F ('Buffalo Bill'), 203
colic, 25
colts, 32, 41
communication, 33–4
Connemara Pony, 55, 180
course designers, 180–1, 207
cowboys, 43, 203, 205, 208–11, 241
cow ponies, 240–1
crib biting, 35
Criollo, 120, 223, 241
cross-country courses, 156, 159,
  161–2, 166–7
cutting, Western riding, 205
Czech Republic, 189

D

Dales Pony, 50
Dancer, Stanley, 190
Danish Warmblood, 78
Darley Arabian, 72, 184
Dartmoor Pony, 52
Davidson, Bruce, 158
Dawn Horse, 18
Day, Pat, 188
Deauville, 186
dentition, 23
Derby, 180
Dettori, Frankie, 188
Diaz, Jerry, 211
digestive system, 23
Dinohippus, 18, 19

discipline, 40–1, 42
display horses, 236–9
Doma Vaquera, 240–1
Domecq School, 239
domestication, 8
dominance, 32–3
Donoghue, Steve, 188
drag hunting, 249
draught horses, 152–3
dressage, 168–75
  circus horses, 240
  driving trials, 198
  eventing, 156, 159–61, 166
driving, 194–201
driving trials, 198–9
drum horses, 234–5
Dutch Draught, 150–1
Dutch Warmblood, 78–9, 171, 200

E

ears, 21, 33
eating habits, 31
Edinburgh, Duke of, 198, 201, 230
electric prods, rodeos, 209
Elizabeth II, Queen, 235
endurance riding, 212–17
Eohippus, 18, 19, 30
equitation, 42–3
Equus, 18–19
eventing, 156–67
evolution, 18–19
exercise, 24–5, 28, 41
Exmoor Pony, 53
eyes, 21

F

farriers, 27, 173
Federation Equestrian International
  (FEI), 12, 158, 161, 170, 176,
  178, 198, 201, 212–13, 218
feeding, 23, 24, 28, 31
feet, 20–1, 27, 33
Fell Pony, 51
fences: showjumping, 178–80
  steeplechasing, 188–9
feral horses, 32–3
fibre, in diet, 24, 31
fields, 26, 27
fillies, 41
films, horses in, 241
Firestone, Alison, 176
fitness programme, 28
flat racing, 184, 187–8
flehmen, 33
flies, 24, 27
flight-or-fight instinct, 31
foals: birth, 23
  body language, 33
  training, 40–1
  weaning, 41
food, 23, 24, 28, 31
fox hunting, 248
France: display horses, 236–7
  endurance riding, 212
  harness racing, 190
  racing, 186, 188

steeplechasing, 189
working horses, 240
French Trotter, 80–1, 190
Friesian, 96–7, 200, 240
Frith, Georgina, 201

G

Galvayne's groove, 23
Garrett, Marvin, 208
gauchos, 43, 241
Gelderlander, 200, 240
geldings, 23
German Warmblood, 79, 171
Germany: display horses, 239
steeplechasing, 188–9
working horses, 240
Godolphin Barb, 72, 184
Grand Prix, showjumping, 179
grass, 31
grassland management, 27
Greece, ancient, 8, 194, 218
Green, Lucinda, 158
grooming, 27
grooms, 38–9
dressage, 172
driving, 201
Guérinière, François Robichon de la,
8, 43, 236–7, 238
Gulf Stream race course, 192–3
gymkhanas, 226, 231

H

Hackney, 201
Haflinger, 60–1, 240
Hanoverian, 84–5, 180, 200, 239
harness, driving, 199–200
harness racing, 190
Haughton, Billy, 190
Haute Ecole, circus horses, 240
hearing, 21
Hedeman, Richard 'Tuff', 211
Hennessey, Walter, 190
herds: discipline, 40–1
hierarchy, 32–3
instincts, 30–1
introducing animals to, 25–6
Hester, Carl, 174–5
Highland Pony, 57, 240
hip joints, 21
Hippidions, 19
hobbles, harness racing, 190
holidays, riding, 207, 250–1
Holstein, 79, 86–7, 180, 200
hooves, 20–1, 27
Household Cavalry, 234–5
hunting, 248–9
Hurlingham Polo Association, 220
Hyracotherium, 18

I

Icelandic Horse, 63
imprint training, 40
India, polo, 220
instincts, 30–1
International League for the Protection
of Horses (ILPH), 10

International Polo Federation (FIP),
220–2
interval training, 28
intestines, 23
Irish Draught, 98–9
Italy, racing, 186–7, 188

J

Jacobson's organ, 33
Jockey Club, 186, 188
jockeys, racing, 190–1
'joining', training, 37, 40
judges: dressage, 172
driving, 201
endurance riding, 215
shows, 247
vaulting, 219
Western riding, 206
jumping: cross-country courses,
156, 159, 161–2, 166–7
showjumping, 156, 162–3, 167,
176–83
Jung, Emil Bernhard, 200

K

Kabardin, 124
Kentucky, 186
King's Troop, Royal Horse Artillery, 234
Kladruber, 200, 240

L

lameness, 25
Lansink, Jos, 176, 182–3
legs, 20–1
leisure activities, 244–51
Liberty horses, circuses, 240
ligaments, 20
Lipizzaner, 100–1
driving, 200
Spanish Riding School, 238
working horses, 240
Loriston-Clarke, Jennie, 44–5
lungeing, 24–5
Lusitano: circus horses, 240
display horses, 237, 239
driving, 200–1

M

McCarron, Chris, 188
manes, 23, 204
mares, 23, 32, 41
Masters of Foxhounds Association
(MFHA), 248
Merychippus, 18
Mesohippus, 18
Metropolitan Police, 235, 242–3
Mexico, display horses, 239
military ceremonies, 234–6
Miller, Del, 190
Miller, Robert, 40
Missouri Fox Trotter, 108–9, 239
Mongolian Pony, 65
Morgan, 106–7
Morny, Duc de, 186
mounted games, 230–1
Mounties, 236

mouthing, body language, 33
mucking out, 27
muscles, 20
Mustang, 110-11

N

Napoleon I, Emperor, 186
Nations Cup, showjumping, 176–8
neckreining, 43, 203
Némethy, Bertalan de, 176
Netherlands, working horses, 240
New Forest Pony, 54
New Zealand Driving Society, 197
New Zealand Warmblood, 79
Norwegian Fjord, 62
nostrils, body language, 33

O

Oldenburg, 88–9, 200
Oliveira, Nuno, 43
Olympic Games: dressage, 168
eventing, 156–8
showjumping, 176, 178
vaulting, 218
onagers, 19
Orlov Trotter, 125, 200
Ouellette, Luc, 190
Overesch, Bettina, 158, 166–7

P

paces, dressage, 168
pacing races, 190
pain, 25, 35
Paint Horse, Western riding, 206
Palomino, 134, 206, 239
parade horses, 239
Parahippus, 18
parasites, 27, 35
Paso, 239
Paso Fino, 121
pawing, body language, 33
Percheron, 148–9
Peslier, Olivier, 188
Pessoa, Rodrigo, 176
Phillips, Mark, 158
physiotherapists, 136–7, 165, 173
Piggott, Lester, 188
Pikes Peak Rodeo, 210–11
Pinto, 135
point to point racing, 189, 249
police horses, 235, 236, 242–3
Polish Warmblood, 79
polo, 220–5
ponies, 48–67
Pony of the Americas, 66–7
Pony Club, 68–9, 158, 226–9, 230
Portugal, display horses, 239
predators, 30, 31, 32
pregnancy, 23, 41
Professional Event Riders' Association
(PERA), 164
Professional Rodeo Cowboys of
America (PRCA), 208, 209, 210
puberty, 41
Puissance, showjumping, 179–80
pulse rate, 28

Q

Quarter Horse, 112–13
  racing, 184
  rodeos, 208
  Western riding, 206

R

racing, 10, 184–93
rallies, Pony Club, 227
ranch vacations, 207
reflex actions, 35
reins: neckreining, 43, 203
  Western riding, 203, 205
Rejoindors, 239
Renaissance, 8, 43
reproduction, 23
Richards, Gordon, 188
riding holidays, 250–1
Riding Pony, 48–9
Robie, Wendell T, 212
rodeos, 203, 208–11
rolling, 35
Roman empire, 8, 194, 218
Ronan, Nadine, 38–9
Rosinbacks, circus horses, 240
Royal Mews, 235
rug tearing, 35
rugs, 24, 27
Russian Trotter, 190
Ryan, Matthew, 158

S

saddle bronc riding, 208, 211
saddles, Western riding, 202–4
scurry driving, 197–8
season, mares, 23, 33
Selby, James, 194
Selle Français, 82–3, 180, 237
senses, 21
Shagya, 240
shelter, 24
Shetland Pony, 56
Shire, 140–1, 240
shoes, 27
showing, 246–7
showjumping, 176–83
  eventing, 156, 162–3, 167
sight, 21
sleep, 34–5
smell, sense of, 21
Spain, 239, 240–1
Spanish Riding School, Vienna, 8, 100, 238–9
speed, 21
sport horses, 10–12, 70–135
sports, 155–231
  dressage, 168–75
  driving, 194–201
  endurance riding, 212–17
  eventing, 156–67
  mounted games, 230–1
  polo, 220–5
  Pony Club, 226–9
  racing, 184–93
  rodeo, 208–11
  showjumping, 176–83

vaulting, 218–19
spurs, rodeos, 209
stable vices, 35
stables, 26, 27, 35
stallions, 23, 32, 33, 41
Standardbred, 116–17, 190
stay apparatus, 21
Stecher, Gabriel, 212
steeplechasing, 184, 188–9, 249
steer roping, rodeos, 208, 210
Stevens, Gary, 188
stud book, 186
studs, 8–10
Suffolk, 142–3, 240
Sutton, Amanda, 136–7
Swedish Warmblood, 79, 200
Swiss Warmblood, 79

T

tails, 23
  body language, 33
  Western riding, 204
Tait, Blyth, 158
taste, sense of, 21
teeth, 23
television, horses on, 241
tendons, 20
Tennessee Walking Horse, 118–19, 239
Tesio, Federico, 187
Tevis Cup, 212, 215
thoracic sling, 21
Thoroughbred, 10, 20, 70–3
  display horses, 237
  dressage, 171
  eventing, 165
  polo, 220, 223
  racing, 184
  showjumping, 180
three-day events, 166–7
Tibbs, Casey, 208
timber racing, 189
Todd, Mark, 158
touch, sense of, 21
trail riding, 204–5
training, 36–43
Training and Efficiency Certificate, 228
Trakehner, 92–3
Triple Crown, racing, 187–8
trotting races, 190

U

United States of America:
  ceremonial horses, 236
  cow ponies, 241
  endurance riding, 212
  hunting, 248
  racing, 186, 187–8, 190
  riding holidays, 251
  shows, 246
  Western riding, 202–7
  working horses, 240, 241
Uphoff, Nicole, 171

V

Vanderbilt, Alfred, 194
vaulting, 218–19

vets, 25, 28
  dressage, 172
  endurance riding, 215, 216–17
  racing, 191
vibrissae, 21
vices, 35
vision, 21

W

Waler, 223
warfare, 8
Warmbloods, 10–11, 76–9
  dressage, 171
  eventing, 165
  showjumping, 180
washing coat, 27
water, drinking, 24
weaning, 41
Weatherby, Sir James, 186
weaving, 35
weighing horses, 28
Welsh Cob, 58–9, 180, 201
Welsh Pony, 58–9, 201
Western riding, 202–9
Westphalian, 90–1, 180
whiskers, 21
Whitaker brothers, 176
Wielkopolski, 200
wind sucking, 35
Windsor Grey, 235
working horses, 10, 138–53, 240–3
World Championships, showjumping, 178
World Cup: dressage, 170–1
  showjumping, 176

X

Xenophon, 8, 36, 168, 218

Y

yearlings, 41
Young's Ram Brewery, Wandsworth, 152–3

Z

zebras, 19

Picture Credits

All photography by Bob Langrish except: 36 Corbis/Bettmann; 64 Corbis UK Ltd/Buddy Mays; 65 Embassy of Mongolia/Ulziibold Gonbojav; 65 bottom Corbis UK Ltd/Dean Conger; 84 Animal Photography/Sally Anne Thompson; 90 top Westphalian Stud/H. Sangmeister; 145 right Animal Photography/Sally Anne Thompson 156 Kruch Imprimeur et Editeur; 187 George Selwyn; 194 Carriage Driving Magazine/Richard James; 196 Carriage Driving Magazine/Richard James; 210 top Gavin Ehringer; 210 centre Gavin Ehringer; 210 bottom Gavin Ehringer; 211 top Gavin Ehringer; 211 centre Gavin Ehringer; 211 bottom Gavin Ehringer; 212 Florac Endurance Race; 219 Horse and Hound/Trevor Meeks; 234 Rex Features